CW01429585

THE VANISHING BOOK

by
Shirley Read-Jahn

Copyright

Contents

Dedication

For my son, Samuel Sutton Kline, and for my sister, Pamela Frances Read-Jahn Bailey.
Sincerest thanks to Horst Reimann, Lynn Rothenberg, and Carl Brush for their patient help and support.

Foreword

The Vanishing Book is based on the author's genealogical tree as documented by her maternal great grandfather, Charles William Sutton, Chief Librarian of the Manchester Free Library in England from 1865 to his death in 1920. The family tree comprises the Pocklington and Sutton families, starting in 1202. The author has incorporated the intimate friendship of Charles Dickens with Thomas Sutton, the father of Charles William Sutton.

Chapter 1
Memoir

I sat at my desk staring at the old, yellowed, genealogical tree. Attached to it were many documents covered in the spidery script of my great grandfather, Charles William Sutton. I knew it was his hand because he had signed some of the papers, attesting to their verity. I'd brought these documents with me in a plastic box when I'd moved to Australia from the United States to marry again. I'd changed my name when I'd married before, but this time around I'd kept my maiden name of Shirley Read-Jahn. Somehow, using my own name on my book covers had given me back a strong sense of self. I had been writing books since I'd retired and moved to Australia, thus I'd decided it was high time I got on with a memoir about the maternal side of my family. I'd hardly looked in the plastic box for a decade, being occupied writing other books for adults plus writing and illustrating books for young children. Besides, I had also been far too busy traveling around exploring my new country and being in love once again. Now it was time, and I was eager to start. I delved further into the big plastic box.

What I saw before me represented fifty-five years of data put together by Great Grandpa Sutton as he'd researched the conjoined Pocklington and Sutton families' history, who they were, what they did, and the culture of their times. Sticking out of an envelope I picked up were photographs, also old and faded, but bringing to life his ancestors and descendants. A cousin of mine had found many of these old pictures, letters, and photos in a trunk under the bed of one of the Sutton relatives after he had died. With this treasure trove, I realised I could create a story surrounding much of my family's history.

That first night, I stayed up way into the wee hours, reading note after note. Great Grandpa referred time and again to a book he was dipping into to create his family tree. He called this book a monasticon. Reaching for my dictionary, I looked the word up. In general, it meant a book describing monasteries and priories in a certain location. When I'd packed the box, I didn't remember putting any book into it. Pushing the documents this way and that on my desk, I looked to see if by any wondrous chance, this monasticon book was part of my treasure trove. It was not. My heart sank. I wondered what had happened to the book? With no way of knowing, I retired. Before nodding off, I thought about what I could do to create what I had in mind without that essential ingredient—the monasticon.

The next day my mind was made up. I would put together a story about my family's background and in doing so, perhaps I'd get an idea of where to search for the book. It was intriguing to me, and as the days passed, it became more and more an insistent, persistent, fascination, an unremitting obsession. If I had the monasticon in my hands, I reckoned I could find out so much more about my family. My great grandfather, Charles William Sutton, had discovered some of the story, but I knew more remained. From the documents I'd been reading, clearly he'd also been obsessed with the monasticon, and I wanted to know why. He'd made notes about a love affair in 1202 between his first known ancestor and the daughter of a knight. This was certainly intriguing, but what else did the book hold within its ancient pages? I had to find out.

With a pot of coffee now next to me, I started to write a narrative about Great Grandpa's working life in 1865 and to entwine it with the branches of the faded genealogical tree. I decided that before Great Grandpa, though, I would go all the way back to the first notation on that tree. Thus, I began with his first entry, from just before the year of 1202.

"Walter Dethic, born in Gascoyne in the time of Henry the Second, came into England, and married the daughter and heir of Sir John Pocklington, of Pocklington, co York, of the race of the Saxons in the county of York"

Herl. Soc. 16. Visit. of York, p.271.

1202 Roger de Pokelinton.

1205 Henry de Pokelinton   MS. Note Book of Rev. J. N. Pocklington

1219 Willelma de Pocklington, witness to deed (Selby), York   Yorks Arch. Ass 13. Selby Records.

1233 Will. de Pokleyn   Oxon   Kennet. Parochial Antiquities

1295   de Pokelinton   MS Note Book

1233 Confirmation of Grant made to Roger son of Roger de Pothalington of 2 crofts belonging to prebend of Bamb' in Pokr   Surtees Soc. 56 p5q.

[1248] Domino Ricardo de Pokelyngtona, Capellano. Datum apud Bugdene quinta idus Martii Pontificatus [Innocent IX] nostri anno quinto." Rolls Series, Mem. en. Inch., Oxrd., p.10.

1243. W. de Pokel. Oxon   Kennet, Parochial Antiquities.

[1250] Domino Ricardo de Pokelyngtone, Capellano. Datum apud Bugdene quinta idus Martii, Pontificatus nostri anno quinto   Rolls Series, Mem. en. Inch., Oxrd., p10.

1252 Rich. de Pokinton ...   MS. Note Book

Chapter 2
1853

In 1202 an ex-Cathar bishop arrived in England from the Gascony area of France, galloping from the south coast up to the walled city of York. He was welcomed into a monastery there, where he stayed until he had grasped the ways of his new country and people. Soon he married the daughter of an English knight, Sir John Pocklington, and later that same year, she gave birth to his first offspring, a boy they called Roger de Pokelinton.

Six hundred and sixty-three years later, not knowing anything at all about this ex-Cathar bishop's adventurous move from France to England in 1202, Charles William Sutton, curator of England's first free library in Manchester, sat at his desk. He had one leg stuck out in front of him while he pondered on his new life. He had no idea either, that through a marriage of his own to come many years onward in his life, that Frenchman from Gascony would become his ancestor through marriage.

A ray of sunlight shone down upon Charles through the mullioned window. Dust motes danced through the light's ray like the thoughts swirling and tumbling through his brain, causing him to cough. The room was lined with old books and manuscripts, hence the dust, he mused ruefully, tapping his fingers on the fine old wooden desk.

It was September of 1865. He'd only just turned seventeen years of age on 14th April, and this was his first job. Like his father Thomas Sutton, Charles had thick dark brown hair. Thomas had a stronger nose than Charles and sported a grey beard and moustache. Charles was a slender young man, rather tall with straight posture. His hands had long white fingers. His eyes were expressive and brown, soulful but rather myopic.

As yet no thick moustache grew on his upper lip. That would come later. Charles' father, Thomas, was an intimate friend of Charles Dickens. The well-known author occasionally came up to the Midlands from London to visit Thomas on his research trips for books he was writing.

As thoughts flew through his head, Charles Sutton flashed on a memory from the Christmas of 1853. He was but five years old when he passed by the living room door in his father's house in Manchester. His father, Thomas Sutton, and Charles Dickens were leaning, one elbow each on the mantlepiece above the fireplace, each man with his other hand stuck into his trouser pocket[1]. Thomas was twenty-eight and Dickens was forty-one at the time. The two old friends spied young Charles listening at the open door. Dickens called out to him, "I've brought a Christmas present for you, young man, appropriate for the season and I know how much you already like to read, you're a clever young fellow. Plus, it's a ghost story, so I think you'll like it even more!" Dickens handed him a signed copy of A Christmas Carol. This significant moment was the beginning of Charles Sutton's foray into the fantastical, mesmerising world of books.

---

[1] There's an old photograph in my house of this event that sadly I have been unable to locate. On the reverse, its spidery writing tells who the two men are, and that Charles Dickens is telling Thomas Sutton about his novella, A Christmas Carol.

Chapter 3
1865

As a youngster, Charles Sutton not only loved books but had a passion for the sport of high-jumping, at which he was very good. He could jump higher than any other fellow at Manchester's Owens College. He was a humble boy, but he was proud of his athletic ability. He was already fascinated by all things in nature, from earthquakes to earwigs. His mother taught him to roll up a newspaper, sprinkle it with water, and leave it outside overnight. In the morning, to his boyish delight, upon unrolling the newspaper he found it filled with the captivating wiggly creatures for him to study.

Another passion of his was his own family's history. While helping his father out in his bookshop, he'd heard many stories about his own line. He hoped, eventually, to compile a family tree, thinking how interesting it might be to his descendants far in the future. That thought certainly made him smile.

It was Charles Dickens who, early in 1865, twelve years later, was visiting young Charles' father. He had taken a break from the public readings of his works in London and in Paris. In 1866 he was planning to go to Scotland for more readings but decided to travel first from London to Manchester to see his old friend, Thomas Sutton, and perhaps give some public readings there.

On this auspicious day, Charles Sutton was striding by the same living room door of his Manchester home when Dickens called out to him once more. "Young man, your father tells me you will have attained your seventeenth year in April. The administrator of our city libraries is our alderman, Sir Thomas Baker. He and the chief librarian, the Italian gentleman, Dr. Andrea Costadoro, have been telling me about you. Sir Thomas has been taken by your similar love of books to his, and we've chatted. We know you're already a clerk to the library committee as well as an assistant. Thus, I've been telling Sir Thomas that in September we will have the perfect permanent job for you as sub-librarian at the library we've established here in Manchester. Charles, this is the first free library of our century in England, and perhaps the first in any of our other English-speaking lands! Your father loves books, I know you love books, indeed, all you Suttons do. You've been booksellers for years, now I think about it."

Turning to young Charles' father, Dickens said, "Thomas, you opened your second-hand bookshop right here in Manchester in 1847, didn't you, just before Charles here was born? Well, what do you say we get your son into our free library here where he can wallow in words, too—words, words, every day of his working life. So, young Charles, what do you think of the idea?"

Charles was thrilled. "Absolutely, Mr. Dickens, a perfectly wonderful opportunity! Many thanks, sir."

"You'll much enjoy the position, young man. There's a reference library, five lending libraries, and they're just opening two juvenile reading rooms and will begin to open all the libraries on Sundays. The total issues circulating are just under a million[2] a year now, but they're multiplying at a rapid rate. Yes, indeed, it will certainly keep you on your toes!"

So here sat Charles in the library in the Campfield area of Manchester, wondering how to start this job that had landed him in an Aladdin's cave of treasures. He'd turn eighteen next April and was filled with vim and vigour to work. The first thought that sprang to mind was cataloguing. Of course! Why not? Nobody had done that yet. Rooms of books filled every corner of the huge old building; stacks of books— hundreds, probably thousands of books. Where had they all come from? Donations, certainly, and obviously he must ask Mr. Dickens; he'd have an idea.

On his free time, "If I ever manage to get any," he ruefully sighed aloud to himself, he'd have plenty of information to peruse for compiling his family tree. Thomas had told him that the Sutton family could be traced back for many, many years and had laid down roots all over the northwest of England in Cheshire, Cumbria, Derbyshire, Lancashire, Merseyside, and Yorkshire, but mostly in the areas around the city of Manchester itself. He'd not only have many books to go through for his research, but also people to talk to—relatives, certainly,

---

[2] When Charles died in 1920, the libraries consisted of 26 branches, with books being issued (loaned out) at nearly 2.75 million per year.

starting with his own immediate family. Then, of course, there was also Charles Dickens, that amazing personality filled to the brim with historical knowledge and bursting with books to write.

As young Sutton stood up, impetuously preparing to go straight to Mr. Dickens, he happened to glance down at his desk, for the first time noticing the head of a horned Satan carved amongst a bed of leaves and flowers right into the side of the table.

"What on earth is that about?" he muttered to himself. "I'll have to ask Boz now I'm off to see him. It seems he knows pretty much everything." Dickens had given Charles leave to call him Boz when Charles was still a young fellow. Dickens said the nickname was taken from Augustus (Moses) Dickens, the youngest of Charles Dickens' brothers. Dickens said Augustus called himself Boses because he always seemed to have a cold and the 'M' had quickly morphed into a nasal 'B'. Dickens took the name Boz to use as a pseudonym in his early literary works, which always gave him a private chuckle.

✦

Charles stopped in at his father's bookshop to ask him for the address where Dickens was temporarily staying while in Manchester. When Charles arrived at Dickens' home, he asked him about the table in his own office with the carving of fruit and flowers and the head of a devil. Dickens said, "Well, it must have been meant to be a dinner table. You know you need to say Grace before eating or Satan could get into the food and spoil your digestion. If you look carefully, Charles, there's probably a carving of an angel next to a cornucopia of edible leaves and flowers on the other side of the table—because everything in the world needs balance." Balancing on Charles Dickens' wrist was a gorgeously-plumed black raven.

"Charles, meet Grip. I take him with me on many of my trips away from home. Grip, this is young Charles Sutton from our library."

"Hullo, hullo, hullo" squawked the raven.

Dickens said, "Reckon I'm right about Satan and Grace and food, Grip?" "That's right, that's right, devil, bad boy!" squawked Grip-the-raven on Charles Dickens' wrist but putting his head to one side and beadily surveying young Charles.

"He talks!" cried Charles Sutton. "Are you talking to me, Grip, you bird-brain? I'm not a devil, nor am I bad!"

"Indeed, Grip talks," said Dickens. "His forbear was called Grip, too, and Old Grip had a huge vocabulary that I taught him myself. He was my favourite raven. Hardly a bird-brain, young Charles. Rather, a highly intelligent bird. One terrible night, let's see, that must have been back in '41, Old Grip suddenly swung upside down on his perch and was a goner. I've been trying to enlarge this raven's vocabulary, but he isn't as clever as his father was."

"Oh, that's very sad, sir, very sad."

"I loved Grip-the-elder, I really did. Indeed, I made him a character in my novel, *Barnaby Rudge: A Tale of the Riots of Eighty*, which I wrote in 1841. Maybe that's what killed poor old Grip, all that attention, you mind." Dickens smiled wryly at Charles, then added, "Well, 'tis all in the past now, isn't it?" After a polite moment of silence, Charles then regaled Mr. Dickens with his plans for cataloguing all the books in the library, and his desire to begin work on his family's genealogical tree.

A pleasant hour passed when Dickens suddenly glanced down at his fob watch and, running a hand through his wavy hair falling over one eye and pulling on his scraggly beard, declared, "A warm goodbye to you for the nonce, dear Charles. Must get back to my writing now. Return to see me whenever you wish, so long as I'm still up here in Manchester."

Thinking still of his favourite deceased raven, Dickens wiped a tear from the corner of his eye while the younger raven on his wrist again put his head to one side, whispering hoarsely, "Goodbye boy, goodbye devil, bad boy!"

Charles returned to the Free Public Library of Manchester with his head spinning about books—reading them, cataloguing them, perhaps one day writing books himself. And ravens. Amazing birds, those ravens. "Yet he must be a bit of a stupid bird," Charles chuckled to himself, "because I'm not a devil. He's wicked to say so, so he is!"

Charles Dickens, 7th February 1812—9th June 1870

Thomas Sutton, 11th March 1825-1883 (day & month unknown), second son of Robert and Susannah Sutton.

Chapter 4
Memoir

Sitting in my office in Australia, what I'd just read in Great Grandpa's notes about Thomas Sutton was interesting to me. I already knew that Thomas, my great-great grandfather, was an intimate friend of Charles Dickens. This snippet of information wasn't going to help me locate the missing monasticon book itself in my world, though, because at that long-ago time, Thomas's son, Charles William Sutton, hadn't even found the book in the library where he was working, or so I gleaned from the notes Charles had left behind. Yet there was a note Great Grandpa had written that said how fond of this 'monasticon' book he was—thus I knew the book existed. I would just have to keep reading through his notes about the library, the jottings on the genealogical tree he'd started putting together, and anything Mr. Dickens had said to Great Grandpa to see what other mentions he'd made of it. Maybe some of this would shed light on what had happened to the mysterious monasticon. Oh my, how I'd love to take a look at it myself; it had obviously been so important to Great Grandpa. Once again, I rifled through all the many documents I'd brought over in my plastic box, but I'd unfortunately been right the first time—no monasticon.

Chapter 5
1865

Seated again at the old table in his office at the library to start cataloguing the books around him, young Charles Sutton pulled out his desk drawer and found some old foolscap. He noticed it had watermarks on it of a fool's coxcomb cap, which a jester would have worn in the Middle Ages. The conical hat had three parts of material poking up from the top with bells sewn onto the ends. The top of the hat was shaped like the ragged crest of a cockerel, that in real life would have been a scarlet red. Charles had read somewhere that it was believed in the Middle Ages that the cockerel thought it was he who made the sun rise when he crowed—such a fool was the cockerel. Charles also knew that teachers would often make their slow or misbehaving students wear a hat like the one in the picture while shamefully standing in a corner of the classroom with their back to the other classroom children.

Speaking to himself aloud, a habit he was to retain all his life, Charles asked the walls, "But why this watermark?" Putting off his cataloguing of the library's books for a little while longer, he happily did some research. Eventually he discovered that the fool's cap watermark was used from the 15th century onwards to specify a particular size of a piece of paper. He couldn't find out exactly why a fool's cap was pressed upon the paper to verify its dimensions, and this annoyed Charles. He'd have to do a bit more research to find that out. He did discover that in the mid-17th century the fool's cap watermark was substituted for the British parliament's papers instead of the royal coat of arms used earlier in Westminster. He liked that idea, finding many parliamentary dignitaries to be fools in general.

After diligently re-starting his cataloguing of the library's books, and working on it for the next three hours, Charles treated himself to his 'free time' beginning work on what would eventually become a mammoth task. This would take him the majority of the free time hours he'd give himself out of the fifty-five years he was to work at the library.

He wrote down dates, names, and the work his ancestors were involved in, comprising many rectors, vicars, booksellers, and freemen. This involved researching hundreds of books in this cave of treasures he felt fortunate to have fallen into, including *The Surtees Society, Drake's Eboracum, The Yorkshire Archaeological and Topographical Journal*, and so many more. As he read, he catalogued, and this was to be the greatest service to the Free Library of Manchester and the readers who came in search of literary enlightenment—for much of what he wrote down wasn't only about his family tree but also information about the subjects' families and their cultural times.

Chapter 6
1867

Charles was working alone on the bookshelves on a day in 1867 when he came across an antique book in his library. This turned out to be the first time Charles had laid eyes on a monasticon so didn't know what kind of book it was; he knew he'd have to find out—being curious was in his nature. As he was looking through the book, it looked like it must have been acquired from a monastery; handwritten in tiny writing in the old style that scribes used, with serifs, curlicues and flourishes. The paper was a very thin parchment, still mostly intact. He'd have to count the unnumbered pages but, although a smallish book in width and length, its breadth was quite fat, and looked to have around 300 or 400 pages. Interestingly, it obviously wasn't being loaned out, not having any sort of library card or paper inside its front or back cover. Charles wondered how, then, it had ended up on this library shelf? No way of knowing that, he reckoned. It was obviously very old—possibly even from the 13th century although Charles wasn't quite sure. He'd need to get a couple of opinions on that. Commanding the fat little book on the bookshelf in front of him, he said, "Don't you dare move, precious book, while I run back to my office to fetch something with which to handle you more safely. You're obviously very old."

Charles put on the thin white cotton gloves he kept in his office specifically to touch ancient books or documents. Returning to the bookshelf, he saw that each page of the book had been lovingly inscribed in now-fading ink, with the pages yellowing with age at the middle and on the edges. The capital letter of the beginning word of each new paragraph or section was illuminated picturesquely and highlighted in gold or silver. He gaped in awe at the book. He almost ran back to his office carrying the book pressed against his chest. He was determined to show it immediately to Charles Dickens, who'd have a good idea of its age.

Having got Dickens to agree to see him immediately when he'd knocked on his temporary lodgings' door—and feeling lucky that the great author was up in Manchester from London again for a spell—Charles marched into Dickens' study, noticing that the writer's desk was facing north.

"Boz, sorry to charge in on you like this, but I want to ask you something, actually a couple of things. Wait a minute, why is your desk facing the dark side of the room? I have mine facing south, so the sun pours in. You'd see far better if you faced south, you know. Just curious!"

"I face it north, young friend, because I believe it aids my creativity. For that matter, I don't mind sharing with you that I always sleep facing north, too. Helps against my constant insomnia, don't you know. AND I always have a compass with me when I travel, to ensure that when I lie down, I'm facing north. Expect you find that rather strange. There's a word for this approach; it's called feng shui, or Chinese geomancy. Surprised you haven't heard of it. The Chinese believe, and I think they're correct, that we humans need to be in harmony with our surrounding environment. The Chinese words mean 'wind-water' and they're just two of the four elements of matter. Oh, and I note you're still calling me by my 'Boz' nickname, and I don't mind, since you're so excited."

"Yes, yes, I do know some of that. Earth, Water, Air, and Fire. I'm sure you're right, Boz. If facing north works well for you then I'm sincerely glad. And yes, I am feeling excited about what I want to ask you."

"Now Charles, aside from all of whatever it is that you want to chat about, please don't neglect to wish good day to this glorious creature once again on my wrist here. He's a bit raucous and aggressive, as you may recall, but is immeasurably more knowing than I am. Aren't his feathers gorgeously black and glossy? Perhaps you recall his name?"

"Hmm, yes well, fascinating as usual, sir. Of course, I remember you and your name, birdie, young fellow. You called me a devil last time we met. Hmmm. Well then. How do, Mr. Grip? Well, what a handsome raven you are, for sure." Mischievously wanting to build up to the excitement he felt Boz would share with him, Charles didn't want to charge right in with his main question about the antique book he'd found. Thus, he said, "Listen Boz, I came to ask you a question: Were the majority of my Sutton ancestors scholars? I suppose I should ask father, but you may well know?" He continued to run on about the discoveries he'd made for his genealogical tree about his paternal family research in great excitement, bringing a smile to Dickens' face.

"Indeed, I know they were, yes, Charles, many were academics, editors, and booksellers," said Dickens. You know your father, Thomas, holds a Master of Arts degree, which I learned from him that you, Charles, are studying toward. And, of course, he has his own bookshop here in Manchester specialising in used books, but you know all of that. He's been at it for years now, as long as I've been writing. I'm thirty-six years your senior, Charles, my boy, you know that?"

"Well, yes, sir, of course you are, that is, fifty-five and I'm but nineteen," Charles gabbled, "and you're learned with it to boot, and, yes, indeed, I am still studying literature for my Master of Arts degree, except not, as you'd say, in an official way, not at the university, that is. Just by my own reading. Now, Boz, by your leave, I have something most important to show you, which I hope you can help me date." Watching Dickens' face with anticipation and glee, he proudly handed over the ancient book he'd found. Charles then sat down in a chair and took Grip from Dickens, placed the raven on his own wrist, and gently chatted to him. After a while, Dickens looked up from the ancient tome and spoke in awe.

"My goodness gracious me, Charles, this could be from the 13th century, s'truth[3]!" Flipping through the pages, Dickens said, "I believe this book is what we'd call a monasticon, Charles. Well, it looks as if it's a monasticon, a book describing the history of monasteries in a certain area, around York, from what I'm seeing, just looking at it casually. Wait a minute, as I'm going through this, however quickly, I can see it's not only about abbeys, priories, etc. around York, but looks like it's also mentioning notable families, important people, and the like, and some of their culture, their times—well, that makes it rather different from the norm, doesn't it?"

"Exactly what I thought, sir. Yes, good, that's the answer I was looking for. I hadn't yet picked up about the leading families in the area, though. Now, I could tell it was old but didn't know what to call it. What a treasure I've found, and just sitting on a bookshelf minding its own

---

[3] s'truth = a contraction of God's truth.

business. Quite astounding, is it not? And, look inside the covers, no library card, so it's not being loaned out. Wonder how it got there?"

"Hmmm, that, my young friend, I'd have no idea about."

As usual, Dickens had let Grip out of his cage. He had been moved from Dickens' wrist to perch on Charles' wrist, but now he fluttered back up to his master's shoulder, then flew to the top of an old wardrobe where he sat preening the underside of one wing. He put his head to one side and looked beadily down upon the two men. Next, he flew up to the top of the chandelier suspended from the room's high ceiling, where he perched for a minute. Watching the two beneath him, Grip chattered to them, throwing in a few delighted squawks and clicks. Croaking with raven delight, he let out a stream of human words, then flew above Charles and let go a stream of another sort.

Before Dickens had commented further on Charles' earlier question, Charles burst out with "Damn and blazes, Boz, the dratted creature just shat on me!"

Grip squawked loudly and flew to the topmost cornice, hung sideways, and glared down at Charles. He was obviously contemplating his next mischievous prank. He then swooshed down from the ledge and settled upon Dickens' wrist. Dickens moved his face close to Grip's, telling him, "You're a wretched, bad bird, Grip. You should apologise to your Charles here, you really should." Grip put his head to one side and glared at his master then let out a gurgling croak, which raised in pitch and intensity and seemed to emanate from the very back of the raven's throat.

As Charles lent forward to take the monasticon back from Dickens, Grip quickly grabbed the book in his strong beak straight out of Dicken's hand and flew to the open window.

"Grip, no!" shouted Dickens at the mischievous bird. Grip ignored his master and flew right out of the window.

"My God," yelled Charles, "he's stolen the monasticon! Oh no, it's going to disappear for sure. Do something, Boz! Stop that dratted bird!"

"Tarnation! Griiiiiiiip, come back here!" shouted Dickens, but the bird was gone.

Charles, really upset, now babbled at Dickens, "Boz! But, buh, buh...how on earth can Grip even carry a book?"

Dickens turned at the window and put his hand on Charles' shoulder, speaking fast as they both moved quickly to the door.

Between huffed breaths, Dickens said, "I'm so sorry, Charles, I really am. In truth, my friend, your book isn't that big or heavy. Ravens can carry up to around one pound five ounces, you know, and I'm certain your book weighs somewhat less, or around that."

They reached the door and rushed outside.

"Aaarrgghhh, such details! You know so much, Boz, but what should we do now?"

"Wait for Grip to fly back to me, of course, and, if we're lucky, with the book in his beak."

Grip, the raven.

Charles Dickens' children with Grip-the-raven.

Both Dickens and Charles, now standing outside, shaded their eyes from the sun as they searched the sky for the escaped raven.

"I still don't understand how Grip can hold the book in his beak, Boz?"

"Well, look, as I said it's a small book, about 6 x 9 inches[4]. They were usually bigger in medieval days but this one happens not to be. Also, its parchment paper is extremely thin, and light, and even with its hardcover I'd say it's around, I imagine, some 350 pages, I don't expect it weighs any more than the one pound five ounces I told you—even though it's quite a fat book. The writing is very small, too; quite cramped, really. Again, as I said, ravens can carry about that weight, but little more."

Charles said, "350 or so of pages, that's what I thought but hadn't yet counted 'em—oh and Grip was holding his beak really wide!"

"That he was, the wretched thief! I love him dearly, but this is too much...ah, there our feathered thief goes..." said Dickens, putting his arm in comfort around Charles' shoulders.

In dismay, they spotted the slow, rhythmic flapping of the raven's wings, the book still in Grip's beak, as he flew over a copse of trees. Just before the raven disappeared, he was a glorious sight to behold. Storm clouds hung ominous in the distance. Grip's black feathers shone gunmetal grey as he passed before the clouds, then picked up an iridescent blue from the sky as he flew lower and lower, then glistened in purple, gold, deep orange, then a glorious shade of deep green as the sun hit his body. He flew even lower, swooshing over a farmer's field of flowers, planted in neat rows ready for the city markets—a glorious, feathered creature was Grip—but a thief, nevertheless, as he vanished into the distance bearing his stolen treasure.

If Dickens and Charles had been able to fly with Grip, they'd have seen beneath them that the bird had spotted a large hay barn with its doors wide open, and feeling peckish from the unexpected exercise, he'd flown inside. Mice often ran around in the hayloft, and Grip enjoyed mice, particularly hunting them. Up he flew. There! He spied a tasty-looking rodent trying to hide from him but peeping out from under a pile of straw at the very top of the barn. Dropping the monasticon, he plunged his beak into the straw, grabbed the squeaking mouse and flew off with his prize. He next flew all the way back to his cage where he liked to eat his meals next to a cup of water obligingly left there by his master. He flew into the open window and settled down to scarf his mouse inside

---

[4] 6 x 9 inches = 15.24 x 22.86 cm.

his cage. By the time that happened, Dickens had already left to give a lecture so had no idea the wretched bird had returned home.

Meanwhile, poor Charles Sutton had gone to the Manchester police station to report the theft and to make the acquaintance of the police constable behind the desk bearing 'PC 39' on his uniform collar.

"'Ow do you do, sir; a pleasure to meet you. Vanished, you say? A valuable book? Oh my, no, this is not good," said Richard Marsden, the police constable. "I 'eard you'd found an antique book. I was chatting with your library's cleaning lady t'other day. She said—believe it or not—it was already all over the library with 'em all quite gobsmacked. Bad news travels fast, don't it? Now, you can't tell me the treasured book really 'as vanished. And took by a bird, eh? A big bird, you say? Hmmmm, very strange, sir, very strange indeed. Not sure as 'ow I'd be able to find where a bird had dropped it, but you never know, now do you, sir?" Sighing, he pulled out his Missing Items List and wrote down all the details.

That evening, on the other side of the same copse, the Squire's son from the village of Upper Wormton-near-Oldham lay stretched out on his back with his knees over a bale of hay in his father's hayloft. A piece of straw stuck out of his mouth, his silk cravat was askew, and his frockcoat was covered in bits of hay and straw. Next to him lay a young girl, a milkmaid who worked at Wormburrow Farm, which his father owned. The young girl's head rested upon her arm as she gazed adoringly into her lover's face. They'd been cuddling together as the sun set outside the barn. The young lord of his father's manor now turned to the milkmaid.

"I must away now, Clara, my love, and you must get back to your father's cottage."

"Kiss me again, my lord, for 'tis still early and the cows are milked, and I do love you so, and...ouch! What's that I'm now lying on? 'Twasn't there before. I must-a rolled onto it some'ow. Ouch, ouch, OUCH!"

Clara twisted away from her young swain to find the source. James stared at her heaving bosom beneath her frilly top pulled low down her shoulders exposing the top of her full breasts. He swiftly pulled her into his arms.

"JAMES! NO! You said we have to go, but help, there's definitely some-at in the straw underneath me and it's 'urting me. It's sticking into me! How come I didn't feel the darned thing before? Pull it out, James, will you?"

James sighed and felt beneath the voluptuous lass's body.

"Clara, it's a book, it's only some old book. Someone must have been lying up here reading it. Wonder who that would have been? You didn't feel it because you were so lost in our kisses! Well, anyway, just ignore it, my dear." He took out his fob watch, noted the time, and added, "Well, no more fun and games for us just now. Look at the time. Late afternoon already. The mood is broken, anyway, m'dear, so I'll needs be off. Besides, in a while I'm to go to a lecture by a famous writer up from London to discuss a couple of his books. A lecture called '*Bleak House or No Thoroughfare? Your Choice*', by Charles Dickens. Sounds a bit dark, don't it? The flyer said he wants our opinion on whether to serialise Bleak House again in the newspapers or do the other book—a public opinion poll or something. He serialised *Bleak House* in the papers back in '52-53—quite a while ago. People loved it so much then, Clara, he's thinking of bringing it back, or do t'other book— and it all helps sell papers, don't you know? Clever of the editors, to my mind. People grab the next issue of the paper just to read some more of the story. But m'dear, you won't have heard of it, or him, but never you mind, my sweet. So it's a fond farewell I proffer you, dearest girl." James dropped the book into his frockcoat's pocket, climbed down the hay loft's ladder, cleaned himself up, put on his top hat, climbed onto his horse, and rode off to the lecture hall.

As James cantered off to Dickens' lecture, he thought how pretty the old book in his pocket was. He fished it out once seated on his horse and flipped through the pages. He admired its illuminated first chapter letters sparkling in the last rays of the day's sun. It was most definitely a handsome item and might even have some value. He'd show it to the famous author at the lecture and see what he thought.

⁓ ᘰ ᘰ⁓

Back in his office the next morning, Charles paced back and forth, pulling at his thick hair, wondering what on earth to do. Not only the raven had vanished but also his most treasured book. Oh, this was insufferable, indeed it was. As they'd both watched the raven start to disappear over the copse of trees the day before, Dickens had assured him Grip would return, that occasionally he 'liked to go for a flutter' as Dickens had said, but he always eventually returned. Dickens had then apologised yet again to Charles, saying, "I'm so sorry, so very sorry that he's taken your book. He's never done anything like that before. He called you a devil, but he's most assuredly the devil in this case!"

What if the vanished book was truly lost? Charles stopped pacing and decided to distract himself by conducting more research. Especially on monasteries. He started perusing the books in the library stacks and felt fortunate to be working there. He came upon a reference to English monasteries and their alleged wealth in the early 16th century. King Henry VIII, who reigned from 1509-1547, had inherited vast wealth himself upon ascending the throne but he'd squandered most of it. The King knew that monasteries in England tended to be rich and he wanted that money. Henry and his henchmen hatched a plan. Thomas Cromwell was the king's chief minister, a lawyer, and a statesman, so people believed what he said. He spread the lie that monasteries were sending vast amounts of money to the Vatican. People believed him.

In 1534 Henry VIII needed to break with the Roman Catholic Church because the pope wouldn't annul his marriage to Catherine of Aragon and Henry wanted to remarry to get a male heir. He had Parliament declare him the supreme head of the Church of England—and it was that event that started the English Reformation.

In 1536, the twenty-seventh year of Henry VIII's reign, there were more than 850 monasteries in England and Wales. Four years later there were none because Henry had dissolved all the monasteries, confiscated their lands and taken all their money. This was the lucrative part of his Reformation of the Church and his break from Rome and Roman Catholicism. He then sold off the monasteries' land and buildings to families who sympathised with his decision to switch from Roman Catholicism to the Anglican Church. And he kept plenty of money for himself. The King had swiftly dismantled the monasteries and nunneries at the fast rate of fifty a month. All the monks, friars and nuns were pensioned off or just given some money to get rid of them.

Charles pulled on his moustache and sighed, muttering out loud to the walls, as was his wont, "Well, look at that! By flouting the supremacy of the Roman Catholic Pope, Henry VIII himself took on the role of Head of the Church of England, a far-reaching move that survives to this day, in that the current monarch of England still holds that title. His action caused bitter rivalry between Catholics and Protestants, still going on today."

Charles sighed. "Monasteries, so much about them in books. I'll just have to do more research. Damn and blazes! If only I had the monasticon."

Charles couldn't concentrate anymore, so decided to stop in on Dickens, who was still in Manchester, to see if the book had shown up yet. He went over to Dickens' lodgings and knocked on the door. It flew open and there stood Charles Dickens with Grip sitting calmly upon his wrist. Surprised, Charles' chin dropped a little as he asked, "Grip? So he's back! And my monasticon, did he bring it back?"

"No, I regret to tell you he did not. Darned bird must have dropped it somewhere and we have no way of discovering where. He came back with a mouse. Must have flown back in through the window I'd left open. I saw the remains of his meal in his cage. You'll see, the book will turn up. Someone will find it. Ye gads, I certainly hope so, Charles. I'm so sorry about all this, dear boy, I really am."

"That's terrible news, sir, what am I to do?"

"Later today I'm giving a second talk on my *Bleak House* and *No Thoroughfare* stories and will then have to get on back down to London. I really don't know what to tell you, Charles. This is a disaster for you, I'm well aware. Wretched bird, oh he's a bad, bad creature."

Charles said a polite farewell to Dickens and marched disconsolately back to his office, kicking at loose cobblestones as he went.

Charles Dickens regaled the crowd at his second lecture with talk again about perhaps serialising his *Bleak House* book for a second run. It had been published in 1852 and serialised into twenty monthly instalments throughout the following year. He wanted to gauge the public's interest so getting another night's poll of the public would be of benefit to him and his publishers and editors. People had loved it at the time, but maybe he'd do better serialising his latest book instead? He once again informed the audience that he'd just published his *No Thoroughfare* book but wasn't sure the public would enjoy it as much as his *Bleak House*. *No Thoroughfare* was a novel and stage play he'd produced with Wilkie Collins, about two foundlings at a hospital given the same name, and the dire consequences with the mix-up that followed. He wanted to ascertain which way to go before convening with his publishing house over the matter and get it settled before leaving for his second American reading tour at Boston's Tremont Temple. Last night's poll lent toward serialising *Bleak House*, so he'd see what this next group of people attending his lecture thought.

Each instalment of *Bleak House* had several chapters and the whole of *Bleak House* was 1,088 pages long. It had wonderfully detailed illustrations drawn by Hablot Knight Browne, known to his friends simply as Phiz. Dickens loved pseudonyms and nicknames, which he used to profusion throughout his books. In his lecture, Dickens spoke about the importance and danger of passion, both in the world of English aristocracy and in the ghastly slums of East London while discussing *Bleak House*. James of Wormburrow Farm had been fascinated by the lecture last night and returned the second evening—particularly because he'd found the old book still in his pocket when undressing at home after getting back from the previous evening's lecture. Lying in bed he'd taken Dickens' words to heart, thinking about the way he was toying with the affections of his father's milkmaid at the farm, his poor little Clara. He recalled the book that had pressed into her ribs when he'd rolled over in the hay to take her in his arms and she'd cuddled closer to him, and how he'd meant to ask Mr. Dickens about it.

At the second lecture, James said to his neighbour, "I brought this old book along last night to show Mr. Dickens and plumb forgot." The neighbour glanced at it and made a comment on its beauty. After the lecture, James awaited his turn to speak to the famous author from London. Pulling the old book from his frockcoat pocket, he said, "Mr. Dickens, sir, my girl and I found this old book in my father's hay loft at Wormburrow Farm t'other night. He runs shorthorns on the place and stores much hay and straw for their feed each winter when the snow is upon the ground and the cattle cannot feed in the fields. I meant to show you the book after last night's lecture but forgot, sir. May I show you the book now, sir? I am sure you know a lot about books in general. It is curious, an antique, is it not?"

"My dear fellow," Dickens cried, "This is the very book that was taken by my pet raven, Grip, only recently. I am absolutely delighted to now discover the book and would be grateful for you to release it to me. I will, in turn, ensure it gets back to its rightful owner, Mr. Charles Sutton, our librarian in Manchester. This book is a monasticon, a tome about many of the monasteries in the environs of York. I can't tell you how relieved, how grateful, Mr. Sutton is going to be. From the bottom of my heart, I thank you."

"You're most welcome, I'm sure, sir."

"Here," said Dickens, "please accept this humble gratuity for your efforts", as he pressed a coin into James' hand.

"My goodness me, sir, you are too kind, but I must demur. Pray take the coin back. It wouldn't do for me to accept the gratuity, but I much appreciate the offer."

Chapter 7
Memoir

From Great Grandpa's notes I read that the monasticon had gone missing and then been found. Lucky Charles! Now, if only my hunt for the monasticon myself in these modern times could be so successful. It certainly would help me write up his story. Where should I start looking for it? I'd have to organise all these bits and pieces of memos, notes, scribbled jottings that my grandfather had written to create a paper-trail of sorts. The prize at the end would be if I found the monasticon itself. How tremendously exciting that would be for me!

I stopped looking through Great Grandpa's papers in my sweet little Shoalhaven Heads home office. Instead, I gazed out of the window at the Australian scenery with the Pacific Ocean off in the distance. The bush was grey, green, and black and extended all the way down to Seven Mile Beach here in New South Wales. How I loved this view. Occasionally, I'd hear the rhythmic pounding of chocolate-coloured wallabies crashing through the bush toward the beach. You could even see them thumping along the sand itself—it you were lucky. I mused on Great Grandpa's notes about finding the ancient book in the library in Manchester where he worked.

A lightbulb suddenly went off in my head—yes, of course, the library in Manchester itself! That's where I should look to see if the monasticon had been returned there. If indeed, someone had found the monasticon, and if they had come across it somewhere in the Manchester area, wouldn't it occur to them to turn it into the place it had been loaned out from? But a note he'd left said it wasn't being loaned out. That was odd, to be in a library and not being loaned out. After all, I imagined, surely it should have had some sort of library card or paper attached in the front or back of it, with the check-out date and the date stamped on it showing when it was returned, wouldn't it? Loan periods were typically three to four weeks. I thought how, if the paper were glued in, that would almost ruin such an antique, but that's what they do in libraries, and have done for years, haven't they?

I remembered checking out library books myself as a child. You'd take a paper card out of what the library called a 'lending pocket' and write your name on it in pen. Then the librarian would date-stamp the card and file it in a wooden bookcase behind his or her desk. Then came a stamp on a form in the back of the book itself showing the due date for it to be returned to the library. Then I wondered if instead of using physical cards and stamp-machines in the book nowadays, maybe it was all done somehow by computer? You probably just took your book to a machine and checked it out using your plastic library card. Regardless, with what I thought of as my 'brilliant' idea, I looked up the email address for the Central Library in Manchester. I knew from Great Grandpa's notes that the library had been moved several times into different buildings. Almost with glee, and sure I was onto a hot trail to find the vanished monasticon, I sent off my email, and sat back, feeling sure I'd soon receive a positive answer. If I had the actual monasticon myself, for sure it would make it much easier for me to write up Great Grandpa's story from all the notes he'd left, that were now either in my container box or spread all over my desk in various piles that needed sorting.

I decided to start sorting again and see if I could continue to make a story out of his bits and bobs.

Chapter 8
1867

Charles stood still in his office and removed his *pince-nez*. He'd needed reading glasses early in life, from reading so many books, and often in half-light or even by candlelight. Holding them high in the air, his head now to one side, he exclaimed to the ceiling, "But of course! My ancient book, with its gorgeous historiated initials, wasn't meant to be read just by any old friar or monk. No, this was a very special manuscript, obviously. I wonder whether the abbot was commissioned to do it for someone in particular. For whom? I wonder..."

He'd already shown it to Dickens and, alas, that's when the book had vanished. "That wretched raven gripping the book in his beak and flying off...maybe that's the reason Boz calls him Grip, ha!" said Charles aloud. "I'd like the opinion of somebody else, too, to confirm it is 13th century and that it is, indeed, a monasticon. I'm sure Boz is right, but...it's always good to have a second opinion—that's what father always says, anyhow."

It came to him that Lord John Morley was a firm supporter of the library. Over the years, he'd also become a good family friend to the point where they were on first names basis. In 1865 the viscount had joined the Libraries Committee and was particularly supportive of all that young Charles Sutton was starting to do to enhance the Manchester library. Not only was the viscount a supporter of the library but was also a writer himself. He devoted much of his time to literature and his literary, ethical and philosophical written criticisms were numerous and valuable. His journalistic work was broad and exhaustive. Plus, he had been nominated for a Nobel Prize in Literature eleven times.

If he ever got the monasticon back, Charles thought he'd be sure to show it to Lord Morley, to get another valuable opinion on its worth and literary value to the library, and particularly on its age. Dickens reckoned it was from the 13th century, and if the viscount agreed, then Charles would be able to understand what was being described in the book a lot easier, surrounded as he was by so many other books in the library, which he could research about that era in England.

Charles wanted to know more about the illuminated initials at the beginning of each of the chapters or sections in the monasticon. When he'd first found the book, he'd flipped carefully through the treasure in his hands and told himself aloud, "What a glorious book! I'm so lucky to have stumbled on such a priceless treasure! I keep wondering how it came to be in my library? And just look at these gorgeous first initials of words in some places, they're so, so beautiful!" One of these medieval initials showed two men with haloes, one showing another gloriously robed man a book. Another was of the Virgin Mary holding Baby Jesus. Another of a man hunting a deer, and yet another of a woman playing a lute.

Always interested in why certain things were as they were, Charles had left his office and marched back to the bookshelves, fixated on researching why the first letter of each chapter and some sections of the book were illuminated in gold or silver. He'd seen this style in old family bibles. Charles reckoned now was the time to delve into this, so off he went to the area in his library marked General History. To his chagrin, he'd forgotten to ask Dickens about that. He'd ask him later, but for now, he could look it up himself. As his mother used to tell him, 'Curiosity got the cat, but satisfaction brought him back'!

His fingers sped along the rows of books in the History Encyclopaedias section of the stacks until he came to a fat tome on the bookshelf that related to the first printing presses and the creation of books by hand well before the days of William Caxton in the mid-15th century. Before Caxton set up his printing press in Westminster, Charles knew, of course, that it was scribes who copied out the contents of books by hand over past centuries. Charles needed to concentrate and enjoyed having solitude while doing his research.

He learned that the enlarged letter at the beginning of a paragraph or chapter often contained a picture. It could have a decorative animal or a human figure within the scene, or just have the letter painted in gold or silver. This type of letter was called an historiated initial. "Doubtless because of the history seen within the letter," Charles said under his breath.

This practice of a decorative initial letter was first seen in the 8th century. Charles read that the first example, referred to as insular art, was in the Saint Petersburg Bede, a manuscript dated from 731-746. It seemed the size of the initial letter revealed its importance. "Well, it would, wouldn't it?" Charles muttered aloud. "What the scene depicted would also show the manuscript was considered important." As Charles stood by the bookshelves, a library assistant much younger than he, wheeled his book-trolley toward him.

"Need any help, sir?"

Charles peered at the youth over his *pince-nez*. "No, everything's in order, not to worry, my boy. Good day to you." Charles had no idea of the young fellow's name, but he could see he was an assistant, thus an employee, and Charles was always polite to his staff.

"I'd better get that monasticon back", said Charles aloud, "so I can show it to dear friend John Morley. He'll be as excited as me and Dickens, I fully expect!"

Chapter 9
Memoir

In my 'real' world, weeks had passed, and I still had no word about the vanished monasticon from the Manchester Library. I was beginning to despair of ever finding it. It would be a major loss for the book I was now starting to write. I was talking to one of my oldest friends in San Francisco over FaceTime one day. She said she was excited to be flying to England to do some research on her latest novel. Serendipitously, she happened to be going to Manchester! Of course, I leapt on the idea to have her chase up my enquiry when she was in the library doing her own research. She was more than happy to oblige, having by now heard me going on about my great grandfather's obsession when we chatted on FaceTime. I told her how I was reading the genealogical tree I'd inherited, dating back to the early 13th century, and that I was now definitely engrossed in finding the monasticon. I caught her up on my hunt for the vanished book, that I was also going through a myriad of paperwork, wills, memoranda—all the work Charles Sutton had done in his research for his family tree, which I had inherited. She said she was now more than excited about her upcoming trip and would let me know as soon as she'd found anything out.

Chapter 10
1867

After his midday meal on the third day after Grip had stolen the monasticon, Charles Sutton received a knock on his door. Charles Dickens stood there and, miracle of miracles, he was holding the missing book in his hand.

Dickens quickly entered the office and took a chair. Spreading his black frock coat carefully on either side of the chair's seat, he smiled at Charles. "Charles, I'm so sorry I couldn't get back to you sooner. I've had two lectures to give then had people to see, and some documents to sign. But here I am, and here's your precious monasticon! I feel very cross with myself that I didn't even send word to you when the book was given to me, but in my justification, it was rather too late to be sending someone over to you or showing up on your doorstep myself. I humbly, most humbly apologise." He pressed the old book into Charles' open hands.

"Now, here's what happened. You know Grip flew off with it." Grinning with delight, Dickens began to tell Charles the story. "It seems Grip flew off over that dark copse of trees we saw to a local manor's hay loft where he must have spotted a mouse, dropped the book, grabbed the mouse and flew back to his cage with the mouse in his beak instead of the book. I told you he'd eventually come back to me. As I told you when you stopped by to see if the book had come back, I know Grip had returned because I saw the remains of the poor little mousey on the floor of his cage."

"The squire's son was apparently cavorting in the hay loft with his father's milkmaid, and she'd felt the edge of the book pressing into her back, or so he intimated to me. Serendipitously, the young lover much enjoys my books and attended my lecture. Trouble is, he apparently forgot to show me the book after the first lecture, so he came back the following evening. Good thing he enjoys my lectures, isn't it! Following the question-and-answer period, said young man handed me the book, thinking it would be of interest to me. Quite a coincidence that he would attend my lectures, wouldn't you say? That's how I found out what had happened to the book. Thus, I'm now absolutely delighted to return it to your safe keeping—I trust!" he added, pulling on his moustache.

Charles, with great relief, informed some of his library staff that his treasured book had been safely returned to him. Now he had the monasticon back, and as he had decided he'd do earlier, he would invite old family friend Lord Morley to give him a second opinion on its age, worth and literary value to the library. This Charles did in short order, sending word asking Lord Morley whether he could stop by his rooms at the viscount's convenience.

The viscount sent Charles back a message, "Most certainly I would. Perhaps you'd care to come by to Blackburn this afternoon?"

Viscount John Morley of Blackburn lived and worked just north of Manchester. Charles took time off from his library work that very afternoon and took himself up to Blackburn. Arriving at Lord Morley's rooms, Charles burst out with, "John, I've found an incredible, ancient book in the library. I must show you!" Charles provided some brief information and the member of parliament said, "Sounds and looks as if it's a monasticon, a book describing the history of monasteries in a certain area, around York, from what I'm seeing and what you're telling me, Charles".

"Yes, I think you could be correct, John. Isn't it simply amazing? That's what Charles Dickens thought, too."

Carefully turning the monasticon over in his hands that Charles Sutton handed to him, Lord Morley examined it closely and riffled through its pages, even held it up to his nose, then said, "Books are wonderful things; you never know what you'll discover. They even smell knowledgeable, don't you think? This monasticon you've been reading with its history of the ancient monasteries, abbeys and their surrounds, and so kindly let me hold, when was it written?"

"I can't tell, John, but look, the front page says in the year of our Lord, then a small part is torn right off the ancient book. See? It's so frustrating, John! I've been trying to find that very detail out for so long!"

"Annoying, certainly. Charles, sit down for a bit, would you? I want to quickly read through the beginning and some of the ending of this book."

"I would imagine it was written sometime in the late 13th century, Charles, from what I'm seeing here. Do you happen to know whether William Dugdale's monasticon referred to your scribe's monasticon?"

"Is that the *Monasticon anglicanum*, John? If so, no, I've not had time to go through all the volumes of that book yet, but I do plan to."

"Well, yes, it does have several volumes. Read everything you can, Charles, my young friend, and one day you may find delight in writing, just as I do, and of course, as does our mutual friend Charles Dickens."

Chapter 11
Memoir

I pushed some documents aside on my desk and saw a note in Great Grandpa's spidery script, 'Boz died 9th June 1870'. Dickens was born in 1812. Oh, my God, that meant he was only 58 when he died. He'd noted the date of Charles Dickens' death beside those two dreadfully emotive words. Goodness me, I thought, that must have been awful, not only to the literary world, but also obviously to Great Grandpa, to Thomas Sutton, Charles' own father, to Lord Morley, and to all those who knew Boz. Charles and Thomas had both become so close to Boz. Stopping my thinking about how to find the monasticon for my own use, I looked for any jottings I could find that Charles had written about what had happened to Dickens; what caused his untimely death. It was good to be distracted from the task I'd set myself to find the monasticon. I came across some scrawled words Great Grandpa had obviously written while distressed. He wrote about the woeful day in 1870 when the Sutton family was informed that Charles Dickens had passed. I imagined that even Grip-the-raven would have been quite distraught. It brought a lump to my throat, so I carefully placed the note aside, thinking I'd insert it at a later date into the book I was writing of Great Grandpa's memories. It shook me that Dickens' death had upset me this way—141 years after the so-sad day

---

I moved all the notes on my desk around in a rather desultorily way, still feeling upset about Dickens' death all those years ago. I read in one of Great Grandpa's notes more about the first vanishing of the monasticon. It seemed that Dickens had been given the monasticon by the son of a local farmer courting a young milkmaid and had returned it to Charles Sutton. Lucky Great Grandpa—I wanted to get it back, too.

A new idea came to me about finding the monasticon. What if I contacted the police station where PC 39 had worked? I knew it was in Manchester. Was I mad? Surely, after all these years, the Missing Items List would have been long gone. But maybe not? The police tended to keep things in boxes for unsolved cold cases.

I wished I'd asked my friend, the author who'd gone to Manchester to do some research on her own novel. I'd heard that she was now back in the States. Why hadn't I thought to ask her not only to enquire whether the monasticon had been returned to the library, but to go into the police station for me, to ask them to search through their cold case storage boxes from long ago? I could have kicked myself that I'd not thought to ask her to do that, too. Maybe I should email her? Or just contact the police station myself?

I pondered on whether to chase it up that way. Yes, I decided, I'd telephone the police station in Manchester and explain what I was looking for. After placing the call and waiting just a short time for the phone to be picked up, a kind young policewoman spent some time writing down what I wanted and said she'd get back to me. She asked if she could reverse the charges when she rang me back. Of course, I agreed; she was going to have to ring me in Australia all the way from England. I didn't mind the expense for my hunt for the monasticon because it would be so useful to have beside me, to look at while I wrote Great Grandpa's story.

For the next ten days, I tried to keep my hopes in check, not get too excited, but, of course, I thought the monasticon could just have been turned in to the police station at some time after Charles Sutton had died. He'd died in 1920. I'd arrived in Australia in late 2011. Almost a century had passed; that was a lot of time to keep things in storage at a police station. Perhaps PC 39 himself had died by 1920. Apparently, from the notes I'd been reading, he was the policeman that Great Grandpa talked to after the loss of the monasticon. PC meant police constable. I remembered that from my youth living in England. If someone had turned it in well after both the constable and the librarian had died, then probably there were no instructions left as to what they ought to do. Perhaps another policeman had just chucked the monasticon into a cold case box and left it to moulder in the police station's basement storage area. Or, for all I knew, the police station itself had changed location or no longer even existed. Who knew? But at least I'd given it a try.

Two weeks to the day after my enquiry, I received a long-distance phone-call on my landline from the Manchester Police Station. The line crackled and the policewoman's voice went in and out, but I got the gist of what she was saying. To her amazement, down in the basement of the police station, she had found the Missing Items List from all those years ago, lying in a cold case box with some other items from the same period, in a dusty corner of the storeroom, just as I'd envisaged. She reckoned, from what I'd told her, that it was possibly placed there originally, by PC 39, a/k/a Chief Constable Richard Marsden at the time of his own death—also long ago. No sign of any old book, though, no sign at all. My heart sank.

A dead-end to my search. Should I give it up? After all, I did have plenty of notes made by Great Grandpa to help me write up his story about the library, his ancestors and descendants, but I had this niggling feeling that wouldn't leave me. There had to be more information in the monasticon about my ancestors. At work, my employer had given me the nickname of bulldog because I wouldn't let go of any task until it was done, done properly, and crossed off my list.

That settled it. I would continue my search. I looked at the papers now sitting in neat piles on the far side of my desk. I saw more scribbles sometimes on torn pieces of notepaper where Great Grandpa's had mentioned a burgeoning romance at the library between two of his employees. Who were they? I wanted to find that out! Tickled by those brief memos he'd made to himself I stopped thinking for now about how to get the actual book back. Instead, I'd work on putting together more of Great Grandpa's story.

I wondered who helped my great grandfather in his work at the library. I found a note about someone he called W.R.

Chapter 12
1870

As the years flowed on Charles threw himself into the creation of a printed catalogue of every book that the library possessed. He was assisted then, and throughout nearly all his working life there, by his deputy librarian, William Robert Credland. Charles called this major catalogue his *Index of Names and Subjects*. He issued the first version in 1879 and would go on to publish an updated edition in 1881, which comprised 1,700 pages. 'W.R.' was his righthand man in the project. W.R. always seemed older than his actual years and people respected him for his seniority in the library, even though quite a young man when he started working for Charles at the age of twenty. Charles was known to have a terse style of writing, but no fluency, thus his literary work was confined entirely to compilation and editing[5]. This was the same in his speaking. He was no orator and avoided speaking to audiences. Later in life he would become a pleasing speaker, best on social or commemorative occasions.

W.R. Credland was born in 1850, two years after Charles Sutton and was to die in 1916, four years before Charles. He worked for Charles all his working life and loved every minute of it. It's no wonder, in that Charles had a charming personality. Charles was the essence of courtesy and usefulness. No-one ever appealed to him in vain. He had an even temper and treated all his staff as valued colleagues. He didn't like reproving any one of them, but if he felt reproval was needed, he didn't

---

[5] Perhaps it was just his lack of fluency in writing that explains why my great grandfather never wrote a story of his ancestors himself; instead, he just jotted down notes on scraps of paper here and there. Or, lack of time in his very busy life.

fail, and his words were never forgotten by the recipient. His memory was phenomenal, not only in bookish matters, but even in details of buildings, for example, that he'd only seen once or twice. His photographic memory was such that he had the ability to remember, and even reproduced, as needed, whole sections of books he'd read.

Credland was also a writer, and had a number of pamphlets and publications under his name[6]. Credland loved writing. He'd dip his pen into his inkwell, put his tongue to one side of his mouth, and create. He called his writing 'creating' because he much enjoyed forming his letters and had an innate ability to make them beautiful. His lines were filled with curves, serifs and flourishes, and occasional curlicues and squiggles better than many an artist could produce in a painting.

He had a job 'in Heaven' as he liked to tell his friends. Not only was his boss good and fair to him, including in remuneration, but Charles seemed to like W.R. personally. Indeed, after work some days they would repair together to The Cat's Whiskers public house for a pint or two of ale before going back to their respective homes. That is, W.R. would often drink two ales, but Charles, abstemious about both food and drink throughout his life, stuck to one.

Sometimes they'd run into other workers from the library. Quite some time later, it was to be a young woman who was preparing to become a nun and a young, rather smarmy chap called Duckworth, whom W.R. avoided whenever he saw him enter the pub.

---

[6] One of W.R. Credland's publications: *Manchester Public Libraries Handbook, Historical and Descriptive*.

Chapter 13
Memoir

Aha! Great Grandpa's mention of two lovers working for him at the library. But a nun? Honestly? Therein must lie a tale! I was really curious about this and moved the piles of my great grandfather's notes around on my desk but didn't find anything more. All it meant was that I'd need patience. There was bound to be more information that would eventually fall out of the piles to satisfy my curiosity. Meanwhile, who else worked closely with him, I wondered?

Chapter 14
1870

Another gentleman of great assistance to Charles Sutton in all matters at the library was Percival Stanley Bastowe. He joined the library as Mr. Sutton's private secretary shortly after moving up to Manchester from London with his family when still in his early teens. Charles had a couple of temporary secretaries work for him prior to Percy's arrival, but once this fellow had come on board, he was most certainly the best.

Percival had a dainty manner and was a shy sixteen-year-old but already well-trained by a year in secretarial school before his library job. He was a short fellow with rather too long blond hair and a few hairs sprouting on his chin of what would eventually become a neatly pointed blond beard. The hairs of his budding moustache were also cut neatly, and you could almost see that when it had fully grown in, it would not quite, but almost, join up with the beard on either side of his mouth. When he spoke, he already had a habit of tugging on his thin moustache on the right side (he was right-handed) in such a way that eventually the right side of his moustache hung lower than it did on the left. In fact, after a decade or so, the right side of his moustache did completely merge with his beard on that side. This gave the little man a lop-sided appearance and would evoke fascinated stares.

Percival was an interesting individual. He talked with a stutter and his sentences went up at the end in a questioning way, as if seeking approval for what he was saying in a manner employed by certain females. He walked mincingly, almost on tiptoe, and once told Mr. Sutton he walked that way because his calf muscles were too tight. When he spoke, he'd give a little chuckle at the end of his speech, thus it became a questioning chuckle. That fascinated all who listened to the gentleman converse.

Percival loved bright colours in his outfits. His frockcoat could almost make you blink or reach for your darkened glasses. Mr. Sutton had told him that an English optician called James Ayscough had created eyeglasses with tinted lenses in the 18th century because he believed the tint could improve vision. Charles said that in 1752, after Dr. Ayscough's lenses, prescription sunglasses were created with blue or green lenses to fix colour-blindness or stereopsis, a condition that affects depth perception.

Even though sunglasses were thought to have been invented in 12th century China, Mr. Sutton told Percy that they were first created around 37 AD. Those weren't actual sunglasses but were emeralds held up to the eyes. Emperor Nero was one of the few people who could afford such a luxury, yet wore them for their functionality, not as a fashion statement. The sunglasses in China were a simple slab of smoked quartz, which was held up against the user's face in a crude frame. It was claimed it could block out the light from the sun.

Percival's frockcoat was striped red and grey, with the grey stripe bearing a glossy sheen. His cravat was a rich silky grey, his tie-pin a sparkling sword-shape, a scimitar from Turkey, he'd chucklingly explain to all who enquired. His shoes had pointed toes and slight heels. It was clear that Mr. Percival Stanley Bastowe felt he was too short in stature.

All in all, Percy, as many in the library called him, was a sight to behold. But, oh yes indeed, he was a very clever, highly intelligent man and a wonderfully helpful and astute assistant to Mr. Sutton. They got along splendidly and worked very well together, those two. It was perhaps a matter of opposites attracting. Charles Sutton was an 'internal' sort of fellow whereas Percival was outspoken, full of *joie de vivre*, and loved to talk. Fortunately, most of what he said was not silly at all. He was smart and had a very jolly disposition and outlook on life.

Percy's desk was in the area right outside Mr. Sutton's office at the library and to the side of Mr. Credland's desk. This way, Percy could vet each person coming to knock on Charles' door or arriving to speak in person to Mr. Credland. People knew Percy as a sort of guardian watchdog they had to get past before reaching one of their bosses.

Almost a decade later, near the end of 1879, Charles was to receive his own telephone in his office as were both W.R. Credland and Percival Bastowe. When someone telephoned Charles or W.R., the library telephone operator knew she had first to connect the call to Percy. If he approved the call, he passed it on to Charles by simply calling out loudly, "Call for you, sir, on the telephone, line one." If the incoming call were for W.R., all Percy had to do was to slightly cover the telephone's speaker with his hand and give a stage whisper to W.R., "Telephone call for you, sir!" There was only one line, but Percy thought it impressed the caller if he overheard the call-outs to his employers.

Charles could hear the call coming through the wall separating him from Percy and W.R. Not only was it loud enough but the top half of the wall separating them was glass, so if he looked up, thinking he heard a shout, he could see Percy waving a limp hand at him and pointing down at the telephone with the other. It all worked quite seamlessly.

Chapter 15
1874

our years passed and by 1874 twenty-six-year-old Charles William Sutton had matured into the decent, always humble, self-respecting, respectful, and thoughtful, man he was to be for the rest of his life. He assisted in his father's bookshop, usually on weekends when he wasn't at the library, and attended social functions here and there, but usually preferred his own company and a quiet life.

Like so many parents of the Victorian—or any— era, Charles' mother and father looked forward to grandchildren. His mother knew that an old Welshman called Joseph Winder Evans and his wife, Catherine Jepson Evans, had a beautiful daughter called Sarah Hannah Winder Evans, born on 14th November 1853 in Chorlton, Manchester. Charles was introduced to Sarah at a family soirée. She was slender with thick plaited dark blond hair curled on top of her head in one of the favoured styles of the day. She was five years his junior. The couple took one look at each other and were smitten.

To their parents' delight, they married shortly after on 14th April 1874. On 11th August 1875, in Barton upon Irwell, Lancashire, when Charles was in his twenty-seventh year, Sarah bore their first son, whom they named Charles Evans Sutton. He was followed by John Francis, known to his intimates as Frank[7]* on 14th August 1877.

In 1877, it had become patently obvious that the old Campfield library building was starting to collapse. Now twenty-nine, and a father for the second time, Charles was put in charge of the hasty removal of the entire library to its new location in the old Town Hall in Manchester.

---

[7] John Francis (Frank) Sutton was my maternal grandfather.

The responsibility of relocating the seventy thousand volumes to the new location would have been daunting to a lesser individual. But for Charles William Sutton, the year 1877 became a cherished milestone in his life.

As it happened, based on the expertise he garnered from this enormously responsible removal job, and compounded by the vast knowledge as a librarian that he'd already accumulated, in 1879 Charles replaced William A. Axon as chief librarian.

Three years passed. Oliver Jepson was born on 29th July 1882 in Barton upon Irwell, in the sub-district of Stretford. The fourth son Sarah gave Charles was Albert Bernard, also born in Barton upon Irwell, on 8th May 1887.

1900s. First Free Reference Library, Manchester. In 1877, when Charles William Sutton was 29, the library was moved from Campfield, Manchester into the old Town Hall in this photo.

Charles William Sutton in 1877 at 29 years of age.
Born 14th April 1848. Died 9th June 1920. Here he's
wearing spectacles rather than *pince-nez*.

Sarah Hannah Winder Evans Sutton,
1853-1889, first wife of Charles
William Sutton.

Chapter 16
Memoir

Reading my Great Grandfather's memos, notes, and jottings on scraps of paper, I was enjoying what he was writing about the people at the library who'd been of much help to him, aside from listing his ancestors on the family tree, stating what they did, whom they'd married, and some of the history of their times. He couldn't have had much time to put his family tree together because cataloguing an entire library of thousands of books must surely have been an enormous task. No wonder he employed quite a staff to help him with the library work. I was finding this quite interesting because I was building a picture of librarian Charles Sutton himself and all the people who surrounded him. I knew what the library building looked like, being familiar with an old photo in colour hanging in my sister's house. Charles had a black and white photograph of his library, which I'd found in the envelope of old photographs amongst my treasures in the box. There were several photos of Charles Sutton himself, which gave me a good idea of his features, plus there were notes telling what he was thinking on different occasions. All of this built me up a picture of my great grandfather.

Every day I checked my email inbox but, to my dismay, there was no news from my friend visiting the library in Manchester as to whether they had the monasticon there. Where, oh where, could it be?

Chapter 17
1879

Charles had noted down what happened to Dickens' wife before Dickens himself had died. There was the scandal of his taking up with a younger woman, then came the divorce from Catherine Dickens. After her marriage to Dickens dissolved, Catherine lived another twenty-one years, until 21st November 1879, thus outliving Dickens by nine years. She was sixty-four years old. She was buried in Highgate Cemetery in London.

Catherine never ceased loving her former husband. They communicated rarely but when Charles did write her a note, he signed it 'Affectionately'. She followed his triumphant reading tours in America and in newspapers at home. Catherine felt some certain relief knowing that her sister, Georgina Hogarth, was living as a platonic friend in Dickens' home in Gad's Hill, taking care of Catherine's children all during the time he was seeing other women after Catherine had moved out—all much younger than Catherine.

Nine years after Dickens died, Catherine Dickens was fighting cancer. In 1879 near the end, she gave all the letters Dickens had written to her to Kate, her daughter, and asked her to give them to the British Museum so that the world would know the famous writer and social critic had once loved her. Catherine was buried in the same grave as her baby daughter Dora, her ninth child, who had died eighteen years earlier in 1861 at only eight months of age.

In her Will Catherine left each of her many children something special and dear to her. The items had little value, for she was not a wealthy widow, but each child knew that their mother had held each one of them in her thoughts as she wrote out her will.

When Dickens died in 1870, he left each of his children copyrights of his books, a far more financially beneficial bequeathment than their mother's. Strangely, he left only three of his ten children most of his £90,000 estate. Conversely, Catherine left most of her not very large estate to her sister but also bequeathed a little something not only to her children but also to all her relatives and principal friends, even her servants.

Charles Sutton's father, Thomas, lived until 1883, outliving Charles Dickens by thirteen years.

∽℃℈℈℈℈℈℈℈℈℈℈∽

Sitting in his chair at work, Charles thought back to twelve years ago, when he'd tapped on Dickens' study door at his rented Manchester apartment, confident the great author wouldn't mind the intrusion. That was later in the frightful day in 1867 when Dickens' bird, Grip-the-raven, had stolen the monasticon. That was the first occasion that the monasticon had vanished. Bile rose in Charles' throat, as he remembered his dismay over the stolen book—all because of a feathered thief. After he'd got the book back from Dickens, he'd been able to visit Lord Morley to have him give him a second opinion on the age of the monasticon and how he'd agreed it was written in the 13th century.

Charles had left a note saying how he'd called out to Percy to get Lord John Morley on the new communication device called a telephone. Percy had been working with Charles since 1870—now Charles saddened, remembering that was the very year Dickens had died. Percy was such a good assistant and knew a lot of extraneous trivia, exactly how to address a viscount, for example. The couple of temporary secretaries Charles had working for him before the arrival of Percy tended not to have a clue in that regard, thus Charles was delighted with Percy's abilities and knowledge.

Telephones had only arrived in Manchester in 1879. Charles still marvelled at modern technology. He recalled how he'd picked up the speaker the day he'd asked Percy to get hold of Lord Morley, held the listening device to his ear, and shouted down the tube. First, he called out his congratulations to Lord Morley—a Liberal Member of Parliament, an Honorary Professor of Ancient Literature at the Royal Academy of Arts, and member of the Historical Manuscripts Commission—for working on his Doctor of Laws degree at the University of St. Andrews[8].

---

[8] Viscount Morley got an honorary Law Degree in 1902.

Next, he'd caught John up on everything that had been happening at the library with the obvious need that the library eventually was going to have to move yet again into larger quarters or have its own building constructed. He told John about whispers starting that a legation was obviously going to have to be formed to go off to the United States to get some ideas on how they were building and running their libraries. A committee would have to make all the arrangements and the Viscount's sound advice would be much appreciated. But, he told the Viscount, that wouldn't be happening for quite a few years yet; all these things took time[9].

"Don't they just," laughed the Viscount. "Everything these days seems to take much longer than expected, even with all this new-fangled technology—telephones, electric lightbulbs...you name it!"

---

[9] As it turned out, the trip to the USA wasn't to eventuate until twenty-nine years later, in 1908.

Chapter 18
Memoir

Four years passed by—it being 1883 in the next note I found amongst all the notes, memos and scribbled jottings in Great Grandpa's spidery writing. I imagined he must have been very busy with all his library work, organising upcoming meetings, and working on his family tree. I was curious about the library having eventually to move again, according to my great grandfather. He'd said it needed to move into new quarters in 1874, which he would organise and accomplish in 1877—moving into the Town Hall. I'd seen the note where he'd told Lord Morley they'd need to move the library again, and that they'd be going to the United States eventually to find out how they organised their libraries. I'd be interested in seeing more of his notes on that, because I knew a lot about the States, having lived there myself from 1970 to 2011. I did find one and put it aside for the moment, in that it said they went to the USA but not until 1908. I laid it on top of the one to do with Dickens' death, which I also planned to get to later.

Staring out my office window at the Australian eucalypts swaying in a breeze, it occurred to me that I still hadn't received word as to whether my friend doing research for her novel at the Manchester Library had found out yet whether the monasticon had ever been turned in there.

Chapter 19
1883

In 1883, Percy had been working at the library for thirteen years. He'd been spending some of his lunch breaks reading travel books in the Foreign and Travel stacks in the Reference Department. He had become mesmerised by America and decided he'd spend all his savings on a fabulous trip to New York City. He'd even offer to pay for his friend Aloysius to go with him.

Quite some years earlier, Percy had moved out of the family home and into a shared basement flat with Al in the Piccadilly area of Manchester. Their building looked onto a park with pretty bedding plants, lawns, a splashing fountain, and a few Victorian statues of naked gods and goddesses with their private parts discreetly covered with marble ivy leaves. Everything was kept neat and tidy in the park. The lawn was manicured and had neat brass signs placed at strategic corners stating, 'Please Keep off the Grass'. The flowerbeds held swathes of purple, pink and white impatiens and red salvias placed in row after row in beds in eye-catching colours. To see the view, the two young men had to go outside and climb up the stone staircase then look over the black iron fencing around their building.

Aloysius Humphrey Knickerbocker was rather proud of the fact that he was considered the black sheep of his old New York family, hence he'd moved to England as soon as he'd left school at fourteen. He'd then had to make his own way in life, his family having cut the purse-strings to the rebellious youth. By the young age of fifteen, he'd already managed to find himself a good job in Manchester and was able to pay half of the cost of the basement flat Percival had rented for them both, thus they'd been rooming together for thirteen years. Al, now twenty-seven in 1883—two years younger than twenty-nine-year-old Percy—

dressed in much the same vein as his flatmate and close friend, but perhaps not at quite the same flamboyant level in dress. In fact, he was but a young shadow of his slightly older friend in character; outgoing and charming. They made a gay twosome as one watched them walking down the street together, both with similar shiny black top-hats and pointed boots with slightly raised heels.

When Percy offered to take Al to America with him, Al was ecstatic, and accepted his offer with alacrity, "My dearest Percy, you are such a brick, such a good friend, I'd love to go with you, absolutely, no question about it! I can pay my own way, as you know." He added drily, "As you can imagine, dear friend, there's no way I'll be looking up any of my, erm[10] moneyed old family while there. They disdain the sort of chap I am, and well I know it. They're such snobs, claiming they can trace their roots back to the 1600s, through the Dutch settlers to New York. I'm sure I've bored you with all of that before, so I won't say more. Regardless, I'll much look forward to seeing my old home town again!"

They both put in for leave from their respective employers and started to plan their trip for their upcoming summer holidays. The day arrived, and they took a streetcar to the Manchester Docks in Salford to set sail for America. The two fellows had a marvellous voyage, travelling in a cabin with two berths, eating well, playing games on deck, and dancing the night away until they steamed into busy New York Harbour.

The friends they'd made on board told the two young men about an exciting circus in New York City run by Phineas Taylor Barnum. As part of its exhibits, the circus reputedly had the largest animal in the world: Jumbo the Elephant. Jumbo was an African elephant taken as a youngster after its mother was killed and her tusks stolen for the black-market ivory trade. Jumbo's mother had been chased and brutally speared and the poor baby elephant must assuredly have witnessed its mother's death.

[10] Erm is Yorkshire-cum-Lancashire dialect for hmm, or um, a sound that people make when they pause in the middle of what they are saying or pause before they speak, often deciding what they'll say next. By this time, Aloysius had cultivated a slight 'oop north' accent, distancing himself further from his American roots

The two men went to the circus specifically to see Jumbo, 'The Giant Elephant' as P.T. Barnum called it. After watching Jumbo give rides to children, they saw his trainer, Matthew Scott, slide off the animal and give him a drink of water. Aloysius, more outgoing even than Percy in some ways, approached Mr. Scott and asked to speak with him. The elephant trainer was quite happy to share a smoke and a chat.

While sucking on his pipe, Mr. Scott said, "If you're wondering about his name, well, Jumbo is Swahili for 'hello'. He arrived in England from Africa as a motherless calf in 1865 where he stayed for eighteen years at the London Zoo. If someone says 'jumbo' to you in one of the fourteen countries where Swahili is spoken—primarily Kenya, Tanzania and Mozambique along the east coast of Africa, and its adjacent islands, it's good form to respond with 'habari yako' meaning 'how are you?'" Mr. Scott went on, "You know, poor Jumbo rages at night, pulling on 'is chain, throwing up 'is trunk, trumpeting and crying, but is quite docile by day."

Percy turned to his friend, whispering under his breath, "Aloysius Humphrey, can you imagine how upset poor Jumbo must be? I reckon it's nightmares after seeing his mother killed, don't you? At least, that's what I think." In response, Al patted Jumbo, fighting tears springing to his eyes, saying, "Oh Percy, that poor, poor animal, I feel so sorry for him."

Seeing their compassion, Matthew Scott went on to tell them, still slightly slurring from the previous night's inebriation, "Earlier this very year, 1884—no, it wasn't, it was 1883, no, I mean to say 1882, that was it, yes, 'twas the year before, 1882—Phineas Taylor Barnum bought Jumbo from his owner at the London Zoo where Jumbo was living, and me living there with the poor beast in his enclosure. I was constantly at his side, see, training him to let me and little children ride him. P.T. paid two thousand quid sterling for the famous giant beast. That's a lot of money, you mind. Same as $10,000 to the Yanks over 'ere, where we both are now."

"Certainly is, sir," said Aloysius, rolling his eyes at Percy. "Imagine, Percy, £2,000!" Both the young men continued patting Jumbo while listening in fascination to Mr. Scott's tale.

Jumbo rubbed his trunk gently against his trainer's face, while Mr. Scott smilingly said to the young men, "See how he loves me? That's partly because me and Jumbo like to pass a lot of the night drinking whisky together. Yes. I spend a lot of me money on whisky for him and me, and ain't that the truth. You know, he'll probably bankrupt me..."

Percy and Al both let out a whistle of amazement.

"What do you mean, why?" asked Percy.

Mr. Scott softly added, "African elephants can live sixty to seventy years. That's a lot of time to drink whisky, innit? But then, whisky calms the great animal while he's going through his night terrors." Then added quietly, "And me, too!"

Chapter 20
1883-1884

On 17th May 1884, P.T. Barnum had arranged a public relations stunt to create excitement and bring crowds to his circus. He had twenty smaller elephants than Jumbo trundle across the Brooklyn Bridge. With them came ten camels, seven dromedaries, and in the rear, his most treasured animal, the enormous Jumbo. The minute the animals all set foot on the bridge it began to sway but did not collapse. The impresario wanted to prove how strong the herculean bridge was, particularly after a terrible accident that had occurred shortly after the bridge was opened on 24th May 1883. People had panicked and stampeded that day on the suspension bridge, which started swaying. *The New York Times* said in an article that when one woman fell down, another screamed, causing the crowd close to her to panic and push their way off the bridge. In only a few minutes, a stampede ensued, with twelve people killed and seven others seriously injured. The swaying bridge incident happened on 24th May 1883, somewhat before Percy and Al were in The Big Apple for their 1883 summer holidays, and a year before P.T.'s public relations stunt on 17th May 1884.

During that summer of 1883, the two young men, Percy and Aloysius, spent a pleasant summer afternoon with Matthew Scott and Jumbo before taking in more tourist sites in one of the greatest cities in the world.

But two years later, when reading the newspaper in the library's staff lounge back in Manchester, Percival came across a sad item. He read that on 15th September 1885, P.T. Barnum's Barnum & Bailey Circus had taken a train to Canada. Jumbo and a very small elephant by the name of

Tom Thumb[11] were about to be loaded into their railway box car on the circus train in Elgin County, when a freight train came thundering along the track toward them. P.T. Barnum claimed that Jumbo stood in the way of the train with the intent of stopping it, thereby saving Tom Thumb and the rest of the circus animals and personnel. Jumbo was killed. An old photograph shows Jumbo lying with his back to the train and Matthew Scott standing against him, caressing the elephant, and looking as if he's bidding him a tender farewell. Jumbo was only twenty-four at the time of his death. Mr. Scott was heartbroken, wept inconsolably and never recovered. P.T. Barnum paid him off to get rid of him. Jumbo's body was eventually stuffed and paraded by the impresario, who never missed an opportunity to refer to his elephant as a major hero.

Years later Jumbo's bones were examined to find out what had really happened. Mr. Scott had always claimed Jumbo was trying to either run away from the approaching freight train or was getting into his railway boxcar when he was struck down. There were no broken bones to be seen on x-rays. The old photograph did show abrasions, though, particularly on his massive rear end. Percival and Aloysius talked that evening, and they both concluded Jumbo probably had died of internal bleeding.

Aside from the train accident, the photograph showed that the teeth in Jumbo's mouth showed damage and rot, which they attributed to sweets the children getting rides gave to the elephant. Percy and Al concluded further that poor Jumbo probably had awful toothaches causing far more pain during the night. They smiled together recalling Mr. Scott's story of how he used to share a glass or two of strong alcohol with Jumbo at night.

"That would have helped him with the toothache pain, don't you think, Al?" said Percy.

"It does for me, when I have any kind of pain in any part of my body," replied Aloysius with a broad grin, reaching over to his dear flatmate and giving him a friendly pat on his knee.

---

[11] P.T. Barnum loved the name 'Tom Thumb'. Tom Thumb is a character of English folklore. Published in 1621, *The History of Tom Thumb* was the first fairy tale printed in English. P.T. Barnum was notorious as a showman. He found a happy, mischievous child of four, who was just over two feet tall and weighed only fifteen pounds—the same size he had been as a seven-month-old baby. P.T. gave the child the name of Tom Thumb and toured him in his circus around the world as a curiosity for people to stare at.

The next day was a work day. Percy knew Charles Sutton was counting on him to help with plans for the creation of reading rooms for youngsters. Wishing Al a warm goodnight, Percy trotted off to bed, thinking about Charles and all his clever ideas for the library.

15th September 1885. Matthew Scott standing in front of dead Jumbo after the freight train accident.

Chapter 21
1885-1892

With Mr. Credland's able assistance plus the help of Percival Bastowe, Charles had opened up juvenile reading rooms in three more of the libraries under his care, fitted out with comfortable little chairs. Then he went on to establish a binding department in the reference library plus a printed catalogue of every book. He was meticulous about ensuring every detail was correct.

The public demanded reading rooms in general so he'd created newspaper reading rooms in 1887 and 1888. By 1894, Charles had created delivery stations at the smaller branches of the library, with a delivery system from those branches delivering books to the larger branches.

As in so many people's lives, tragedy came to Charles Sutton. At the age of only thirty-five, his wife, Sarah, was knocked down in an accident by a runaway horse and cart. At thirty-six years old, on 29th September 1889, and after very great suffering, she died in Barton upon Irwell, leaving their four children in Charles' care.

Often many people mourn for three years and only then do they feel ready for a new life partner, and so it was for Charles. Three years after Sarah's demise, Charles Sutton, now forty-four years old, had the good fortune to meet the kindest of women, one Maria Pocklington. Charles married Maria on 13th February 1892.

Maria was born in 1862 in Sherbourne, Dorset. She was a jolly woman, always smiling, and fourteen years Charles' junior. She was rather pleasantly plump and wore her lustrous light brown hair parted in the middle and plaited in a bun at the back of her head. She needed to keep her hair out of the way now she was helping Charles raise all his four children. She bore Charles another son, the only child of her own.

He was George William Pocklington Sutton[12], born almost a year after her marriage to Charles.

Maria Pocklington Sutton, 1862-1911.

---

[12] My great-uncle.

Chapter 22
1892

The day Charles married Maria Pocklington in 1892 was the day he made a momentous discovery.

"Maria! I just realised that your family is mentioned in my monasticon book!"

Maria sat down heavily onto a chair in their salon. "What on earth do you mean, dearest Charles?"

"Listen, my love; this is quite extraordinary. I've had this book since I found it in the library in 1867 and I've married you today, 13th February 1892—that's twenty-five years. That is, I've had the book except when it vanished, swiped by dear Dicken's raven, Grip. That means all these past twenty-five years, I've not had occasion to think this Walter Pocklington in the book was in any way related to anybody I knew, but now, only now do I put two and two together and realise that he is your ancestor, my dearest wife. And that makes him, through marriage, my ancestor, too!"

"Good heavens, dear husband, you must read everything about him to me; you are much better at reading than am I. Your eyes are stronger than mine, as you already know—albeit I'm fourteen years younger than you. I know you wear your spectacles, or those funny *pince-nez* for reading, and I don't use anything like that, but still and all, you do read much better and faster than me."

"Yes, yes, all true, and don't you fret; I'll enjoy reading it aloud to you. Now listen, to start, dearest, it's your forbear, Walter Bishop, who came over from France in 1202 and married the daughter of a knighted Pocklington and took her family's name. Ah, now I shall research your family line with gusto!"

"Oh, how exciting that will be for both of us," Maria smilingly said. "I wonder why he took his wife's name?"

"Well, back then in 1202, he'd been a bishop and that's how people referred to him, by the sound of it. Walter Bishop. So, I imagine when he married a Pocklington, he just switched names! Taking on the name of a daughter of a knight might have been rather attractive to the fellow!"

Up until that moment, Charles had read so much in the monasticon about the Pocklingtons, but it hadn't had much impact on him, as he'd just told Maria. Why would it? It was just a name. But, even when he first met Maria and learned her surname, he still hadn't put two and two together. He now slapped his hand on his forehead and burst into a low, satisfied, laugh. "Amazing it's taken me a little while to work it all out! What a nincompoop I was! I should have realised Walter was your ancestor when I first met you, but, my darling, I had so much else on my mind about you, that your surname was the last thing I was thinking about."

"Nincompoop?"

"Yes, my dearest Maria, and I so enjoy your fascination with words, just like mine. You can trace its origin back to the mid-1700s. It comes from *non compos mentis*, meaning not of sound mind in Latin. I'll bet you didn't know that!"

"Charles! So my forbears really are in that book you love so much?"

"Indeed they are, and I'll have much to re-read and tell you about. Pocklington's an unusual name; comes from the area they were living in, called Poke."

"Charles," Maria slowly said. "Something's come to mind. My grandmother used to tell me that her grandmother told her that our family came from France originally. She's the one who taught me French words here and there."

"Well, well, how about that, then!" smiled Charles to his new soulmate.

Having taken a few days off work for his honeymoon, Charles settled into the loveseat in their home the following day with Maria right next to him. He held the book that had become his constant companion in recent days: *The Yorkshire Archaeological and Topographical Journal, Volume Nine*. Charles kept it tucked into his pocket for easy accessibility whenever he needed to clarify obtuse references that he often stumbled upon in the monasticon. He kept having to read a sentence repeatedly because his darling new wife insisted on cuddling and kissing him, causing total distraction to the lucky man.

Charles now turned back to the monasticon and read aloud to Maria that her forbear, John de Pocklyngton, was principal of Balliol College at Oxford 1332, then became Master of University College at Oxford in 1362. Aware of Oxford University's historic roots since its founding in 1096, up to now Charles had not known about Maria's scholarly forbears. He wondered where his own Sutton family's love of books and academia came from. He wished he could talk to Boz about all of this, but the dear man had died in 1870, twenty-two years earlier. Charles smiled, recalling his father's and his pet name of Boz for Dickens. He also remembered that he had managed to pick Dickens' brains a little about his own paternal Sutton side of his family. Dickens had remembered quite a lot about his old friend Thomas Sutton's family and had been happy to impart the information to Thomas' son Charles. Knowing that the Pocklingtons in the monasticon were ancestors of his new wife was now putting a whole new slant on the way he read and digested the contents of the monasticon.

Maria was interested in what Charles was reading out to her but, to tell the truth, she was rather more interested in whisking her husband upstairs to their cosy bedchamber. "My dearest dear, please don't tire out your poor eyes from reading in this candlelight," she told him diplomatically and considerately. "Besides, we are on our honeymoon, my darling Charles!" She then jumped up from the loveseat, grabbed his hand with one of hers, the candlestick with the other, and literally pulled him upstairs, all the while he was mildly and laughingly complaining but not pulling back from her eager movements for one instant.

<hr/>

Charles returned to the library after another pleasant interlude of conversation about the monasticon one day with Lord Morley, then, on the omnibus going home after work that evening, Charles sat on the upper level, in the very front row. He enjoyed sitting up high, looking down upon the horse-and-carriages, the odd smoky motorcar crawling along, carts with huge wheels being pushed by street-boys wearing slouch caps, and all the pedestrians, strolling, running, often narrowly being missed by a horse-drawn omnibus such as the one in which he rode. He recalled that his father had taken him on his first horse-drawn double-decker bus in Manchester when he was still a young lad. Thomas Sutton said he'd met the chap called John Greenwood who had opened the first omnibus line in Manchester in 1824. Mr. Greenwood had pioneered this great service which, unlike the old stagecoaches, needed no prior booking. Thomas said the omnibus pioneer was thirty-six in 1824, and Thomas only eight years old when he'd met the man in 1833. At that time the omnibus service had been in existence for nine years. Thomas told Charles how impressed he'd been by this fellow who expressed great excitement about his transportation vehicles.

"Son, imagine this. You'd stand at the side of the street and wave your hand, the driver would pull his horses up, and you'd hop on. That's what Mr. Greenwood told me and my father."

"Father, what if you wanted to get off just a bit later?"

"Why, you'd tell the driver to stop the horses and you'd hop off!"

"Wherever you liked?"

"Yes, wherever. Quite a service, wasn't it? Now there are special places to get on or off, as you know. The driver and the poor horses would have got sick and tired of constantly having to stop or go at the whim of the riders!"

Smiling to himself at the memory, Charles took the old book out of his pocket, adjusted his *pince-nez,* and proceeded to take a good look once again at his treasure. He simply never tired of reading it. The book was gorgeous, but it was the content that gripped him. He recognized that it was not a religious tome but rather a history of monasteries in and around the area of York, just as Dickens had told him over two decades ago. There were names—St. Mary's Abbey, Whitby Abbey, and a few friaries such as Blackfriars, Greyfriars, Austin, and one whose name delighted him called Friars of the Sack. And there were the nunneries, including the small nunnery of St. Clement's Priory with only a Prioress and eight nuns.

Fascinated, probably for the hundredth time, Charles re-read the monk's stylised writing. He knew the story by now pretty much by heart but got a thrill each time he read the tale.

Walter, a bishop of the church, told my abbot his life story, at the time he returned to our monastery as an old man, there to pass his days in quiet reflection until the day he returned to our Lord. My abbot commanded me to include the bishop's tale in my tome of our local history of this area's monasteries.

Walter informed that early in 1202 he fled Gascony in southwestern France with one attendant manservant. They disembarked from a small ship below the white lime cliffs of Dover, bought horses from a local stable, left the south coast, riding through the middle of England and up to the area of York. Entering through the walls of the city, they galloped up to the heavy wooden gate of our monastery, set just inside those encircling city walls. Walter was gorgeously dressed in a riding habit of forest green strong cloth collared and edged with fur of white ermine. It was in our monastery that they rested for many, many weeks until revived from their journey and until Walter was satisfied that the learned good abbot had prepared him for a new life in this foreign land.

As Charles read on, Walter had given up his high standing in the church once he had settled in England. He despised religious wars and

63

the pain they caused humanity. He had been a bishop of the Cathars in France, an heretical Christian sect that believed in the principles of a neo-Manichaean dualism in the world of both good and evil, holding the belief that the material world is radically evil. Charles pondered on that anew. He knew that Manichaeism was a dualistic cosmology with a spiritual world of light (all things good) against a world of darkness (the evil material world). He smiled to himself, as he thought of a simpler way to explain this cosmology to, say, one's child: in stories, a knight riding a white horse is always depicted as the good knight but the knight riding on the black horse is always seen as the evil fellow. Come to think of it, he thought, that would be a good way to explain it to any young person who had asked him to tell them what lay inside the covers of this ancient book.

When Charles had originally read this passage in the monasticon, he'd learned that Walter believed up to then that one gained salvation through the gnosis, that is, the knowledge of spiritual truths or mysteries, that in the earthly world, life is filled with pain, suffering, and evil. Walter's many long discussions with the abbot had given him fresh insight into the meaning of good and evil and now understood that the material world is not evil, but certain people in the world are evil. Walter much preferred that line of spiritual thinking. As a result of this epiphany, Walter had decided to live a simple life. He would no longer be a bishop, but he would attend church on Sundays and holy days, work hard, and read more of the books he'd brought with him to England in his saddlebags, along with books the good abbot at the monastery had given him. Walter was a learned man, proficient in Latin and his native French and, being a quick learner, up to speed in English as well. Thus, he was ready to leave the monastery and begin his new life.

Charles sighed, rereading the story again. He reckoned he'd much enjoy talking to this Walter, an ex-bishop, and someone who'd been a Cathar. Cathars had their headquarters in the French town of Albi, hence were sometimes known as 'Albigensians'. Charles wondered what it would have been like to believe, as they did, in two gods, one who was so full of goodness and the other an evil deity. So, Charles mused on, it was just a different way of Christian belief. Christians believed not only in the good Lord but also in the evil Satan.

As the omnibus swayed along the street, Charles went over the next section where in his writings the monk recalled the abbot telling him that after Walter left France, he should explain that it was propitious Walter had left when he did because in 1209 Pope Innocent II had initiated a Roman Catholic Crusade against the heretical Cathars. The staunch Catholics in northern France swept down upon the heretics, and this

Albigensian Crusade (1209-1229), although unsuccessful in eliminating Catharism, did eventually make it easier for the French king to establish authority over the south of France, where the nobles had tolerated and even supported the Cathars.

Charles Sutton peered at the gorgeous little book he held in his hands, smiling with satisfaction for the hundredth time that it really was his. He'd had the book since finding it in the library in 1867 when he was only 19. My goodness me, he thought, that meant he'd had it for twenty-five years already. He'd read it over and over; no wonder he knew it virtually by heart. It hadn't got a library card affixed inside its covers, so it hadn't been loaned out. His intention had always been to hang on to the glorious book; perhaps selfish of him, he recognised, but it was far too valuable to let any Tom, Dick or Harry get hold of it. Staring out and down at the people walking in the street, he remembered as a young fellow looking up in the Oxford English Dictionary where the expression of 'Tom, Dick and Harry' emanated. He laughed aloud, remembering it told him that it came from the lyrics of a 1734 song that went: 'Farewell, Tom, Dick, and Harry, Farewell, Moll, Nell, and Sue.' The man in the seat behind him snorted at Charles' out loud roar of laughter, tapped him on the shoulder, and asked him to share the joke. Of course, being very polite, Charles turned around and complied, resulting in the two of them laughing aloud together, trying out different tunes to the song lyrics. The gentleman he'd been laughing with now left the bus.

Settling back into his seat to face the front again, and already knowing that Pocklington, his second wife Maria's surname, had a long-storied ancestry, imagine his excitement when he read the following. This person the scribe was telling about was an actual ancestor of his new wife. "Wait till I tell her all this detail!" he muttered to himself. "Now I know she's of this Pocklington line, this makes everything I'm reading so much more interesting and exciting. Maria will just love it, I'm sure!"

1202[13]. After departing the monastery during that year, this bishop, now known in England as Walter Bishop, born in Gascony in the time of Henry II,

---

[13] I only possess Charles William Sutton's genealogical tree from 1202 for the Pocklington side of the family, but unfortunately not the earlier Suttons' entire family tree, created by Charles William Sutton, except for a tree listing Robert Sutton onwards, born in 1789. I have a note written by CWS that he'd put together such a tree. After research, I discovered the Suttons had originated in France, as did the Pocklingtons. The first Sutton name noted in England was in 1066 after the Norman Conquest.

who had come into England, speedily married the daughter and heir of Sir John Pocklington, of Pocklington, county of York, of the race of the Saxons in the County of York. Now living in England, Walter then took the name of his wife, daughter of a knighted gentleman, but spelled it Pokelinton. The happy couple later in the same year of 1202 produced a son. Walter, still French to the marrow, named the boy Roger de Pokelinton.

Three years later another son arrived, Henry de Pokelinton, followed in 1219 by Willelmo de Pocklington, now returned to an earlier spelling of the surname. By 1233 young Roger had married and produced his own heir, another Roger, and it was this young man who was granted two crofts belonging to the prebend of Bamb, in the district of Poke, north of Manchester, land of the knighted Pokelinton gentleman. The prebend received his stipend from income drawn from the local cathedral's estates. The two crofts were lovely cottages with thatched roofs. As the years passed, the male descendants of the Pocklingtons became 'cappellanos,' (chaplains in our English tongue) one being titled 'domino Ricardo de Pokelyngtone'. By the mid-13th century, there were two in the family who had achieved high status in the church and named after St. Remigius.

Probably amused by what he was told to write, and smiling to himself, the monk had added:

Old Walter, once a bishop himself, must have smiled inwardly as he realised life had come full circle with his descendants becoming chaplains of our great church.

Charles noted that at first, the abbot's version of Walter's life was rather sparse but then, the story ripened, as if the abbot had allowed his imagination to deepen Walter's abbreviated version. Or, thought Charles, perhaps it was the scribe who had the imagination. No, that can't be true, Charles realised, for the abbot would surely have read over what his scribe had written. It must have been that the abbot had a rather salacious imagination, although this did seem unlikely since he'd presumably never experienced a woman's love himself. But perhaps, Charles thought, lust-filled envy would have been sufficient to spark the abbot's imagination. Charles imagined him pacing the floor, dictating to his scribe, and the scribe licking his lips as he dipped his pen again and again into the inkpot to capture the abbot's lurid account.

Walter himself, it seemed, had had no experience with women when he was a bishop in France. Charles found it rather odd that the most salacious parts were written in first-person, as though Walter were writing, and the abbot no longer dictating. Mesmerised once more by the story of Walter's romantic life, Charles saw the ex-bishop had gone back to his arrival in England with a fuller description:

When I came with my manservant to the lime cliffs upon disembarking from the ship that brought me from France, I betook myself to a stables and there hired two horses. A girl appeared leading the two beasts. My heart somersaulted as I saw she was not just a serving wench but for sure the daughter of the owner of the stables. She wore a barbette of a pretty band of woven leather below her chin holding a fillet safely upon her head. This fillet encircled her head like a round band and was decorated with shining blue beads. Her dress was a long, simple, piece of blue fabric, matching the beads in her fillet and the blue of her wide-open eyes. Those eyes drilled into my very soul. My servant dared to punch his elbow into my ribs, chortling to me that I had finally fallen in love. This wench was of the age to marry, for sure, being about twelve or thirteen I gauged. She flirted prettily with me, bringing her blond braid of hair from behind and laying it over the breast of her dress, where she played with it, curling the hairs at the end of the braid with a slim white finger, making me react with desire, to my shame. My shame? Nay, I bethought myself that I was no longer a bishop, no longer bound to celibacy, no longer a slave to the austere and authoritarian church.

She took my hand, dipped a curtsy to me, and said her name was Matilda. Then she stroked my riding habit of forest green strong cloth edged with the fur of white ermine and asked if her father could provide a room for the night for my man and me at the local inn. I was loath, indeed most undisposed, to part from the stables and from her, but dusk was nigh, and York was calling to me. My manservant and I took the horses and paid the young lass. I galloped from those stables, looking back over my shoulder at Matilda, my heart and body lusting for a girl for the first time that I could remember. The wind blowing hard in my face helped to distract me, allowing me to conquer the desire that had risen in my body. I galloped faster, knowing I was now free from the shackles of my old confining religion. Life was calling to me. I was excited to be in England. Thinking these thoughts, the whole way up to York, stopping at inns to eat and rest upon the way, I was a new man, a happy man.

"Goodness me, he's a man alright, is this Walter!" Charles said aloud. "And he ended up around Poke, eh? And got himself married in short order to the daughter of a knight? That's how they got the name Pokelinton, from the town of Poke, of course! The knight would have taken the name from his village. Oh, and maybe it was Walter Pokelinton himself who commissioned the abbot to put this book together. It must have been, surely? Heavens, what a lot I'll have to tell Maria when I get home and show her my precious treasure I've been reading for so many years!"

The bus conductor ran up the few steps to the roofless upper deck of the omnibus, cheekily calling out, "Your stop, Mr. Sutton, get your nose out of that book and come down!"

Discombobulated from the disruption to his reading, Charles put the book down next to him, grabbed his umbrella, hurried down the stairwell, and hopped off the bus. The minute he landed on the pavement, and watched the omnibus disappear around the corner behind its two, white, clip-clopping horses, he said,

"My book, oh my Lord, I've left it on the bus! What if it rains tonight?"

***

Charles had to get his monasticon back. As he continued on his walk home, he thought, I'll go straight to the omnibus company first thing in the morning and hope against hope that nobody has taken my little treasure. No good going there right now, because the bus still has a long way to go on its route. Once back at the bus station, the draught horses pulling the bus will have to be watered, fed and stabled for the night. That would be done first. Nobody at the omnibus station's going to find the bus I've been on and look for my book until tomorrow. I only hope the book hasn't vanished for good. Oh, his heart gave a lurch at that thought.

I'll leave earlier than usual tomorrow morning, Charles decided, and make my way to the omnibus station and, if I have to, I'll look in every omnibus on-site myself.

What am I going to tell my wife? I'll tell my deputy, W. R. Credland, but I know already that he's going to heave one of his drawn-out sighs but will commiserate with me. Good man, Mr. Credland.

***

Mesmerised by what he'd been reading on the omnibus, Charles wished he could share it with Maria that evening at dinner.

Now that the book has vanished for the second time, he thought, I can only tell her what I've read about her ancestors. Never mind. Maybe the book isn't really lost but will reappear. It might well still be on the bus where I was sitting. Oh, it had better still be there. Oh dear, what a fool I am!

He expected Maria would call him a foolish man for losing the book, but he also knew she was already fascinated that she hailed from French stock. It was she who'd told him that her grandmother had told her that the family originated from France. She loved the French language; he knew that already. He struggled with how to deal with this loss as he walked toward his home and his dearest Maria.

While Charles and Maria were walking out together, she always liked using French words here and there and liked to point out that many English words were derived from the French as well as German. She commonly referred to the water closet as the 'loo'. As she liked to tell her husband, "Listen, Charles dear. I happen to know that in the Middle Ages the women threw the night's slops from a wooden bucket out their window. There'd be a channel running down the middle of the narrow, cobbled street, between the two rows of houses on either side. They'd aim the slops at that channel, chanting as they did, *'Gardez-l'eau'*. That means 'Watch out for the water', but I expect you know that, dear Charles. Funny, though, how we English used French words, and still do! Over the years, the chant became 'gardee loo' and eventually just 'loo'." With a broad grin, Maria would stick out her ample chest, put her arms on her wide hips, and say, *"Voilà!"* [So there!]. Even though Charles did know that history and had heard her tell it a hundred times or more over their courtship, he always smiled kindly because he adored his Maria.

He remembered something else Maria liked to tell people about those long-ago times. One winter morning, while cleaning out the previous evening's grate from the warm fire they'd sat in front of, Maria had said, "Charles, dearest, I know something else about the French. On her knees, she swept up the burnt pieces of wood, and said, *"Couvre-feu!"*

"Cover-fire? What do you mean?"

"Well, that word got corrupted over time, you know, just like 'loo'. Back in the old days people had to cover their fires in the fireplace to prevent conflagrations. You know, Charles, 'cause many houses were made of timber back then."

"Ah, of course, *couvre-feu*, so 'curfew' came from that, when you can't have a fire after a certain time, which turned into you can't do a certain this or a certain that after a certain hour of night. Very good, dear Maria!"

Feeling the full weight of her plump body, Maria rose heavily from the floor and planted a grateful kiss on Charles' cheek. She always liked his compliments.

Thinking about all of that, his mind then went back to the loss of his book. The omnibus had dropped Charles at the bus stop closest to his home, but he still had a long walk ahead of him. The scribe's words were running through his mind as he walked, and due to his keen ability to remember nearly every word of what he read when something particularly interested him, the narrative was still acutely alive, unlikely to fade soon.

Morning dawned with a crash of thunder and pouring rain. Well, it would, wouldn't it, to match my worried mind, Charles thought, as he grabbed his umbrella on his way out the door. When he arrived at the omnibus station, he asked if his book had been turned in. It had not. Sighing with disappointment, Charles asked which was the bus he would have taken on his route home last night. He ran toward the vehicle pointed out. Clambering up the staircase, he walked to the front of the upper deck. No book on the seat!

"Damn and blazes! It really isn't here," he cried in frustration. Down the stairwell he flew, back to the omnibus station office. There he hesitated. What to do now? I'd better go straight to the police station to report its loss, and this he did poste-haste.

Behind the counter stood a rather fat police constable. They'd met before so Charles reminded the policeman of his name as PC 39 shook his hand, reminding Charles his name was Police Constable Number 39, or rather, Superintendent Constable Richard Marsden by now, adding, "You'll recall I met you some years ago, sir, when I was just a regular police constable walking the beat. That was the first time, years ago now, back in 1867, methinks, when that dratted raven of Mr. Dickens' stole your book and you reported it to me. Yes, a lot's happened in them past twenty-five years, 'asn't it, sir? To us both, I'm sure. I so enjoy your library, Mr. Sutton sir, as does me boy and his mother. Mind you, me boy's all grown up now. We all enjoy reading a good book, you mind." Then, in a book entitled, 'Missing Items List,' PC 39 wrote down all the details of the loss and said he'd look into the matter. With no other recourse, Charles walked slowly back to the bus station. He had to find his book!

Leaning against the omnibus station's counter, picking his teeth, was a young chap wearing a stable hand's slouch hat. Charles approached him and said, using the local northern vernacular to the boy, "Nah then, do you happen to know the 812 omnibus, my boy?"

"'Ey oop[14], mister. Aye, that I do. I takes care of 'er 'orses after they come back from 'er daily route. Me and Jimmy minds all the 'orses 'round 'ere."

Mancunian slang definitions [Mancunian = of Manchester]:
[14] Ey oop = hello.

The young man proceeded to explain in detail how he had to water, feed, rub down the bus number 812 draught horses and finally stable them for the night. Charles asked if he and this Jimmy knew anything about a book left on the upper deck of the No. 812.

"I doesn't," said the fellow, "but th'owd lad[15] Jimmy may. 'E's a reader, 'e is. 'E learnt 'is ABCs but not me. Me mam[16] said I 'ad no need of such hi-falutin' bobbins[17]."

Charles asked him to kindly find his mate Jimmy. Another youth with a pimply face full of sore-looking red spots arrived, looking worried. In broad Mancunian dialect, this youth claimed,

"Ecky thump[18]! I ain't done nuffin, sir, really I ain't. It's a pretty book wiv gold and silver pictures in places. 'Ooever was sat up front of the bus musta forgot it. Finders keepers, me mam says. I took it in outta the rain, see. Good thing it's stopped now, innit? So I ain't partin' wiv t'book, guv. An' if I did, it woulda given me the morbs[19]!"

Charles had an idea. He pulled the young man outside the bus station's office where the manager lounged, looking bored and smoking his pipe. Charles took out half-a-crown[20] from his pocket and, making sure the manager didn't see, he offered it to the stable hand. He didn't want to get the boy in trouble. Continuing to use the local dialect to make the lad feel comfortable, Charles said, "Please be so kind as to give us back t'book and you can 'ave this money for yer trouble, young fella."

"Ta, mister. Ta'ra."[21]

The exchange made, Charles hastened away, feeling a huge sense of relief and a certain smugness that he'd managed quite easily to find the vanished book and get it back into his own hands. He'd tell Maria about it after work tonight. She'd be very pleased and, although half-a-crown was a lot of money for the boy, the monasticon's recovery was well worth it. He held the precious book up to his cheek, then sniffed it with pleasure. He flipped its pages, one after the other, enjoying the glint of the gold and silver of the illuminated first letters of each chapter. Thank goodness it hadn't got damaged by the rain showers.

---

[15] th'owd lad = the devil (or 'old mate').

[16] me mam = my mother.

[17] bobbins = rubbish.

[18] Ecky thump = an exclamation of surprise.

[19] Morbs = a sad or depressive mood (from 19th century British).

[20] half-a-crown = 2 shillings & sixpence. (12 .5p in modern day decimal currency. [The British crown was a denomination of sterling coinage worth 1/4 of one pound, or 5 shillings, or 60 (old) pence.]

[21] Ta = thank you; Ta'ra = goodbye.

Then Charles thought, wait, I'd better hasten back to the police station to tell PC 39 he can stop looking for my book. Cross it off his Missing Items List. Yes! A lucky, most fortuitous find, indeed! Not only must I do that, though, but I've got to work out a way to keep it really safe. His eyes widened as he blurted out, "safe!" That's it, he now inwardly told himself, I'll buy a safe with a key for my office and keep it locked up in there! After that satisfying thought, he carried on to share his good news and decision with PC 39, who would surely agree with his clever idea.

Chapter 23
Memoir

I'd just put down one of Charles Sutton's memoranda where he was writing about going to go home to Maria after leaving the book on the bus then going to the bus station the following day to look for it. Coincidentally, it was this very day that I got a call from my old friend, now in Manchester doing her own book research in the Central Library and ringing me on my landline.

"Shirley," she said, her voice coming in and out over such a great distance between England and Australia. "I've got lots to tell you. The Manchester Library is phenomenal. Listen to this. I've found so many books to help my research for my novel and you know what else, there are masses of people there, all willing and able to help me look things up, and then there's a whole room devoted to periodicals, and you know what? I've met the most charming gentleman who asked me out to dinner, can you believe it? And then..."

She talked more about her own research and this new love interest until my curiosity got the better of me and I impatiently interrupted her, asking, "But did you find the monasticon? Is it there? Can you take it out of the library and post it to me here in Australia, by registered and certified mail, of course?"

There was silence on the line for rather a long while, then I heard her utter a deep sigh. "I'm so sorry, Shirley, but they didn't have it. Nobody ever turned it back in."

"Do they even have a record of it?"

"Yes, an old, rather washed-out card was in their card file. It said it had been taken out decades ago by the then chief librarian and never actually returned. They said it wasn't a book that went out on loan actually and the card wasn't affixed inside the book cover as they usually are. The card was just stuck inside the book and it said the chief librarian had it for safe-keeping and it wouldn't be returned and wasn't ever to be loaned out. There was a note on the card itself saying he'd written up a card just to keep in the library's card-file to show the book existed but was now to be kept by the chief librarian. They asked me to kindly let you know, so don't expect a call from them. Again, I'm so sorry, Shirley."

After more friendly chatter, mostly about her work, I placed my phone back on its cradle. I confess I shed a tear, not only of sadness, but also of dismay and, yes, deep frustration. Now I'd have to think of somewhere else the monasticon might have ended up.

Going back to Great Grandpa's paperwork, I thought, lucky man, at least one of us had got the precious book in their hands...hopefully it wouldn't vanish again!

Chapter 24
1892

Charles was fascinated, now he'd married a Pocklington, to read everything the monasticon said about that family. He'd been talking with Lord Morley one afternoon in one of their friendly get-togethers about the years of the plague in England. Charles hadn't been able to find any mention in the monasticon of any Pocklingtons dying of the plague in the 14th or 15th century, but then, the book did have an additional entry near the end written by a newer scribe some years after the original abbot and scribe would have died. A scribe by the name of Friar Alberic, Charles recalled, and that was about the plague.

Charles now did more research and learned that in the days of the General Arrests in the middle of the 13th century, a century before the plague hit the land, another kind of disaster did hit Maria's ancestors (and now his, by marriage, Charles smiled to himself). Roger Pocklington's crofts were burned. One night Roger had returned from his church to find his family gone and both his crofts' roofs were shooting orange flames high into the black sky. He'd heard there were those who called him a heretic. He knew he'd better get away before he was caught, imprisoned, and maybe even burnt, as were his crofts. He fled all the way to Garway in Herefordshire but was tracked down and arrested there for his 'heresy' and sent to languish in the Tower of London, built by William the Conqueror in the 1070s. Charles, thought, I wonder what the specific details of his alleged heresy were?

This led him to muse on William the Bastard, thinking, wretched king, William I. I suppose there were good things about him but mostly not, in my opinion. William the Conqueror insisted everyone speak a mixture of French and English, something I'd call franglais, Charles thought inwardly. William was illegitimate so probably shouldn't have even been king. He was the son of Duke Robert I of Normandy and Arlette, the daughter of a French tanner. And William the Conqueror's forbears were Vikings! Fancy that! His reign was corrupt and violent and imagine what he did to the church! He completely reorganised it—with the Pope's blessing. And he doled out English land to the Norman elite after the Battle of Hastings in 1066. Well, that made England and France inseparable for a long time afterwards. As some historians claimed, William I may have been a great diplomat, but he was ruthless.

The tie with France was how so many French phrases crept into our vernacular; "that Maria loves to use", Charles muttered aloud. He suddenly remembered something to share with Maria, who might tell him she already knew it, he smiled, but he'd tell her, anyway. The Beefeaters at the Tower of London had history in their name. The word came from a corruption of the old French word of *bueffetier*, meaning food taster. Edward 1 (Edward Longshanks) had more reason than most to fear assassination—he'd already been struck in the arm by a poisoned dagger, which weakened his health from then on. The Yeoman Warders were employed as bodyguards and food tasters. The word *beaufet*, meaning well-made, was an elaborately decorated sideboard on which you placed your most valuable plate and dishes. Charles muttered aloud, "buffet—that's what Maria will say!" He decided he'd tell her that the closest servants serving the king and guarding his displayed treasures of plate were the *beaufetiers*—the beefeaters. The Yeoman Warders only got vegetable scraps and non-meat leftovers from the king's table to eat, but the good beef meat scraps were for the beefeaters to enjoy. When he'd finished his explanation, he'd smilingly say "*voilà!*" to her, just like she loved to say!

As he strode home after getting off at his bus stop, he then mused on Maria's ancestor, Roger Pocklington, and his opinion about the church. According to what Charles had read, Roger believed that Heaven and Hell were real, but he did not believe in the Roman Catholic religion or the Pope. "Aha, that's what his heresy must have been!" When Charles read this in the monasticon, he'd wondered whether Walter Pocklington knew that his descendant had been considered a heretic, just as he had been considered, when he'd been a Cathar before leaving France.

When Roger's crofts were burned in 1260, Walter was assuredly still alive, Charles thought. He must have been, to relate his life to the abbot who then had his scribe transcribe the story.

Charles stopped to let a horse and cart cross in front of him. As it slowly clomped by, he remembered something else that had popped up in the monasticon, out of order. It was as if the abbot, or scribe, had himself remembered what old Walter had told of his courtship and marriage to the daughter of the 'Pokelinton' knight and dropped in his recollections wherever he wanted in the monasticon. He must remember to tell Maria about that. It was all about sex and marriage in the 13th and early 14th centuries. Really, having this kind of information inside a tome about the monasteries in and around the area of York was surprising, to say the least. It made the book much more interesting to the reader. Charles laughed hollowly—such a relief to have got the book back into my own hands again! What a stupid ass I was to leave the book on the bus. Maria would be quite right to call me a fool, but she'll be pleased about my idea to get a safe to keep it in.

Charles stopped musing about the monasticon's loss and lucky recovery as the words he'd read about Walter's romantic forays sprang back into his head. He knew he was one of those fortunate beings who have what scientists referred to as a photographic memory. It was this ability of his that gave him much pleasure and had observers wondering why he was often to be seen just staring off into the distance. What he was doing, of course, was running over in his mind conversations he'd heard or stories he'd read, recalling all of them almost word-for-word. He appreciated he was one lucky fellow indeed.

The abbot kept me well-fed and well-accommodated at his monastery for quite some weeks until a good command of the English language was achieved and my knowledge of the ways of these strange folk, the English, were understood by me in nearly all manners. I already spoke some of this complex language, so it wasn't too difficult for me to achieve a comfortableness in expressing myself, although my French accent persisted.

I found myself thinking often of Matilda at the stables and my nights were not blessed with sleep as I tossed and turned imagining how her golden locks would look if loosened from their restraining braid. I thought of her form revealed beneath the long blue gown. I thought of many things and realised I needed to be wed. I spoke with the abbot about this matter, and he told me of a knight who dwelt in his manor house not far from York in a village called Poke who was the blessed father of a beauteous daughter. Leaving the monastery without my manservant, I rode to this village and in the distance saw a large house surrounded with fortifications appearing on the horizon. I was bedecked in my finest outfit, the green riding habit with the ermine collar and edging, and knew I looked well. Tugging at the bell-pull by the entrance gate, a youth appeared and took the letter of recommendation given to me by my abbot as a way of introduction.

I was brought into the Great Hall and told to wait for the knight. Looking around, I saw heads of slain boar and deer mounted on plaques upon the walls, next to sconces for rush lights or flaming torches, set well forward to avoid a conflagration of the wooden walls and beams behind and above them. There was a large plaque also hanging upon one wall which showed the knight's provenance—a shield bearing his name with a deer on one side and a boar upon the other, intertwined with flowers and the word 'Poke'. A table of dark oak that could seat at least twenty people stood in the centre of the Great Hall with a fireplace at one end that was filled with the entire trunk of a tree of some twenty feet in length, with kindling beneath, all prepared to be burnt to heat this enormous room.

Hearing soft footfalls, I swung around to face the most enchanting vision of womanhood I had ever seen. Following her was an older gentleman, still wearing some of his chainmail across his chest. He welcomed me most genteelly saying he was Sir John Pokelinton and this lady, his gentle daughter, Eleanor. He had just come from a bout of jousting and pointed out a suit of armour standing on one side of the entranceway to the Great Hall. He said he only ever wore the complete suit in battle, not that it had been used much lately, and chuckled a little.

As he spoke, I could barely remove my eyes from the vision of loveliness standing now slightly behind him, appraising me with violet eyes. Her lustrous dark brown hair was mostly confined by a crespinette or caul. Her hairnet was made of some sort of golden thread. Her long gown was of purple, with ties of gold criss-crossing her youthful breasts. She held her hands across those breasts, as if shielding them from my gaze. Her long fingers bore rings of gold and silver, one with a stone of purple amethyst. Not since Matilda had I warmed so much toward a young woman, and this girl was young indeed, yet somewhat older than Matilda, I gauged. She couldn't have been more than fourteen, perhaps fifteen. The abbot had told me that these days in England girls and boys who reached puberty were considered ripe for marriage, at twelve and fourteen, respectively. He also told me that nowadays in England marriage was simply a matter of saying 'I do' to each other. To my great amusement, he said a wedding could take place in a public house, at a friend's house, or even in bed! Couples didn't need permission of their families to marry or have a priest to officiate, but of course, being wed in a church did give greater spiritual weight to the proceeding.

The abbot told me, too, that having sexual intercourse was only permitted if one were married. Couples only had to consent by using words or actions. If they had sex, that meant they had consented to marry. He said consent could also be deemed as a promise to marry if the man gave a 'wed' to his intended, a wed often being a ring. A 'wedding' meant the woman had accepted his gift and the marriage was thus created. The abbot laughingly advised me not to give any kind of ring made even of reeds or other natural material in jest to a girl I wanted to fornicate with, or, unwittingly, I would be placing myself pledged to the responsibilities and burdens of marriage. He said a church marriage statute was planned to be issued by the English church, but it hadn't yet come into its own; he thought it could be ratified by 1217 or 1219, thus perhaps not for another 10 or even 15 years hence. There was still much theologian talk about the important subject. He also pointed out that in the 12ᵗʰ century, church theologians decided marriage was, and should be, a holy sacrament because the union of a man and a woman represented the union of Jesus Christ with the church, yet this belief was still not accepted by most English citizens. A church service was available but only used by the minority of couples. Many couples did like the spiritual connection to the church so got married just outside the church doors. Architects then built rather ornate entrances to some churches, specifically for couples to get married beneath. I had heard elsewhere that these lychgates were not only for a wedding to be held beneath, but also to shield a corpse from inclement weather. The dead often in those times awaited the arrival of the clergyman for their burial dressed only in a shroud or occasionally in a coffin, if moneyed, thus a lychgate served its purposes well.

The abbot also mentioned that in some places, couples were expected to ask permission of the lord of the manor to marry, but those were exceptions. And the lord did occasionally insist on his right to sleep with the lass before the bridegroom could consummate his marriage to his bride. I was dismayed to hear that. He added that in those very few places where couples were being pressured to get permission to marry, they could, and did, travel away from England. For example, there was a village²² across the border in Scotland where no such permission was needed.

Knowing all this, I knew this girl I wanted was going to be my wife. For but a brief moment did I imagine asking her to consent to being my bride that very day. I felt it the second I gazed at those soft, yet wise, violet eyes. I wanted this lass, this Eleanor, with every fibre of my being. When she dropped her hands away from shielding her breasts, I knew she would welcome me into her life.

---

²² The village of Gretna Green only officially started holding weddings in the mid-18ᵗʰ century. The village blacksmith repaired and constructed tools for farmers and also forged new shoes for their horses, eventually forging marriages for eloping couples, starting in 1754.

Interestingly, the word 'forge' comes from Middle English for 'make' or 'construct,' from Old French *forger* and Latin's *fabricare*, meaning to create in a workshop, usually a smithy. In the 14ᵗʰ century Old French used the word *faverge* for a smithy's shop where the blacksmith heated an object in a fire or furnace then hammered it out, such as horseshoes. A forger of bank notes, for example, is somebody who creates fraudulent, counterfeit, or imitation currency. At Gretna Green, marriages were forged, or created, with the sense of something enduring or successful being built from a beginning point.

When she started touching her hair and twirling a loose curl falling over one ear, I suspected she was interested in me. I saw her eyes appraise my broad shoulders then stray down my whole form. I was almost done for at that point. Fortunately, her father took my elbow and led me to a chair and offered me a tankard of mead.

That part of the tale ended and continued with the story of Walter's life, the quick marriage, and the children borne of it, but Charles had been titillated by the romantic angle of the story and looked forward to relating it all to his Maria tonight.

Charles arrived at his house, opened the garden gate, and, taking a deep breath, marched up to the front door to let himself in.

Chapter 25
Memoir

Sitting at my desk in Australia and thinking back to Walter and Eleanor's romance in the 13th century, I recalled Walter had arrived in England from the Gascony area of France in 1202. He'd lived a long life, described by the abbot's scribe in the monasticon. I wondered whether in the latter part of the book there would have been any mention of the bubonic plague. The fascinating part to me about the plague is that it had arrived from Gascony in June 1348, certainly long after our Walter had left Gascony for England, lived his life, and passed on. Modern research discovered that it was brought to England by a seaman whose ship landed in Weymouth, Dorset. That is the first recorded case. It's known that the disease was carried by fleas on rats.

I looked it up and discovered that from 1348 to 1665 records show there were repeated plague epidemics with many plague deaths listed. We now know the pandemic was caused by the Yersinia pestis bacteria. Around 40-60 percent of the country became infected over the years. By 1665 people were calling it the Black Death. The decrease in population caused a halt to the Hundred Years War. With less people for soldiering, and less men to work in the fields, a huge resentment sprang up and in 1381 the peasants revolted, which in effect, even though the rebellion was put down, caused the end of serfdom in the land. The plague had come and gone over the 14th and 15th centuries, with the last known outbreak in 1665-1666, called the Great Plague of London.

If only I had the monasticon book, but by the time the plague had struck England, I knew the abbot and his scribe would have been long gone. I did have a passing thought about how marvellous it would be if another scribe had made an addition at the end to record the further culture of the times. I could but hope, yet at the same time seriously doubted it. To find out, I had to find the precious book! And just as I was thinking that, I came across a scribbled note by Great Grandpa telling about a new scribe writing about the plague quite near the end of the monasticon. That spurred me on to settle my thinking cap on my head even more firmly to find out where the 'dratted book' (as Maria Pocklington would say!) was lurking.

Meanwhile, I picked up another document covered in Great Grandpa's lacy writing. He had copied out something he'd read in one of his books, which had obviously saddened him greatly. After reading what he'd written, I wondered whether it had affected the Pocklingtons. Most certainly it would have, for after the Black Death had hit, from one-third to one-half of the citizens of England had fallen victim, which had changed the history of the country in so many ways. Yet, when I scrolled through the pages of the genealogical tree, there was no mention of such a fate befalling any of Maria's, and now my own ancestors.

With all these jottings, memoranda, and notes Great Grandpa had made, I thought he could have written a book himself about the family— if he'd only had time—so here I was, writing it for him. A Cheshire Cat grin spread over my face; I hoped he'd approve.

Chapter 26
1892-1896

W hen sitting on the omnibus on his way home, Charles had flipped the pages of the monasticon, then looked at a section very close to the end of the book. What he read saddened him greatly. The year was 1348, 146 years after Walter had first set foot in England from Gascony. Another scribe had taken up his pen to add a few sentences after the abbot's scribe had cut off his reporting of the abbot's words about Walter. By this time, all three, the abbot, his scribe, and Walter, were long dead.

My name is Friar Alberic and I write these lines in our monastery's scriptorium. I write at the end of this our terrible year, the year of our Lord 1348, when God saw fit to inflict upon our monastery the direst of evils. Nay, not our Saviour, but the Evil One himself, I do now think. The monks as usual attended to the needs of the townsfolk of York, bringing them succour in all ways. Upon their return to their cells, they fell ill of the most hideous disease, I know not what at this time. They were in mortal pain, their foreheads wet from the fever, their skin bursting with foul-smelling buboes. These boils swelled up like apples, emitting a stench of disgusting horror, with pus the colour of purple, blue, and a necrotic black. The surrounding skin rotted away, with vast amounts of pus exploding from the buboes, causing the patient to cry out in agony.

We had the death-cart come to take our poor dead monks away for burial, for our abbot cannot bury them in our own graveyard, according to the strict rules of our district. All we were permitted to do was enshroud them in white cloth and lay them upon the cart. As the cart departed our gates, the driver rang a bell, warning passers-by to step aside. This they did, holding a cloth across their nose and mouth in the hope of not falling prey to this ghastly plague that has befallen the land. Our people are to be laid to rest in plague pits, for 'tis said there are too many victims of this Great Pestilence to lie in individual graves. Our abbot will accompany the cart and speak blessings upon the mass grave once it is sealed. I fear for his safety and have begged him to stay safely behind in our monastery.

Charles sighed, shed a tear, and wiped his reading glasses. There were no more entries about the plague. He wondered if the scribe's fears had come to pass, that this newer abbot himself had fallen victim to the Great Mortality.

With vast excitement that evening, Charles opened his front door. Holding the monasticon out in front of him, he ran into Maria's arms.

"Look what I've got, my dear, look, it's vanished no longer but here in my hand."

His wife was as relieved as he, feeling his emotions as if her own. She loved Charles with all her heart and was desolated when he was sad. With a broad smile, she kissed her husband and asked him to read her the passages after dinner that pertained to her own Pocklington ancestors. She would light a fire and they'd sit together, while Charles recounted what he'd read about her family history.

Charles stayed up late that night after Maria had given a huge yawn, grabbed her candlestick and gone upstairs to bed. He'd keep the salacious parts for another evening when she wasn't so tired. They were still in the first year of their marriage. As much as he wished to run upstairs and climb into their enticing bed, he was a kind and respectful individual. He saw how tired his new wife became after caring for his and Sarah's sons on a daily basis. This particular evening she'd seemed more tired than usual, but also much contented. Her body, as comfortably plump as it was, had started taking on a little more weight in her midriff. He had seen that occur four times with his late wife, and he wondered whether Maria was now carrying a new child for him. He'd wait till she was ready to tell him the news, if his suspicion was correct that she was, indeed, pregnant[23].

As Charles continued to read downstairs, he learned that as the 13th century came to an end, the Pocklingtons moved away from being church leaders to simple churchgoers, just as Walter Bishop Pokelinton had done. Many of them became mercers and dealt in the burgeoning textile industry of fine materials such as silk, fur, and velvet. Knowing

---

[23] Maria was pregnant. She gave birth to my great-uncle George on 10th January 1893.

that the royal household wore these fine materials, in the middle of the century Adam de Pocklington managed to become a camerarius, a chamberlain in charge of the royal household, where his mercer skills were appreciated.

Edward I, referred to by the locals as Edward Longshanks, was now king of England. Edward I reigned from June 1272 to July 1307. Adam de Pocklington made Longshanks' outfits out of the richest materials and especially long to fit those long royal legs. He also had his workers sew gorgeous silk dresses for Longshanks' wife, Eleanor of Castile, and silk dresses and ermine coats sewn for the king's second wife, Margaret of France, whom Edward married in 1299. Many of the Pocklington family had carried on speaking at least some of the French language ever since Walter had arrived in England from Gascony at the beginning of the 13th century. Adam was one of those who still enjoyed speaking French, thus was a favourite of Queen Margaret's court. Adam made quite a lot of money as a mercer.

Adam's descendants, going back to 1299, were mostly mercers in the royal and noble courts. The monk transcribing Walter Bishop Pokelinton's life story (dictated to by the monastery's then abbot), listed the boys' names in Latin, including Galfridus, Walterus, Jacobus, and even Dionisia, the wife of Reginaldi de Pokelington. Dionisia was an expert in delicate embroidery and sewing ermine fur onto rich velvet cloth.

Tired out from his exciting day, and all the reading he'd been doing, Charles held his candlestick as he walked upstairs to join his wife in their double bed with its old-fashioned heavy curtains to keep the draughts out. He fell asleep thinking of draught horses, drafts of wind whistling under his bedroom door, abbots, monks, scribes, and all the Pocklingtons. His eyelids closed and soon he was snoring just as loudly as his adored pleasantly plump wife, Maria.

Charles had made himself stop researching his genealogical tree. He'd set himself that task, to create a family tree. But then, there was also his principal work to be accomplished, which he'd been employed to do at the library. Thus, at work the following day, and sighing gustily but happily enough, he spent the next few hours cataloguing the library's books, a mammoth ongoing task that was to take him much of his working time, even with help from older children he hired from the local orphanage. He was a kind and courteous fellow, always willing to aid those less fortunate than he, characteristics that were to continue throughout his seventy-two years of life.

One of the orphanage helpers was a girl of sixteen years of age. She told him she was already a novice and would soon be entering the local convent to continue her initiation to become a nun.

Sister Winifred Agnes had been through a terrible youth. Whether or not it was a good thing that her immediate family had died in an accident was an unresolved question. When she was found, having walked away from the wrecked motorcar—the only family member to have survived—she was placed in an orphanage. She was twelve years old at the time of the accident in 1892. Prior to that awful day, Edith Alice (as was her name then) had suffered horribly at home. She complained to her mother that her older brother came into her bedroom at night. Her mother called her brother her 'golden boy', who could do no wrong. She called Edith Alice a liar and a young girl just looking for attention.

"Besides, you shouldn't strut around trying to look so grown-up, Edie, my dear." Edith Alice had muttered under her breath, "I don't, and I can't help it if I do look womanly already." Out loud, she told her mother, "It's not my fault, you should stop him!" She received a slap for her impertinence.

Edith Alice kept trying to tell her mother what was going on, that it wasn't her fault, but her mother wouldn't believe her and chose to shut her eyes to the obvious incestuous lust in the young man's eyes.

Then came the day of the accident. Father was driving the family automobile, his pride and joy, with mother next to him and the youngsters in the back. He worked at the East Riding Cycle and Motor Company in Kingston upon Hull in Yorkshire. He had been given 'a right good deal on the old banger', he liked to tell everyone. The 'old banger' was not old whatsoever, rather being a brand-new motorcar, one of the first manufactured by the company. It had a soft top but no windows, and it had a spare tyre affixed to the outside of the driver's door. Father enjoyed his job helping to manufacture these exciting new vehicles. He took his lunch break sitting outside the factory near the Humber Estuary, whatever the weather. He was a tough chap and worked long hours so wasn't home much to see what was going on at his house.

Her brother kept touching Edith Alice in the back seat of the motorcar and, as much as she could, Edith Alice wriggled away to her side of the car. In those days they didn't have seat belts so when a dog rushed in front of the car and father swerved, it was too late. The car was driving along at its usual quite slow rate, but the impact with the dog was enough to make it skid off to the side of the road and roll down the embankment. It landed upside down on its soft roof. Mother had been crooning a popular waltz song of the day at the top of her voice. Smoke now snaked up from the engine. Mother's voice stopped in mid-crescendo. Edith Alice had closed her eyes as the car skidded off the road, and when she opened them and looked around, she saw her mother, father, and brother lying in funny, twisted, positions, half in and half out of the motorcar. She felt herself all over and her hands came away covered in blood, but she felt alright. She wondered where the blood was coming from and thought maybe it was her head.

Edith Alice turned herself the right way up as much as she could and crab-crawled out. By some miracle, it looked to her as if the dog had sustained no injuries. He probably hadn't even been hit—just ran in front of the car causing father to swerve. He was now just sitting next to the car, panting, with his tongue lolling out. His sad eyes surveyed her, and he began to howl. He was an old beagle; a dog Edith Alice had always loved. She found she could stand up but didn't know what to do so she looked around. The dog stopped howling and set off across the field next to the embankment. He kept turning around to look at her as if to say, 'follow me'. They crossed a ploughed field and came to a farmhouse.

"There you are, Rexie, I wondered where you'd gone. And who's this with you? Oh, my dear child, you're covered in blood! Oh Lordy, you've a cut on your forehead, poor girl. Here, let me wash it and bandage it up for you. The head bleeds more than anywhere, from what I've learned. Oh my, I do hope it doesn't hurt too much, my dear?"

The farmer's wife cleaned up Edith Alice, chattering on about what must have happened while the farmer ran across his field to the car. Upon his return, he told his wife and Edith Alice that there'd been a nasty car accident, that nobody else had survived, that he'd sent word for the constables to come, that an ambulance was on its way to take the bodies away and what-on-earth-was-he-expected-to-do-with-this-girl-now, eh? They fed her and had her stay the night. There were no relatives to phone, even if they'd owned a telephone. And so, young Edith Alice ended up in the local orphanage. She told the farmer's wife there was no other family because they'd moved up to the Manchester area when she was a baby and father always said he couldn't stand 'that other lot' so Edith Alice never learned who they were anyway.

During the next four years, as she matured, Edith Alice realised that she distrusted, even hated boys. No surprise there. But well after she'd reached puberty—and she'd indeed been an early bloomer, as her brother had noticed—she had gradually started to change her mind about boys. All those horrible goings-on with her older brother were fading.

There was a convent in the Salford area, and the abbess often took the bus to the orphanage to 'do her good deeds'. Edith Alice wasn't quite sure what that meant but she liked the abbess, who was very motherly toward her. The abbess suggested that Edith Alice might be interested in becoming a novice and enter a year of novitiate training, especially since she always said she couldn't stand boys. Edith Alice didn't say she might, just might, be changing her mind about that. Anyway, it was all too confusing. Then the abbess told the orphanage director that the girl should also be thinking of going to work. The O.D. said that Edith Alice loved to read, so at sixteen in 1896, that's how the young woman ended up working at Charles Sutton's library.

Edith Alice also loved to sing and joined the abbess's convent nuns at Compline. They loved listening to her clear contralto soaring up and down, savouring the holy words. Eventually, she agreed to become a novice and in 1896 took the new name handed to her by the motherly abbess, who gave her leave to call her Mother Superior.

The newly-named Sister Winifred Agnes was a lovely young woman, with translucent skin, merry eyes, and a ready smile. She was spending her canonical novitiate year in much prayer and 'doing good works like Mother Superior,' as she described it to Charles Sutton at the library. She wanted to know everything she could about the religious life and the unique spirit of the order of nuns with which she was affiliating herself. During her canonical year, she was delighted to work in an institution that served the public.

Sister Winifred wore a white tunic and a short veil over her lustrous red hair. Laughing, she was constantly tucking stray strands and curls poking out from under her veil. Eventually, she told Charles, she would wear all black, plus, at the ceremony where she would be 'taking the veil', she would have a wedding band placed upon the ring finger of her right hand and she would become 'a Bride of Christ'. She wouldn't wear the ring on her left hand for that was reserved for secular marriages. Her complete renunciation of the world and the adoption of a nun's life would take place during that ceremony.

Sister Winifred Agnes was much looking forward to leaving the orphanage and eventually moving into a cell in the house of her Order of Augustinian Anglican nuns. The building owned by the Order was large, spacious, and quite beautiful. It had been built two centuries earlier with cloisters on all four sides of an interior courtyard that was filled with plants and a tinkling water fountain that attracted birds. Some of the nuns tossed crumbs to the birds.

"Reminiscent of St. Francis of Assisi, don't you think?" said her employer.

"Indeed, it is, Mr. Sutton. When you walk along the cloisters with their beautiful decorative arches, you can hear not only the chattering of the birds but the nuns as they chant their Matins songs. Oh, sir, you should hear them. Their voices rise up to Heaven in pure harmony and sweetness."

"Must be a most calming and gentle experience. May you move in very soon, Sister Winifred Agnes!"

Mr. Sutton sat down with the novice to listen further to her rapturous take on the order she was to join in another year as a nun. In 1897, when her canonical year ended and the girl became a full nun, Charles would have attained his forty-ninth year. It pleased him greatly to have 'young blood', as he called it, working with him in the library with its old, often musty, books. The young people giggled and laughed and lent a happy feeling to the work environment, which Charles much savoured. He enjoyed listening to what they had to say and saw himself as a teacher to them in some respects, helping them to discover much of what his treasured books harboured.

The young girl said that in the 6th century, there was a monk who, around 597 or 598, became the first Archbishop of Canterbury. The nuns told her he was known as Augustine of Canterbury and that he was much venerated in the church. Augustine was chosen by Pope Gregory the Great in 595 to lead a mission from Rome to convert the pagan Anglo-Saxons in England to the Christian faith. King Aethelberht of Kent converted to Christianity, and it was in Kent that Augustine settled.

The Sister said, "Sir, it really was about the lust of a king."

Charles replied, "How so, Sister?"

"Well, sir, the Church of England became the land's main arm of Christianity when King Henry VIII changed the country in 1534 from Catholicism to Protestantism so he could get an annulment from his current wife to marry another that he preferred, and with whom he hoped to have a son and heir. That is, he knew the pope wouldn't let him divorce or get his marriage annulled, so he basically said he was going to ignore the pope and do what he wanted, becoming head of the new church in England himself. You know that to this day the Archbishop of Canterbury is still the most senior cleric in the Church of England."

Sister Winifred Agnes took a gulp of air and said she'd learned even more from the nuns. "Prior to the Reformation there was no distinction between Catholicism and Protestantism. Protestantism really began prior to 1534. It was when a monk named Martin Luther nailed his '95 Theses' to the door of the Cathedral of Wittenberg in Germany in 1517. He also translated the Bible into proper German rather than Latin, thus enabling more and more of the common people to read it. As a result, people began to question many of the doctrines and edicts of the Roman church, which were seen as not biblical at all. The word Catholic means universal, sir, the unified one and only church with the pope being its father (its papa), the representative of Christ on earth, thus assuming heavenly power over all the earth. Protestantism was the word taken by those people who protested Catholicism."

To himself, Charles thought, goodness me, this young woman is quite well informed for her age. She obviously listens very well to what the nuns tell her.

Charles then asked the young novice, "Do you know what the '95 Theses' was?" The young Sister took another gulp of air, and said all in a big rush, "Well, sir, I think it was about the Bible being the central religious authority. Only we mortal beings are able to be saved by our faith and not our deeds, you see, and people protested that."

"Quite so, I believe that's correct, Sister. And that's what really sparked the Protestant Reformation, you're quite right—when the common people protested that Catholic edict."

"Thank you for listening to me, Mr. Sutton." The young Sister stood up, smoothed down her tunic and hastened away, wondering if she'd bored her poor employer silly. In turn, Charles watched her retreating back, thinking how lucky he was to have such an informed, intelligent young lady working for him in the library.

Chapter 27
Memoir

Ah, so that's the nun who's going to have a love affair with somebody at the library! I shuffled the paperwork around on my desk until I found the next note scribbled hastily by Great Grandpa. It simply said, 'Tell Richard/safe/stash monasticon/only one key.' I expected Richard Marsden, a/k/a PC 39 would have been extremely pleased, and relieved, to hear that Charles was going to further lengths to protect his prized possession. It would be an expense, but worth it. Besides, he could keep other valuable manuscripts in the safe, or even the payroll. I wondered if his accounting department had its own safe—probably not—if it was Charles' intent to purchase such an item.

Then I sat there imagining Maria's face when he'd come home with the book after finding it at the omnibus station. I felt relieved myself that he'd got it back. I found it fascinating to be reading Great Grandpa's short jottings, notes and memoranda about life at the library. For the hundredth time, I wish I'd known him. My grandfather, Frank Sutton, used to occasionally talk about his father almost reverently. "Such a good fellow, Shirley my dear, such a clever man, so thoughtful, so caring", he'd told me. My mother was only ten when her grandfather Charles died. She adored her own father, Frank, and often said how like his father Frank was. She was always humming an old tune, 'Oh mine papa, to me you were so wonderful...'. I know I'd have adored Great Grandpa as much as I had loved my own grandfather Frank, too. Meanwhile, I wanted to know what was going to happen with that nun at the library. And, what about the monasticon hunt I was on? I'd only received that email from my friend researching her novel at the Manchester library saying the monasticon wasn't to be found there. I took a turn around my flower garden pondering on how to keep my hunt for the book going.

Chapter 28
1896-1898

Upon the young novice shyly entering his office another day, Charles bade her take a seat. It was one of her early days at work in the library and he wished to make the sixteen-year-old feel welcome. Charles told her about the monasticon book he'd found in the library in 1867, twenty-nine years ago, long before she was born, when he was only nineteen—just three years older than she was now. He told her all about the monasticon, how it had vanished twice already, but always seemed to show up again at some point later. She was thrilled to have his whole attention, and more excited when he said, "My dear Sister Winifred Agnes, I know you'd enjoy reading about the abbeys, priories, convents, and how a scribe in a monastery in York had written down the life story of an ex-Cathar bishop ancestor of my own wife, Maria Pocklington, whom you've not yet had the pleasure of meeting."

"Oh, sir, I'd much enjoy reading the book from cover to cover, if you'd ever permit me. From what you say, with it vanishing here and there, sir, I'd be happy to even just sit in the staff lounge to read it on my breaks, and not carry it away from the library whatsoever. And, sir," she said with a pretty blush, "I'd be honoured to be permitted to make the acquaintance of Mrs. Sutton."

"I'm sure we could work it out, Sister. I know you'd find the monasticon quite fascinating and you're right, I'm afraid I cannot permit it to be taken out by the library assistants. It's not even going to be in the public domain for borrowing. It's far too valuable to me."

"Oh, good, and yes please, I'll be anxious to read every detail! Please let me know when it will be possible for me to make a start on the precious monasticon? I'm sure it's going to take me some time to read it.

I don't expect it will be today," she said with a cheeky grin, "so before I leave today, I'd much like to tell you something, sir, about the Augustinian Order I'm planning on joining. Will that be alright? You want to hear, don't you, sir? I know you'll find it interesting, won't you, sir? And sir, once I've read the monasticon, I'd so much enjoy conversations with you about it all."

She'd taken a seat across from him at his work desk. He was itching to carry on with his own work, but Charles, always interested in his staff—particularly a young novice such as this girl—agreed to listen to what she had to say about her future life as a nun. This was the first novice he'd encountered and was quite curious as to why a pretty, intelligent girl such as this Sister Winifred Agnes, would even consider leaving the sectarian life to become a nun.

It appeared that the Augustinian nuns had told her that there was an old Saxon church dedicated to St. Botolph originally on the site of the Augustinian priory in Colchester, England. There were several small Augustinian monasteries, convents and priories scattered around the UK, with the one she was drawn to situated in the environs of Manchester on the way to Salford.

According to the nuns, a priest from Kent called Norman had taken religious studies from a man called Anselm of Canterbury in France. When Norman returned to England, he settled in Colchester, and joined a college of St. Botolph church secular priests. Norman advised this college to join the Augustinian Order. They needed to establish a house of this Order in England and, to do that, they got Norman to write a letter from himself to present to some abbots in France, particularly in Chartres and Mont-Saint-Eloi. They took the letter to the French abbots, and it was they who taught them the Rule of St. Augustine. It was Anselm who became the original prior of the first Augustinian institution in England, around 1116.

Internal fighting and disputes followed, primarily centred on control of the church. The nuns then told Sister Winifred Agnes that in 1380 a complaint was made to King Richard II that several people were pretending they were the attorneys and proctors of the Augustine priories and churches. These fake electors were even collecting money from their unsuspecting victims by showing them forged letters telling them they had to pay up. The king had his men find the miscreants, had them arrested and tossed into Newgate gaol, and the forged letters were handed over to the Archbishop of Canterbury.

"Oh," exclaimed Sister Winifred Agnes in righteous indignation, "Mr. Sutton, sir, there is so very much more I've learned from the nuns, even about the Act of Suppression in 1536—just two years after Henry

VIII had changed the country from Catholicism to Protestanism. You know, in 1536, when small monasteries and convents were closed, and the Crown took all their money, buildings, and land. And not three years later came the Second Suppression Act, when the Crown dissolved the larger monasteries and religious houses. It was all frightful and unfair."

Charles was quite impressed with all the knowledge Sister Winifred Agnes had obviously acquired from the nuns and was now imparting to him. "Yes, I do know about some of that history, my dear, but not all. It's fascinating to have you fill in some of the gaps."

"Well then, did you know that there are Augustinian nuns in both the Roman Catholic and Anglican churches? In fact, we Sisters don't belong to just a single Order of St. Augustine, but we've got quite a few communities living under the Rule of St. Augustine." She went on to say, "So I'll enter an Anglican Church Order after my canonical year's novitiate training comes to an end. There are quite a few congregations of sisters following the Augustinian Rule in the Anglican Communion, different from the Roman Catholics, with their single Order only." Putting her head to one side and fingering her white tunic, she smilingly added, "The Anglican sisters all have different modes of dress, depending on which convent we enter. I already know which Order I'd choose to enter, and it's the one with the very kind Mother Superior, situated near Salford on the outskirts of Manchester. Do you know it, sir?"

"I don't, Sister, but I have an idea I'll soon be getting to know it well once you move in!"

Charles was interested, of course, in everything Sister Winifred Agnes was telling him. She was obviously devoted to the idea of becoming a nun in one of the Orders, but, for now, he was feeling impatient and wanted to carry on with making entries of names, dates and the work they did, on his genealogical tree. He sent her on her way to assist in another area of the library and she left him cheekily saying, "Now don't forget to tell me, sir, when you'll be ready to let me have a read of your very special book!"

The next day, a library assistant called Tommy Duckworth loaded a pile of library books onto his trolley-cart and, whistling softly to himself, pushed the heavy load along the aisles of the stacks of bookshelves.

Wonder where that new girl in the funny outfit who's been helping Old Man Sutton went, Tommy mused. He certainly employs some cuckoos to work here, and that's for sure. Wonder why she covers up her red hair? I know it's red because bits were sticking out. Pretty girl, even with that stupid long tunic and veil. Maybe I'll ask her out for a cuppa one of these days. Or take her down the pub...maybe after a pint or two I'll get a kiss...yes, that's a much better idea! Thinking these rather salacious thoughts, he pushed his trolley on along the bookshelves and disappeared around a corner to reach the Archaeology section.

"Let's see, I can read my ABCs enough to know which section this lot go into. A for Archaeology. Yes, 'ere we are." Standing in front of books about Egypt was the red-haired lass in the funny outfit. He immediately noticed her with her locks of red hair trying to escape her veil. He thought to himself, Good, I'll take this opportunity to ask the girl out. She's bound to say yes to a brawny chap like me.

Sister Winifred Agnes noticed the young man wheeling his trolley up to her. She wasn't supposed to look at young men, or so the nuns told her. She wasn't supposed to even notice them. After all, she was to become a Bride of Christ. Oh dear, but look at his lovely hazel eyes, and broad shoulders. No, I'm not going to even pass the time of day with him.

"Hullo, young lass. And what's your name? I've seen you helping our Mr. Sutton earlier today. This is your first week 'ere, innit? You're from the orphanage, aren't you?"

Anxiously, Sister Winifred Agnes thought, Oh dear, I really mustn't even talk to him. Wish he wouldn't talk to me; it's unfair. He should see I'm a novice. How does he know where I live?

"I can't talk to you. I'm going to be a nun."

"A nun?! Is that why you're wearing that strange outfit? It don't suit you. You've got smashing red 'air, I can see some curls peeping out."

The novice sat down suddenly on a small stepladder next to the bookshelf. She'd suddenly come over all funny.

"You shouldn't talk to me; it's not allowed."

"Not talk to you? A pretty girl like you? That's stuff 'n nonsense. Pure rubbish. I'd like to get to know you. Want to 'ave a cuppa with me? Or, better still, let's go for an ale at The Cat's Whiskers pub. It's just round the corner. Want to? Would be fun!"

"You really mustn't talk to me. It's not allowed. In a year I shall be a Bride of Christ."

"Christ! Whoops, shouldn't swear, shouldn't take the name of the Lord in vain, eh? But a Bride of Christ? Listen, lovely, Christ ain't married. He don't take brides. Don't you know that? Everyone in my church knows that! I don't listen to the sermons much but me mam makes me go with 'er sometimes of a Sunday."

"Oh, please go away!"

"What's your name, lovely? Mine's Tommy, Tommy Duckworth. I like you and I'd like to know your name."

"I'm not supposed to talk to men."

"But why? Sounds daft to me. So what do I call you?"

"I'm a Sister."

"Sister? Well, blow me down with a feather. I don't want to call you sister. I mean, I'm a brother 'cause I got a sister, but I don't go around calling meself brother. That's daft, innit?"

Sister Edith Agnes got to her feet, bravely turned her back on Tommy and hurried away. He stared after her, puzzled, then shrugged and wheeled his book trolley off back to the stacks.

The very next day, Tommy spied the luscious lass bending over to push some books onto the lowest shelf of a bookcase. He caught his breath as he took in her rounded buttocks. Drawn to her, he hurriedly wheeled his book trolley down the stacks until he was next to her once again.

"Look, luv, I really do want to get to know you, but I still need to know your name. I asked the girls in the staff lounge and they said to call you sister. I told 'em I can't do that; it's plain daft."

Edith Alice let out a sigh as she straightened up to stare at the young man. Why, oh why does he pursue me? she thought. Maybe if I tell him my name he'll leave me alone, but then, he's so attractive...

"It's Sister Winifred Agnes."

"Phew, you really are a nun then!"

"Well, it used to be Edith Alice until I became a novice."

"Edith Alice, eh? Pretty name. Why do you cover your lovely 'air? What's a novice?"

"A novice is a girl studying to become a nun, but first she has to spend a year in novitiate training. We cover our hair so as not to be attractive to men."

"Is that right? Well, it don't work. I still think you're pretty, and I want to take you out for a drink!"

"Nuns don't have anything to do with men. Don't you know that? You must have nuns visit your church. You must know what we are. We're married to God!"

With that, she stood up and marched away from Tommy Duckworth. He gazed after her retreating back, scheming up a plan.

What a loss to mankind if she became this nun thing. Married to God? Daft as a brush[24], this Edith Alice.

In turn, she felt his eyes burning into her back. Oh Lord, help me ignore this man. He's made my heart beat faster. He's got me all in a mither[25]. It's not allowed, what am I to do? When she got back to the orphanage, she fell to her knees in her dormitory room, praying hard for God not to test her this way, to remove this Tommy Duckworth from her mind entirely.

Tommy Duckworth sat down to his tea that evening, scheming about how to get this ever so pretty girl to go out with him. What did he care about her decision to become a nun, married to God, for Heaven's sake? Ha! He thought, look at that, he'd just made a wee pun. She wouldn't be of any use to Heaven unless she were dead, and she most certainly was not dead. She was alive, vibrant, and gorgeous, not dead in any way at all. These nuns wanted her to be dead to men. Outrageous. Girls were put on earth to be with men, and men with girls. It was the order of things. He'd not felt this way about any of the other lasses he'd met. He was already eighteen and he'd now decided that this Edith Alice was the one for him. Sister Winifred Agnes? No way. Daft name! Chomping on his fish n' chips, he came up with a scheme. He'd heard the Sister was on the roster to work at the library the next day, so he'd lay it on her.

The next morning arrived in a show of glorious sunshine, birds tweeting, his mum's dahlias all nodding their flowery faces at him as he

---

[24] Daft as a brush: when using a wet brush, you dab. When using a dry brush, you daff. After much use or daffing, the bristle splay out in all directions and the brush is then said to have become 'daft' or useless. Someone daft as a brush is said to be unable to concentrate on the matter in hand. In Victorian days, children were used as chimney sweeps because of their small size that made them able to crawl up or down a chimney to clean it with a brush. They were often held upside down in a chimney to do this task. Injuries resulted, especially to the brain. Thus 'daft' became synonymous with being silly, as in, unable to concentrate. The original expression used to be 'daft as a brush and not half as useful'.

[25] mither is the regional Manchester slang for bother, trouble, or aggravation.

strode out of the house to work. All good omens, and Tommy believed in omens.

He punched his time-card into the machine inside the library entranceway. Why he had to do that, he didn't know. Old Man Sutton had told him those time-clock machines were newish, invented in 1888, he'd said. He'd also said that the administrative girl in the back office checked the time-cards every day, to ensure he'd arrived and left work on time. Creepy, that was—people watching when he arrived and when he left. No, he didn't like that one bit. The boss had said if he didn't punch his card in and out, he wouldn't get paid properly. He also said all the staff had to comply. Bloody new-fangled machines. He thought the boss ought to just trust him. Muttering under his breath, he marched straight to his locker and put on his brown protective coat over his shirt and trousers. Looking into the long mirror he thought himself a fine specimen of a man, indeed. Thick, wavy, dark brown hair, hazel eyes, and the small moustache on his top lip growing quite well, it was. He had to shave his chin already and all around that pencil-thin moustache. Nothing like the lustrous moustache sported by Old Man Sutton, not at all. His was huge. In fact, he'd seen him drinking his tea from a cup apparently provided by his missus. That cup had a china strip on the front of the cup where you'd drink from, and the strip held the moustache out of the tea. Ha, what a clever idea, Tommy thought, but he wasn't going to let his moustache get like an old man's. No sir. He was young and a tidy pencil-thin moustache on his top lip was all the fashion for chaps his age. He knew he wasn't well-schooled, but well enough, he reckoned. He still had his accent from before his family moved up north from London when he was a young fellow. Not posh, certainly, but at least he didn't talk like some of these lads in the library, with their 'ee ba gum and you've got me in a reet[26] mither. Even Edith Alice said that mither word sometimes, which made him smile, the sweet young thing.

Striding upstairs to an upper level, he saw Edith Alice with three other girls. She was the only one in that ridiculous outfit. He stared at her. Sensing his stare, she swung around and blushed. He noted the colour rise up her neck and flood those pretty cheeks. She raised her hands to her face and hurriedly turned away from him.

Gotcha! Tommy said to himself. He saw that she liked him. She wouldn't have blushed, now would she? She moved away from the other girls and walked down one of the aisles of bookshelves, obviously pretending to search for a book. She trailed her hand across the spines

---

[26] reet = right.

of each book. Such pretty hands. Long, white fingers and neatly-trimmed nails. He followed at a distance, watching her every move. Oh, those ankles. Look at how nicely they're turned. That tunic didn't cover the ankles, stopping just above them. He couldn't make out all her body lines but what he could see pleased him.

"Mornin', Miss Edith Alice, and 'ow are you today?"

"Oh, hullo Mr. Duckworth, you startled me, I didn't see you there. Please don't say Edith Alice. My name is Sister Winifred Agnes."

I'll bet, thought Tommy. You saw me alright and you liked what you saw, so you blushed. You are such a sweet young thing, you!

"Well, erm, Edith Alice, I've given our conversation from yesterday a bit ov thought. It occurs to me that if you're to become this nun-thing you told me about, you need to know what temptations to resist, now don't you?"

"Temptations, Tommy? What temptations?"

"Ah well, getting to know a man, going for a drink, what a pub's all about, that sort of thing. I mean, if you don't know 'ow to recognise a temptation, 'ow are you going to know 'ow to resist one, eh?"

There, he'd said it. He found he wasn't feeling smug at all. His heart had leapt into his throat. He wanted her to smile at him.

"I've given it a bit of thought myself, Tommy," she smiled. She smiled! She actually smiled at him. Success was coming his way!

"I prayed about it and came to the same conclusion, Tommy. I need to know how to resist temptations. I've a lot to learn still."

"So you'll go for a drink wiv me?"

"I don't drink alcohol, but I'll be happy to have a ginger beer with you, if you like. And, listen, Tommy, you really oughtn't call me anything but my novitiate name."

Giving her a cheeky grin and a sly wink, Tommy replied,

"Right-oh, Miss Edith Alice. I'll come by the orphanage at seven o'clock, after you've 'ad your tea. I 'eard you live there. I know where it is, and I'll be there on time. You'll see."

Sister Winifred Agnes started to shake as she watched this attractive man walk off down the aisle between Bound Periodicals and Course Reserves in the Reference Department of the library. What a nerve he had! She was rather attracted to that. Another young man came around the corner of the stacks, carrying an armful of periodicals.

"Not in these stacks," the novice whispered to him, frowning at his obvious ignorance of how the library was organised. "You're holding individual, current, periodicals. These stacks are for the bound ones." She already knew that and this was still her first week at work!

"Ta, miss. Miss, you look unwell. A bit pale. Need any help?"

"No, I'm alright, thank you; go on, off to the Periodicals stacks."

Sister Winifred Agnes felt a sense of foreboding. Things were getting all mixed up in her head. She shouldn't be going out with this Tommy Duckworth. To distract herself, she decided to go to Mr. Sutton's office to ask if she may be permitted to read some of the monasticon yet?

With excitement later that day, Tommy arrived bang on seven o'clock to pick Edith Alice up and take her to the pub. Sitting in The Cat's Whiskers, nursing her ginger beer, Sister Winfred Agnes herself told Tommy Duckworth all about the monasticon. That is, all Mr. Sutton had shared with her.

"Sounds like it's worth a bob or two, innit, Edith Alice?"

"Well, I imagine it is, Tommy. It's frightfully old, probably a collector's piece, if you ask me. If our convent owned a book like that, why, we'd be the talk of the whole Order!"

Tommy pondered, staring deep into his golden ale and swirling it around in his tankard. The amber coloured ale brewed with pale malt sent a delicious aroma to his nostrils of fruit, floral, and citrus trapped in the hops. Another scheme was forming in his brain. He wanted to curry this girl's favour. If she wanted that old book for her convent, well, why didn't he try to get it for her?

He needn't tell her what he was doing. Next year, when she arrived at the convent to become this darned nun-thing, she'd find the book there to greet her—if he'd sold it to the abbess. What a wonderful surprise that would be! He'd tell the Mother Superior, the abbess, or whoever it was Edith Alice called the head of the convent, that she'd have to fork over some good money for the monasticon. She'd do it, for sure, because no other convent would have such a book. Mr. Sutton needn't know about it. There were hundreds, if not thousands, of other old books in his library for him to enjoy. Yes, the young man was hatching a plan.

And maybe, just maybe, Edith Alice would stop messing around being a sort of nun, this novitiate nonsense, by the time he'd managed to get her lusting after him. He was already known by the local girls as a good kisser. One girl said she felt like swooning whenever he pressed his lips against hers. Yes, his masculinity would undermine her silly desire to get married to God. For Heaven's sake, no woman could realistically believe God would marry her. How on earth would they even consummate such a marriage? The very idea boggled his mind. Before Tommy's father died, he always told Tommy that women were crazy, all mixed up, and they needed a man to set 'em straight. He was beginning to understand what his father was on about.

Yes, he'd set his plan in motion as soon as he could. It meant getting into Mr. Sutton's office after hours. That would be hard; he knew the librarian always locked his door when he left for the night. This needed careful planning, but he already had the beginnings of a plan in his head, and it was a right good one. Miss Edith Alice would end up being so impressed with him that she'd throw herself into his arms—if he pulled it all off right. But first, the dratted book would have to be removed from the safe in Mr. Sutton's office.

Tommy Duckworth could think of nothing but Edith Alice. Her novitiate year had come to an end. They'd been walking out together for some months now. After talking to the abbess and her closest friends, Sister Winifred Agnes decided against the nunnery. As she tried to explain to the Mother Superior of the convent, she could not resist the temptations being given to her, particularly the handsome, brawny young fellow called Tommy Duckworth. She knew he had fallen in love with her—or was it lust? Said she, "Oh, Mother Superior, I think I'm in love with him. My heart thumps in my chest each time he comes near me. Is that love?"

"I can't tell you that, child, for I've never been in that situation myself and I've not met the young man in question. What I do know, though, is that if you'd truly felt the calling of God, nothing would get in the way of your taking the veil."

For her part, the young girl was convinced she was now deeply in love with Tommy. As she'd tried to tell the abbess, her heart fluttered whenever she saw Tommy, her breath caught in her throat, and her tummy did somersaults. She felt bereft if a day passed without catching a glimpse of the young man. From what he'd whisper to her when they were working at the stacks together, he felt the very same way. Then there was The Kiss. Oh, dear Lord, how could a kiss send one to Heaven like that? When Tommy embraced her and his eager lips closed over hers, the whole world flew away, she felt she and he were enclosed in a kaleidoscopic bubble of rainbow colours, the very walls of the library holding her in a warm, passionate embrace.

People saw what was happening to the young couple and knew there was no way Sister Winifred Agnes was going to become a nun. People talked; of course, they did.

Then came the day when Edith Alice showed up for work in a plain grey skirt and blouse, wearing hose and sensible walking shoes. But it was her hair, her glorious mane of red tresses falling freely around her face that made them realise that something was up. Her working girlfriends gathered around her, touching her long wavy hair, whispering encouragements, endearments, and throwing endless questions at her.

As she wiped tears off her face with a white handkerchief, she told them she'd given up the idea of becoming a nun. Yes, she loved Mr. Duckworth. Who wouldn't? I mean, all you need do is look at him! Her colleagues had all noticed that the two lovers were walking out together. She told them she was sure he now wanted to marry her!

"But I can't," she wailed, "He hasn't asked me yet, but I'm still unsure of my decision, if he were to ask me. Mother Superior said I'd know for certain if I'd made the right decision to take the veil, that nothing, no temptation would steer me off-course. But I don't know for sure," she added with a choking sob. "I'd better be sure, hadn't I? I mean, you can't just marry a man when perhaps you should be marrying God, can you? Oh girls, it's all so confusing. I wish I'd never come to work here, never met Tommy Duckworth, that's what I wish, I really do!"

One of the girls knocked on Charles Sutton's office door. She asked him if he knew what had happened, that Sister Winifred Agnes had given up her novitiate training and was in a bit of a state. Charles did know, of course he did. He was a keen observer and a sensitive person to others' emotions. He'd seen this coming but had decided not to interfere. As he told the young woman now in his office, those two young people needed to sort out their own feelings and make their own decisions. Personally, he had discussed it with Maria and, as usual, she'd agreed that he shouldn't interfere.

Maria had told him, "It'll all come out right in the end, all come out in the wash, as 'tis said, however they decide to lead their lives, together or separate. But Charles dear, I've met that Duckworth chappie and I must say, there's something about his smarmy good looks that I don't quite like. Can't put my finger on it, but 'tis something and that's for sure."

"Erm, you're usually quite right and an astute judge of character, my dear. I tend to give him the benefit of the doubt whenever he does a small something or other that makes me question him. Remember when I told you about that money disappearing from the pot in the staff lounge? The money to buy the biscuits, tea, and coffee? The tea lady complained to me about it, as I'd told you. Nobody could prove it was Tommy who'd pinched it, but I did wonder. Yet he always looks so guileless, so innocent, that I feel I have to trust it wasn't him. Ermmmm," he added for the second time, but more meaningfully.

"And what does your Mr. Credland think about all this?"

"He says it's not our business so best to stay out of it, my dear. I agreed with him. What will be, will be!"

Tommy Duckworth was in love. Not only that, but he saw the way to impress his girl was still the same idea he'd had before. He'd ensure he'd get that monasticon from Old Man Sutton and sell it to the abbess. THAT would impress his girl and both she and the abbess would be happy the book would now belong to the convent. Edith Alice was holding back from marrying him; not that he'd actually asked her yet, but he just knew. Same stuff and nonsense about maybe, just maybe, still wanting to become a nun. He couldn't have that, no, he couldn't. He wanted her. He lusted for her. He ached for the lass. He wanted to marry her, keep her at home, make babies with her. Soon the house would be full of little Tommys and little Edith Alices. His mum and dad liked her, of that he was sure, but not sure about Mr. Sutton or old Credland. He wasn't sure, either, of the secretary, that Percy fellow. He was off with the fairies a lot anyhow. But Sutton and Credland? Tommy sometimes caught both of 'em giving him a searching sidelong glance. Nothing concrete, but Tommy sensed Mr. Sutton wasn't too sure of him. And yet, his boss had called him into his office one day and promoted him to senior assistant librarian and placed him in charge of acquisitions at the library. Well, that is, he still had to consult with the man about the purchase of any book for his precious library.

Tommy lay musing beside Edith Alice on the shore of the Mersey River in the south of Manchester where they'd gone for a picnic.

"Old Man Sutton must realise 'ow good I am with money, you see, and that's why 'e put me in charge of acquisitions," he said.

"Why do you call him old, Tommy dear? He's only 49—a girl in Accounts told me so. Oh, and Mr. Credland's only a couple of years younger than Mr. Sutton."

"Well, he seems old to me; 'es a lot older than you, or me, for that matter!"

"He knows a lot more about everything than we do, and that's for sure."

"That's 'cause 'e's always got 'is nose stuck in a book, innit? I don't 'ave time for all that sort of reading Old Man Sutton does. Some of us 'ave got to work!"

With his girl's head resting on his outstretched arm, he thought more about that good idea he'd had and that he was now going over in his mind, an idea he now felt ready to put into action. He'd get Old Sutton's monasticon out of his office. Yes! He'd sell it to the abbess who'd have no clue from whence it came. He'd once asked Edith Alice innocently if she'd ever mentioned the ancient book to the abbess and she'd replied, "No, why would I? It's the property of Mr. Sutton and what would Mother Superior want with it? I mean, yes, of course, if it belonged to our Order, it would be grand, but there's no way that would happen, Tommy dear." There it was again, Tommy had thought, she'd love to own the monasticon.

So, he pondered on, once he'd got the money from the abbess, and the good Lord knows (haha, another wee pun, he inwardly chuckled)— the convent had plenty of money from what he'd learned from Edith Alice—he'd go down to Boodles, that old fancy Tudor-fronted jewellery store on King Street in Manchester and buy his girl a whopping big diamond engagement ring. She often took the bus over Salford way, to stop in at the convent to visit her precious Mother Superior, so eventually she'd discover the monasticon was now there. It would impress her that it was he who had arranged for the monasticon to become the property of the convent. Oh yes, he'd really make Edith Alice admire him. He recalled she'd said her convent would be the talk of the Order if they owned that book. Sucking on a blade of grass, a thought flashed through his mind. What if Edith Alice felt sorry for Mr. Sutton? She knew how much he valued it. But no, she valued her convent and its abbess far more. Mr. Sutton was just her employer. Yes, she'd been with the library over a year now, since she was sixteen and I was only eighteen then, wasn't I, and now we're both older and wiser, hahaha. The question was, how was he going to get the book out of Old Man Sutton's office?

Skulking around one evening, Tommy noticed that Mr. Sutton always locked his office door at the end of the day and dropped the key into his frockcoat pocket. That was a huge problem. As he pondered how to solve it, he planted a deep, soulful kiss on Edith Alice's lips until she moaned with pleasure, then he pulled away. Make her want more of me, always more. That's how I'll keep her mine.

❦

Young Tommy Duckworth hadn't been happy to hear the news the next day from the assistant librarians having a tea-break in the library's staff lounge. Not happy whatsoever. They confirmed what he'd heard from Edith Alice. The dratted monasticon was now always kept in a locked safe in Mr. Sutton's office.

So when he'd sneakily watched the old man lock his door and put the key in his frockcoat pocket, he was probably putting the safe key in there, too. Hell and damnation! No, worse than that. Bloody hell and bugger it all. Cussing those nasty words made him feel a lot better.

He really needed to think hard now how to get it out of there.

He puffed out his chest, slyly telling the other assistant librarians, "Well now, ain't that the greatest news!"

After a good night's sleep, another sly smile spread across Tommy's face as he realised the time had now come for him to put his nefarious plan into action. He'd worked out his plan. It would be he who would make the monasticon vanish again. He would sell it to the convent. He would become the hero in his sweet girl's eyes. Yes, he thought, a good plan; now how to do it?

Alone in his bedroom at home the previous night, Tommy had mused on the problem. Yes, I've got it, he thought! Obviously, I'll get a copy of Old Man Sutton's office door key made, and not only that key, but I'm glad I heard those gossipers let slip that the boss is now keeping the book locked in that safe I saw in his office all the time. Damn him! He's the most annoying man keeping the book in the safe and I don't care whatsoever that it's that important to him. That doesn't serve me; I want it to go to the convent so Edith Alice will fall for me properly. That's what I want and that's what matters.

In the morning he was still going over his plan to steal the monasticon. He said to himself, I'll have to get impressions of both keys, for when I happened to go into his office this morning to deliver some books to him, I noticed it was a safe with a keyhole rather than numbers to turn. Blast the man's canniness! He's giving me even more trouble now. But then, he's really made it easier for me, 'cause I don't know how to open a safe with numbers but at least I can get a copy of a key made. Look on the bright side, Tommy me old mate, he chuckled to himself. Alright, ha! I know how I'll do it! Of course. I'll lift it from Old Man Sutton's jacket pocket on a warm day when he removes his frockcoat— something he rarely does, the annoying man. All I'll have to do is keep wax ready in my pocket to make both the keys' impressions.

One such summer day arrived. Tommy ensured he was always around his employer's office area, keeping an eye on him and awaiting his chance. Mr. Sutton came out of his office, hung his frockcoat on the wooden coat rack just inside the door where his top-hat hung. Tommy had often watched his employer arrive of a morning and toss the hat in the general direction of the coat rack. Mr. Sutton would give a little smile when the hat landed precisely on one of the curved arms of the old oak rack.

"Yes!" was Charles's usual exclamation. That's all, just a 'Yes'. And, amazingly, the man never missed. Tommy had heard of Mr. Sutton's prowess in high-jump as a youth but hadn't known how good he was at tossing.

Tommy watched his employer march off to the lavatory, humming a tune as he went. Glory be! Percival and Mr. Credland weren't at their desks. Who knew where they were...probably got the day off for some reason. What a boon! The young thief slid into the office, slipped his hand into the frockcoat's pocket and drew out the two keys on one ring. Taking a block of softened wax from his own pocket, he hurriedly pressed the keys one after the other into the malleable wax, giving the keys a wipe with his handkerchief before returning the keyring to his employer's correct pocket. Tommy disappeared as quietly as he'd slipped into the office.

Now he'd get keys cut from the wax impressions. He knew a chap down one of the old, cobbled lanes by one of the Manchester canals who'd do the deed for the princely sum of a crown, but it was going to be worth it and pay off in spades.

Obviously, Mr. Sutton occasionally had to leave his office during the daytime, sometimes for a Libraries Committee meeting, which was held in another part of the library, or sometimes for a myriad of other meetings, for he served on a large number of committees in general. Tommy had impatiently skulked around the bookstacks nearest his employer's office, wondering what on earth the man was thinking, as he watched his silent musing seated at his desk, staring out into the distance, seemingly accomplishing nothing. Tommy was not to know that Charles had been thinking extensively, and satisfactorily, about his many accomplishments over the past year. He had been thinking how Christmas had come and gone and here they were in another new year, 1898 already. His monasticon was safely tucked up in his office safe, so all was well with the world.

Tommy was careful not to be noticed by Charles' secretary, Percival Bastowe, or Mr. W.R. Credland. Now, to his delight, through the window in the wall Tommy saw Old Man Sutton suddenly rise from his chair and head to his office door. Peeping out from behind one of the bookstacks, he heard Charles wish goodnight to his W.R. and Percival, as they shrugged on their frockcoats and disappeared toward the staircase down to the library's lower floor.

Gotcha! Tommy grinned as he watched Charles saunter away from his office, after locking the door behind him and, glory be, without the monasticon. Ha! Out came Tommy's key-ring. Looking left and then right, no sign of anyone pushing a book-trolley along the stacks, he unlocked the door and in he sidled. With speed, he opened the safe's door with his copy of the key he'd had made. Ah, there it was. The monasticon! Bloody marvellous. Tommy slipped the book into the large pocket of his brown protective work coat. He locked the safe again. Now to put my clever plan into action. The old man won't even realise it's gone because I heard gossip that he doesn't look at it that much these days; afraid to take it out of the safe, they say. Besides, he's probably read it from cover to cover a million times already.

The last hour of his workday shift was spent quietly by Tommy at his own desk, so all was proceeding well to plan. He removed his brown work coat, happily punched in his time-card and sauntered on home.

For the rest of the next day Tommy waited to hear whether Mr. Sutton had discovered his book was missing but apparently he couldn't have returned to his office the previous evening to discover its loss—if he even were to check the safe. He must have gone straight from the lavatory and run down the staircase sometime after Percy and W.R. and gone home themselves.

At the end of the next work day, Tommy left the library. Cautiously, he entered a public telephone box on the corner of the street, ensuring he wasn't being watched by anyone from the library, not that they'd know what he was up to. It was an impressive telephone booth, painted bright red. A sign screwed inside the booth stated that it was in 1884 that Britain's first telephone booth was installed in Manchester under license to the Post Office. The Postmaster General at the time, Mr. Henry Fawcett, allowed Britain's fledgling telephone companies to establish Public Call Offices. Manchester, Salford, Stockport, Oldham and Bolton all received Public Telephone Booths that used wiring solutions which then were adopted across the entire country. How about that, then? Tommy smiled, while next looking up the number of the convent in the bedraggled telephone directory attached to the inside of the recess made to hold the book of telephone numbers. He dropped in his coins and dialled the convent.

Putting on what he hoped was a rather good imitation of an upper-class British accent, he said to the nun answering the telephone, "Erm, good afternoon, madam. This is Arthur Higginbotham. Yes, Higginbotham. I'm with the Manchester Auction House. Erm, I'd like to speak to your abbess if you don't mind."

"One moment, I'll see if she's out of Compline yet. She always leads Compline of an evening."

Tapping his fingers nervously on the receiver of the telephone, he waited. What the Hell was Compline? Some sort of prayers, I imagine. Bloody nuns, always praying. Her prayers were about to be answered now, though, weren't they!

"Good evening, Mr. Higginbotham. Do I know you?"

"Not yet, Abbess, but you will, you will. I have something very special for you and your convent. May I stop by for a chat?"

"That sounds mysterious. What is it? Well, I suppose I'll find out shortly. Our evening meal is not for yet-awhile, so I suppose that would be alright. Do you know where we are?"

Tommy excitedly left the telephone box and hurried along the street toward the omnibus stop. He hopped on one going toward Salford. Arriving at the old convent door, he rang the pull-bell beside a small window. Eventually a panel slid open across the window and a nun in a coif pushed her face into the little gap of the door's window.

"Mr. Higginbotham, is it? Mother Superior's awaiting you. Do come in."

The little nun led him into a stark office where the old abbess sat. She waved him toward a chair on the other side of her plain oak desk.

Coughing discreetly, then using his hopefully cultivated voice, Tommy said, "Good evening, Mother Superior. I am very pleased to meet you. Arthur Higginbotham. How do you do? And do I call you abbess?"

"Sit, Mr Higginbotham. No, Mother Superior is alright. Now, how may I be of service? I'm curious to know what it is you said you have for me and my convent?"

Tommy knew she hadn't a clue who he really was. Edith Alice didn't own a photograph of him, and he had never gone with her to the convent to visit the old lady there. With a theatrical flourish, he drew out the monasticon.

"When this extraordinary book came into our possession at the Auction House, Madam, we immediately thought it might be of interest to a religious order such as yours. Were we right? Well, of course we were. I can see by your intrigued expression that you have an interest in this ancient tome."

The abbess went through the monasticon page by page, exclaiming with subdued delight over the historiated initials of each section and chapter.

"I really should be wearing white gloves to touch this antique, as should you, my son!"

Some fifteen long minutes ticked slowly by, mostly in silence, except for the gentle rustle of pages as Mother Superior read, and an occasional sigh when she noted the decorative initials. While she read, Tommy chewed on his lip in exasperation. Why was she taking so long? Bloody 'ell! The old woman looked like some sort of crone or blackbird in her black robe. He kept his face expressionless as she raised her own coifed face from the book to stare straight at him.

"Is this a gift, Mr. Higginbotham?"

Oh my, now there's a conundrum. What do I say now? How am I going to phrase this? Hadn't given the wording for that any thought at all—in case she asked. He was gobsmacked that the abbess might even presume it could be hers for free. Damn and blazes. No, didn't expect she'd even think of it as a darned gift. Should have assumed she might have thought that, though. Gawd, what a dunderhead I am. Quick, I've got to think of something...

"Ah, no Madam, not in the sense of pecuniary matters, that is. Erm, no, not at all, dear lady. But one could say, oh yes, ahem, indeed one could, that in a sense 'tis a gift from God in that we, erm, ah, I, in particular, at the Auction House, dear Mother Superior, immediately thought, as I mentioned before, of your Order as being the recipient of such a, erm, ahem, valuable item that no other Augustinian Order would be in possession of."

Whipping a large white handkerchief from his top pocket, Tommy coughed politely into it, put the handkerchief away and beamed at the abbess.

"I see. Thank you. And how much will it cost my Order?"

Boy oh boy, she was a direct old lass, wasn't she? But Tommy had thought about what he'd say, if the abbess were to agree to pay for the monasticon. He'd searched through books in the library to see if he could get a clue as to what such a medieval book might carry in value but hadn't been very successful. He then had a private chat with a crony of his who worked in a bookshop, pretending it was just a general sort of question, nothing about any special book he had in mind whatsoever. That fellow had a casual chat with somebody else he knew, with the outcome that Tommy now had a pretty good idea of the sum of money to ask the old abbess to cough up for the book. Tommy leaned forward and quickly blurted out the sum in pounds sterling that he had been dreaming of for so long. A smile slowly spread across the abbess's face. She was a canny haggler and rather enjoyed getting a good bargain. The haggling began. With the business eventually consummated, and the money safely in his pocket, Tommy left the monasticon with the abbess and scuttled off home.

While Charles was happily filling in his genealogical tree, and continuing with his daily work at the library, Edith Alice and Tommy Duckworth were continuing their love affair at the library and walking out together in their free time. They'd known each other for almost two whole years now and they both adored each other.

Edith Alice liked, no, loved, her Tommy Duckworth. She trusted him completely and was so much in love that she just couldn't see the man's poor character. She'd never been in love before. He seemed to her to be the most wonderful creature on earth. She gazed at him with total adoration. He gazed at her with lust and desire. He hadn't a clue how to be a decent human being; he had no idea that she'd be repelled by the nefarious plan he had put into action. He only knew what he wanted, and he was determined to get it. He had no idea that she would absolutely loathe his recent actions. He obviously didn't know the young woman whatsoever. He'd been acting strangely lately, happier than normal and mysterious to boot. She couldn't put her finger on it but knew something was up.

Late one Saturday when they were both working, Tommy picked Edith Alice up from her department in circulation at the library and took her out to the local Lyons Corner House for a bite to eat on their lunch break. The waitresses, smartly dressed in their Lyons' uniforms, served the couple a light meal, followed by the company's famous Treacle Tarts.

After eating, Tommy got up, walked around to Edith Alice's side of the table, and fell to one knee. He fished out a small black velvet box, opened it, and said,

"Edith Alice, will you do me the honour of becoming my wife?"

Silence quickly spread from one end of the cafeteria to the other. The whole place must have heard him or seen him drop to one knee. That meant only one thing and the clientele knew it. The waitresses stopped serving and stood still. Everyone awaited Edith Alice's answer. Finally! Edith thought to herself, finally my love is proposing to me!

"Oh yes, oh yes, dear heart, my Tommy, of course I will!" He slid the huge sparkling diamond ring upon the fourth finger of her left hand. The whole cafeteria burst into applause, the men wolf-whistling, the ladies dabbing at their eyes with lace-edged handkerchiefs. The hustle and bustle could be heard once more, and things went back to normal. But not for the romantic couple. Edith Alice stood up, Tommy stood up. He took her hand, raised it to his lips and kissed it. Closing her eyes, she lifted her chin and felt the gentle quick kiss he planted upon her lips. Nothing passionate, for they were in public. At least he knew a little about how to behave in public.

Edith Alice was the happiest woman alive. They spent that evening at their favourite pub, The Cat's Whiskers. The following day was Sunday, so no work for either of them. Edith Alice was beside herself with excitement. Before accompanying her girlfriends to church, she told them the happy news. They could barely sit still in their pews, they were so thrilled for her. Today she planned to tell the Mother Superior of the convent. Edith Alice knew the abbess was dismayed about her dropping her novitiate status, but she believed Mother Superior would also be so happy with the news of her engagement. Edith Alice knew Mother Superior thought of her almost as a daughter and thus only wanted happiness for her.

"Come with me, dear Tommy. The abbess will be thrilled, I know, and desirous of meeting you."

Tommy's heart started pounding as he anxiously thought to himself, Oh Lord, now this is a conundrum once again. I can't go to see the abbess because when last she saw me, I was Arthur Higginbotham from the Manchester Auction House. No, it wouldn't do at all for me to accompany Edith Alice. How to get out of this?

After Edith Alice had returned from church, the happy couple was walking along the towpath of the Bridgewater Canal from the city centre, hoping to make it all the way to Salford. Edith Alice's plan was to stop in at the convent on the way to Salford and regale the Mother Superior with her splendid news. It was a very pretty walk, passing under bridges built many years before. They watched barges slowly making their way along the canal. They passed Tudor homes with lawns coming right down to the still water of the canal. They'd each got up early that Sunday at their respective homes to take this long walk together, with Edith Alice attending the early church service with her girlfriends, then meeting up with her Tommy at the towpath. There were pubs along the way where they were planning to stop at noon for a Ploughman's Lunch.

Edith Alice hoped they'd get as far as Salford, at least as far as the convent. She could think of nothing but imparting her news to her 'second mother'.

Hand-in-hand, they strolled along, Tommy now in silence as he pondered how to get out of visiting the abbess. An idea started for form in his head.

"I'm not feeling so good, Edith Alice, my dear heart. I must have eaten something bad yesterday at Lyons. Something must have been a little off. My tummy has been churning and I've not been feeling up to snuff."

"Oh no, Tommy, that's not good. I so want you to meet my dear abbess. I know she'd love to make your acquaintance."

"I don't think that can happen, dearest, at least, not today. Oh God, I feel I may have to be sick." He ran convincingly behind a bush beside the towpath. Bending over, he made retching noises. Edith Alice stood alarmed with her hand over mouth, wondering what to do. Tommy came around from the bush holding his large white handkerchief to his mouth. He put a sick expression on his face. It seemed to have worked. He decided to pretend he was getting even worse. Bending over and clutching his stomach, he inwardly told himself, I'll tell her I'll catch a bus home and she should go on without me. That way, I can stop in at any old pub near home for a bite of lunch and she'll be none the wiser. I love her, but I just can't let her know I sold the book to the convent. I want her to see it when she's there, so when she does find out, she'll be impressed with my cleverness. She already loves that expensive diamond ring! She'll be so happy her beloved abbess has the book. Surely, she wouldn't give a hoot about Mr. Sutton no longer owning it. Besides, it's just a stupid book.

The plan did work, just as Tommy thought it would. He left his beloved on the towpath, and, continuing to hold the crumpled handkerchief over his mouth, he made a show of stumbling away from the canal up to the nearest road to look for an omnibus to take his poor, sick, carcass home to bed. It wasn't nice of him to trick Edith Alice like that, but it was all in a good cause, wasn't it? He'd come out smelling like roses. They'd get married and live happily ever after. That's what he thought. How mistaken can a person be?

Edith Alice could barely contain herself in her excitement to tell her Mother Superior at the convent about her darling Tommy Duckworth. She continued along the towpath on her own, regretting the absence of her fiancé. Once she'd arrived at the convent, she received bad news. Mother Superior had gone into her bi-annual 'Period of Silence' and would not be available to receive visitors for a little while.

Looking into his safe one day, Charles discovered that his precious treasure, his monasticon, had vanished. Dematerialised from the face of the earth. Vanished for the third time, and out of his office safe, to boot!

How on earth could that have happened? He was the only one with a key. Not even W.R. or Percy had a key.

By now, he had his own telephone in his office, so he grabbed hold of it and dialled the police station.

"Give me PC 39, please. On his way back from a meeting? Be back in a minute? Yes, I'll wait, but I must speak to him the minute he comes back in, if you don't mind. Alright, I'll hold, but do please tell him I'm waiting on the telephone the minute he comes in!"

"Richard, hullo! It's gone again. Yes, again. The third time! My precious antique monasticon. What do I want you to do about it? Yes, I KNOW it always comes back, but I must report its theft, mustn't I? You police constables must have an idea who'd pinch a book like that, and where they'd try to sell it? Alright, alright. It's definitely been stolen; taken right out of my office safe. Can you believe it? How on earth? Any idea who the local safe-breakers are these days? No? Who'd even want it, Richard? Alright, alright, Richard. You go ahead and look into it, make your report and do please get back to me as soon as you hear anything. Yes, I know, you told me that you're sometimes out on your beat and sometimes working the desk at the station. Aren't you too high up now to be walking the beat? Well, alright, Richard, yes. Add it to your Missing Items List and work on trying to find it when you can. Yes, and I like your idea, ask people when you're walking your beat. Good idea, Richard. Good. Thank you, Richard, thank you very much." Charles wasn't often as annoyed-sounding as this to anyone, but he was irritated; he'd had it. Why hadn't he checked in his office safe earlier? He hadn't a clue how long it may have been gone for this time so couldn't tell Richard that. He had assumed it was lying exactly where he'd placed it after he'd found it that last time at the omnibus station, shown it to Maria, then brought it back to work and put it in his safe.

Charles placed the phone on its cradle, stared into space, and out of sheer habit, just for a second or two, he decided to tell Charles Dickens the annoying, horrible news. Sadness quickly replaced that thought and regret washed over him as he thought about his dear friend's death long before in 1870. He decided instead that he'd ring his eldest son, Charles Evans Sutton. He really needed to impart the news to somebody close to him. He knew Charlie had a telephone and would be interested in the news.

Picking up the phone, he placed a long-distance call.

"Seriously? It's gone, again?" Charlie said. "What's going on with that monasticon? I'm sorry to hear this news, Father, most sorry indeed." Charlie let his father ramble on, making appropriate tut-tutting noises here and there. He loved his father very much and was conflicted over his own thoughts. He regretted how upset Charles got whenever the monasticon vanished. He also regretted that his father laid such importance on a book, a mere book! On the other hand, he knew how old the book was, and how his father felt about it—he couldn't, therefore, fault him for those feelings.

Having unburdened himself for a good fifteen minutes, and not wanting to take up more of his son's time, Charles put the telephone back into its cradle. Besides, those long-distance phone calls were very expensive. He was pleased to have spoken to Charlie, but he knew talking to Dickens would have been quite different. Dickens would have truly appreciated what the loss of the book meant to Charles. Charlie couldn't be expected to really understand; he wasn't that bookish, and like most young people, a book about monasteries wasn't going to be very exciting for him. Charles knew most people wouldn't really understand, but one person would have. Charles sat at his desk thinking about his friendship with the late Charles Dickens. How his father, Thomas, had got to know the man and how, as a youngster, Charles himself had grown up hearing about, then meeting, the famous author himself. Boz would have certainly understood Charles' attachment to the monasticon.

Then his thoughts turned to PC 39. Already twice before he'd had to telephone the poor police constable about the theft of his precious and valuable book meant that the man was virtually a friend by now. Charles had had occasion to meet him a few times but not for a while. The police constable was a tall but rather portly gentleman, rather like his supervisor, the police chief. PC 39's real name was, of course, Richard Marsden, but Charles had become accustomed to referring to him by the number on his jacket collar. PC 39 had two jobs at the police station. One was to man the front desk and the other was to walk the beat, as he'd explained to Charles. As a matter of fact, Richard had been promoted and wore different insignia on his uniform collar by now, but Charles hadn't seen him in person for years, so had no idea. Apparently, he still walked the beat now and again, although his promotion meant that he didn't have to. More junior constables could do that, but Richard liked the job. That's when he'd work out what was going on in the neighbourhood, who was up to no good, whom he ought to keep an eye on. Richard would pick up local gossip from chatty people passing the time of day with him as he walked along, checking all was well, and dealing with situations and incidents that required police attention.

Charles had researched the Manchester police department, as he would—his life revolved around research on everything and everyone. By 1900 the United Kingdom (but not including Ireland) had 46,800 policemen working out of 243 constabularies. In England and Wales alone were 44,904 policemen, a ratio of one to every 724 people. Charles loved facts, figures, and statistics of all sorts.

Ever curious, Charles looked up where the word 'bobby' came from, the term everyone used for a policeman. In 1829, an aristocrat named Sir Robert Peel had established the London Metropolitan Police Force, with certain policies and rules that the members (now affectionately known as bobbies) had to follow. It was Peel who eventually became known as the Father of Modern Policing.

Charles found PC 39 to be somewhat ponderous and cautious, but that was not only part of his character, but also part of the way policing was practised. PC 39 was also gruff. He sported a drooping greyish-red moustache, had tired, watery eyes, and wore a leather belt that encircled his rather fat belly. The belt held his truncheon. On his head was the regulation custodian helmet, otherwise known as a 'Bobby Helmet'. As he walked his beat, he removed his truncheon from his belt and held it in his right hand, banging it rhythmically into the palm of his left hand. Children, hearing the approaching thwack, thwack beat a very hasty retreat in the opposite direction.

That night Charles told Maria what had happened. She assured him the erstwhile book would show up; after all, it always did, didn't it? She gave him his supper with a glass of strong ale. Emotionally exhausted, he decided to have an early night. With an aching heart he went upstairs to their bedchamber, lighting the way with his candlestick. Maria stayed downstairs to clean up, allowing him to grieve his treasure's loss alone for a while. "Damnation, it's all too much, it really is," sighed Charles. He climbed into bed and, shivering from upset, he drew the curtains around the bed to shut out the draught and soon felt his body start to warm. When Maria parted the curtains to climb into bed, Charles was breathing slowly and regularly. What a relief, he'd fallen asleep. It was, indeed, all getting to be too much, she reckoned. Dare she say it? Yes, she would. She'd said it before and she'd say it again: "That dratted book!"

⸙

One week later, after Sunday morning church, Edith Alice telephoned the convent and discovered that Mother Superior was out of her 'Period of Silence' and ready to receive visitors. The young woman now proceeded along the towpath on another long walk until she saw the towers of the old convent this side of Salford. She'd invited her lover to accompany her but, when he heard her mission, he declined, saying his stomach still wasn't quite right so he wouldn't want to risk being away from home. Hurrying up to the big oak door of the convent, she rang the bell-pull. The panel across the little window slid open and a nun's coifed face appeared.

"Sister Winifred Agnes, is that really you? Oh, how delighted Mother Superior will be to see you!" The heavy oak door creaked slowly open, and Edith Alice stepped inside.

With delight, she regaled the old abbess with her happy story of her engagement to her sweetheart, Tommy Duckworth. They shared a celebratory tiny glass each of liqueur, provided periodically to the convent by the Benedictine monks in France. The abbess kept in touch with those monks on purpose. She much enjoyed receiving the occasional bottle or two of this exquisite, strong, alcoholic drink. Besides, it was good for controlling one's intestinal workings when taken before a meal.

She toasted Edith Alice by saying, "To God most good, most great. You'll recall, child, that that's what the DOM means in Latin, don't you, as in *Deo Optimo Maximo*? You know, in the name of the liqueur, Bénédictine DOM. Oh it's a wonderful elixir, isn't it, and will sustain us both for yet awhile. Do you know, it has twenty-seven different herbs and spices in it but those rascally Bénédictine monks refuse to give me their recipe!"

Edith Alice took a sip and smiled.

"Not that you'd even have any idea how to make the elixir, Mother!"

"Such cheek, you sweetest of girls!"

Now feeling quite relaxed and happy to impart her own news, the abbess opened a drawer in her desk and took out the monasticon with a flourish. Edith Alice's hands flew to her throat, and she gasped in amazement. She placed her glass of Bénédictine down on the table with a plonk causing the contents to fly up the sides with a little splashing over the top.

She gasped out, "Why, that's Mr. Sutton's vanished monasticon. Let me see. Yes, oh yes, most certainly it is. How did you come by it, dear Mother Superior?"

The abbess told the young woman her story about Arthur Higginbotham selling it to her.

Edith Alice went quite white. She wasn't stupid. An awful, horrible feeling swept up from the bottom of her stomach to her mouth. Running from the room into the tiny lavatory next to the abbess' office, she saw her pale face in the mirror and thought she might have to vomit. She wiped her forehead with a wet handkerchief and took some deep breaths to calm herself.

Returning to the abbess, now quite in control of her emotions, Edith Alice asked the old lady to describe the man from the Manchester Auction House. She knew it. She now removed the diamond engagement ring from her finger and handed it to the abbess.

"He's not getting this back, no he's not," she told the old lady, after explaining who the man really was.

"You must sell this ring, Mother Superior, to replace the whole amount of money you spent to purchase this book. I shall return the book, with your kind permission, to its rightful owner—my dear employer, the chief librarian of our Manchester Free Library. Mr. Charles Sutton has been bereft since his precious book vanished apparently, he said, for the third time. It is, indeed, a police matter. I shall report Mr. Duckworth to PC 39, who always follows the case when this valuable book vanishes, again and again, it would seem. It must be exceedingly valuable. Actually, he's been promoted but I don't know what else to call him."

With that, Edith Alice took the book and departed.

The abbess sat quite still for the longest time. She then went into the convent chapel and fell to her knees and prayed. What did she pray for? For gratefulness to God who had used this incident to teach her a valuable lesson—not to be proud. Owning such a book would have been a chance to show her fellow nuns and other convent abbesses how superior her convent was. That was a vice. Pride was a vice. But God was good in that she now had a valuable diamond ring to sell. She'd use the money from the sale to replace the large amount of money she had pridefully borrowed from the convent's coffers just to acquire a material book, religious or not. She prayed that God would forgive that young man and make him see the error of his ways. She prayed that God would forgive her for her greed, albeit to acquire such a wonderful book for her Order. She prayed that her dear Edith Alice would return to the convent fold. Men were evil creatures; God had just proved it. She stood up, went straight back into her office, and knocked back not one, but two glasses of Bénédictine liqueur.

Edith Alice left the convent in a hurry. She was white with fury, disappointment, dismay, and, indeed, the worst feeling of all—feeling duped. She'd almost married the bounder!

That's it, no more men for me. Rotten, evil bounders. That's what they are! It's over. I should never have left my novitiate. I shall tell dear Mother Superior after talking with my dear girlfriends and the convent nuns that I shall, no, that I WILL take the veil. I will become a Bride of Christ. But first, I shall slap that Duckworth's smug face, the bounder, the rotten, horrid, mean, nasty bounder. HOW COULD HE DO THIS? The only good thing will be when I return the monasticon to poor Mr. Sutton who has suffered so each time it has vanished. Oh yes, and the ring, that whopping diamond ring. Well, Mother Superior will get a good price for it to recompense her. Oh, that bounder, oh, he's broken my heart...

With all those thoughts teeming through her brain, she got on an omnibus and returned home. Monday morning saw her knocking on Mr. Sutton's door to deliver what his heart desired the most. The monasticon had been missing for quite a long time. With heartfelt appreciation, the kind gentleman embraced the young lass and promoted her on the spot.

Richard Marsden, a/k/a PC 39, received a telephone call from the chief librarian, excitedly telling him the monasticon had been returned and asking him to remove it from his 'Missing Items List'. PC 39 took down all the details, particularly in reference to the bounder who'd stolen the book from Charles Sutton. Noting the name of Mr. Thomas Duckworth, he hung up the phone and spoke to his Superintendent. He then gathered up another police constable. The three men arrived at the library and asked for directions to the acquisitions department. It was a simple matter, really. They accused Duckworth. His face flared crimson. His fists balled, but they had him, and he knew it. They put the handcuffs on him and took him away, the wretched thief that he was. As he was led toward the exit of the building, propelled forward by the portly superintendent, and with a police constable on either side, the burly fat one holding tightly onto his handcuffs, he saw his beloved standing in a doorway. Her mouth turned down, her eyes but slits as she glared at him. He glanced at the left hand holding her lacy white handkerchief to her chin. No ring. Where was his diamond ring? She saw his glance, and a smile flitted across her mouth: he knew. He wasn't ever going to see his expensive diamond ring again. As he stopped for a minute to stare at Edith Alice, she stepped forward and, quick as lightning, slapped Tommy across his face, leaving a white handprint on his burning right cheek. He started back in surprise and dismay, then, with a sinking feeling, but without any compassion for the bereft, cheated lass, he stumbled as he was pushed through the library's main exit by the superintendent and the two burly police constables in bobby helmets, tall as giants next to his suddenly shrunken, sad, and wretched self.

And Edith Alice? Having obtained permission from the abbess to re-enter her novitiate, she took back her title of Sister Winifred Agnes and moved into the convent at the abbess's invitation. She was given a rather nice but appropriately sparse cell looking onto the courtyard. She knew nuns needed no worldly comforts. And yet, at night, through her little window, she could hear the ever-running gentle splashing of the water fountain, and that, too, was good and yes, quite comforting. To enter her little cell, Sister Winifred Agnes bowed her head before God. The lintels above the cell doorways were all purposely built extra low. Even if you were a rather short person, you still had to duck your head to honour the good Lord. All of this was very good to Sister Winifred Agnes.

The novice began to calm down in all ways. She still worked at the library where she helped her dear Mr. Sutton whenever asked, but more and more, she spent time in the convent chapel, on her knees, praying and giving thanks to her God for this second chance to become a nun. Life was becoming good and stable once again.

Chapter 29
Memoir

Oh, my goodness, how my heart went out to Great Grandpa. He had to be feeling a mixture of relief to get the book back, plus disappointment, dismay, and maybe even a modicum of anger about Tommy's pinching the monasticon—although it appeared to me that Charles didn't possess any genetic propensity for feeling the kind of fury I reckoned I'd be feeling, with the repeated loss of my favourite book. I sat in my office thinking about the third time the monasticon had vanished. All because of that Tommy Duckworth! What a money-grubbing, revolting, smarmy, young, egocentric, creep he'd been. How on earth hadn't Edith Alice seen through him? She wasn't stupid. Ah, love is indeed blind. When I'd been reading Great Grandpa's notes about the young couple's love for each other, I'd had a horrible suspicion Edith Alice was going to get hurt. I could see it coming. What was it that Queen Elizabeth II had said, 'Grief is the price we pay for love.' So true. My heart now went out to Edith Alice once again. I just hadn't bought it that Tommy had been truly in love with her. He was simply a horrible young chap with no integrity, decency, honour, or ethics. I recalled hoping, when reading more of Great Grandpa's jottings, I'd discover that Tommy had turned out to be not so bad after all, 'though I'd doubted it. Anyhow, the wretch had got his just desserts and ended up in gaol. Good thing, said I to myself.

I stirred up all the paperwork on my desk, looking for some sort of note that would tell me what happened next. This time the vanished book had been found in pretty short order. Of course, I now wondered about my own hunt for the vanishing book in my world. Where on earth WAS it these days? Surely it wouldn't have been thrown away in the garbage? I most certainly hoped not!

Now Charles had the book back, what would he do next? And what should I do next in my own hunt for the book?

Chapter 30
1902

harles sat back down at his desk in his library office, musing about his family tree. In his middle years now, he sported a full brown moustache. By the time he was fifty-four in 1902, newspaper journalists were having fun drawing caricatures of him for their newspapers, because of his influence at the library and in Manchester in general. He was considered a 'man of mark'. Charles raised his teacup to his lips. White bone china decorated with exquisite pink rosebuds, a gift from Maria. Hardly manly, he thought, but made him think fondly of his Maria every time he drank from it. It had a china ledge across it where he sipped, which cleverly held his rather thick moustache out of the tea. Every time he drank from the teacup, he found the ledge to be a clever idea by its maker, and a most thoughtful gift from Maria. He then rose and stared out of his mullioned window. After many chats with Maria and her parents, Charles had learned a lot about the more recent Pocklingtons on her side of the family.

He recalled years back having a chat with Dickens about the Suttons—indeed, that was the day his dratted raven had stolen the monasticon. How he wished the family's dear friend Boz had remained alive so he could have asked him about Maria's family, and now his—all those Pocklingtons to learn about. When Boz had flipped through the monasticon—prior to that evil bird, Grip, flying off with the book— neither Boz nor he himself, had realised that the Walter Bishop, then Walter Pocklington, had been an ancestor of Maria's. How would they? Charles was still young and hadn't even met Maria at that time. It was only much later, well after Boz's death in 1870, when Charles had married Maria on that sparkling February day in the spring of 1892, that he'd read the words in the monasticon that referred back to her ancestor.

How did those words go? He had the book back but had locked it in the safe, but he could remember well enough to bring the words back to him. Something to do with the book being written after the old ex-bishop Walter Bishop, a/k/a Walter Pocklington, returned at the end of his life to the abbey in York where he had told his story to the abbot. Both the abbot and his scribe must have been very old men by then. How fascinating it was, indeed, that this Walter Pocklington was an ancestor of my wife, Maria, Charles had thought. Oh, and then there were the rather salacious bits added into the story. Charles and Maria both had wondered what the scribe was thinking when he had been commanded to transcribe what the abbot was telling him. They found it quite extraordinary that Walter would have revealed his romantic exploits to the abbot!

Staring into the distance, he mused about the Suttons, too, and knew they were an old, old family from the Lancashire area, and beyond. Charles William Sutton himself was born in Manchester. His great-grandfather, Robert Sutton, had married a lady called Susannah Bentley. Their second son was called Thomas Sutton, and he was to become young Charles' father. Thomas was born on 11th March 1825. He married Martha Eyres, the second daughter of Robert and Mary Eyres, at the Collegiate Church of Manchester on 25th September 1845. They had eight children. Their first son was Charles William Sutton himself, born 14th April 1848. "Yes, me!" Charles smiled to himself. "And," he said under his breath, still staring out the sunny window, "it was my father, Thomas, who was Charles Dickens's good friend, but that's only to do with the Sutton side of the family. I need to pursue the Pocklingtons' history further before researching more of my paternal line. I do find the Pocklington story engrossing, and I'm much enjoying reading about who they all were, so the Suttons' story will have to wait."

Looking over his notes, he spoke to himself, as was his wont, "Hmm, that Pocklington begat this Pocklington, who begat that one, who then, good Lord, begat this other one, and then...this is ridiculous, it's getting to be like the Old Testament in the Bible with all the begats!" He started in surprise, as a thought leapt out at him from the page. Aloud, he stated clearly to nobody in the room, "Thomas and Martha had a son before me, called Robert, born on 3rd October 1845. They were married on 25th September 1845, so, wait a minute, that meant they had to get married. Well, well, naughty father and mother, eh!" Musing on, he noticed they'd had a second son, also called Robert, born on 18th September 1846 but who died only five months later, on 25th February 1847. "And then I came along one year later, and how happy they must have been that I lived, as did my six subsequent siblings," he continued, whispering softly to himself.

Charles had spent many a happy hour researching Maria's and his family tree. In talking with Maria and her family, he told her that his Sutton family, through marriage with the Pocklington people, was joined with people who could be traced all the way back to 1202. When he'd told her that little detail, she'd let out a whistle of amazement. "Hardly womanly, my dear, whistling like a man!" Maria knew he never criticised her in earnest, so in response, she just threw her plump arms around his neck and gave him a loving hug and a kiss.

Now smiling at such a warm memory, Charles got up from his chair and paced around his office. "But," he told the walls, "so much must have happened in those six hundred and sixty-three years between that first dated entry of 1202 I put in the family tree, and when I started my library work in 1865, so very much..." He sat back down and tugged on his moustache. He then burst out with, "Well, I've most assuredly got my work cut out for me, now haven't I?" W.R. and Percy raised their heads to stare at the window separating Charles' office from theirs. They both then looked back at each other, shaking their heads in fond amusement at their employer's outburst.

This family research project might take him all his life, but, oh joy! What a job this was turning out to be, finding out who all Maria's forbears were, who now were his, simply through his second marriage. The history the Pocklingtons had lived through! His heart began beating faster. Leaping up from the old chair, he stretched his arms up high in pure delight, spun around in a pirouette, then clapped his hands together in elated anticipation of what more he hoped he was about to discover. Plopping back down into his chair, he had to smile, realising he was hardly young anymore, yet could still act like a youngster and react in youthful glee.

Breathing heavily from that exertion, he suddenly remembered a book he'd noticed in one of the stacks. He'd made a mental note to look at it once he'd finished researching the Pocklington side of the family. The book he'd briefly skimmed through addressed the origins of the Sutton family name. He'd decided that this book would be a good place to start on the Suttons' genealogy. He'd already discovered the first time his own branch of the Sutton name was mentioned in family records, and that was for a Robert Sutton born in 1789. This Robert Sutton was his own grandfather. Charles had already penned Robert's name on the family tree, with his wife, Susannah, entered beside him. Now, thoroughly intrigued, and impatient to know more right away, Charles leapt up from his chair.

"The Pocklingtons are going to have to wait while I look up the Suttons," he smilingly told W.R. and Percy as he marched out of his office. They gave each other another meaningful look, then bent their heads back to their work. Charles marched quickly to the bookstacks and took down the book he'd seen earlier on the shelf. Returning to his office, and flipping through the pages, he was soon glued to the book, reading about the origins of his paternal Sutton name.

"My goodness," Charles again burst out aloud. "Here's information from even before 1202...I wonder if I should enter it on the family tree? Ah, probably not; I don't want to tread on the Pocklington toes, now do I! I'll just leave the tree starting with old Walter Bishop-cum-Pocklington, that's what I'll do." Then, sighing gustily, he said aloud, "Meanwhile, I really want to research the beginnings of the Suttons some more, so yes, that's what I'll do right now."

OUR LIBRARIAN.

MR. C. W. SUTTON.

MANCHESTER EVENING CHRONICLE

Dec. 20ᵗ 1902
54 years of age.

The Suttons in general went back a long way in history, even a little over a century before Walter Bishop (now Pocklington) had arrived in England. Charles reckoned that, of course, his own Sutton branch would have at some stage descended from these original Suttons. Following the Norman Conquest of 1066, Charles read that the Suttons lived in a village called Sutton Montagu in Somerset (also known as Sutton Montis). The family was descended from one Dreu de Montaigu who'd arrived in England in 1066, following a personage by the name of the Count of Mortain. Sutton Montagu was where Dreu settled first, then moved up north to Tuxford in Nottinghamshire in the Midlands of England, where the Suttons became lords of the manor at Sutton-on-Trent. Charles saw that the family acquired the Sutton name from the place they lived in— a toponymic surname—which was normal in those days. Sutton meant 'south farmstead or village'. He also noted that the book claimed that every English county has one or more placenames with a prefix of Sutton, and that the Domesday Book had various spellings listed for the Sutton name.

"They certainly got around, did the Suttons," Charles said, with a laugh out loud.

The first Sutton listed was called Roland, the son of Hervey, a man living in the reign of Henry III (1216-1272). This Roland married Alice, the daughter and heiress of Richard de Lexington. Nottinghamshire became the established family seat, particularly around the parish of Averham.

"This is similar to how the Pocklingtons got their name," Charles said. Percival heard his employer talking aloud, with nobody in his office.

"I tell you, Mr. Credland, our boss is at it again. I always think somebody's slipped past me into his office, but no, it's just our Mr. Sutton talking to himself", Percy sighed. Mr. Credland simply smiled fondly at Percy's words and carried on working.

Finding all this new information fascinating, Charles read on. It seemed that an earlier Robert Sutton, also known variously as Lord Lexington or the Baron of Averham, had a manor house in Averham, where the family had dwelled since the year 1250. Many skirmishes and battles were fought in the area and by the time of the siege of Newark-on-Trent in 1644, the manor house was destroyed.

"Probably set fire to...I wonder where the Suttons went...must have left the area...probably ending up in various other villages..." Charles whispered, thoughtfully pulling on his moustache.

Charles was intrigued to read further on that there were relics and old memorials to the Suttons in the churches of Averham and Kelham.

Some of the windows in the ancient churches dated back to 1220. In one of the churches could be seen a memorial, decorated with cherubs and armorial bearings, to the memory of the 'Right Honourable Robert Lord Lexington,' who, it said, 'descended from 'ye ancient family of ye Suttons'.'

"Well, what do you know, a probable forbear of my own was a 'Right Honourable' and 'a lord' to boot...must be...and yet, who knows which branch of the Suttons I hail from, what with Suttons, whoever they were, having moved all over the place, from what I've been reading in this book about the origin of their name."

There was also a line in the book stating that Kelham Hall was the family seat of the Suttons since its construction in the 1860s. "Ah, I know that place. A huge red brick manor house, a bit like a castle, with its own clock-tower, and surrounded by green lawns. Nice, very nice indeed."

"So," Charles muttered further to himself, "we Suttons have been in this area of England for many, many years. Both the Pocklingtons and the Suttons have lived up here in the Midlands. Not only that, but both families came over to England originally from France. Fascinating, yes, quite interesting, indeed. I'll be sure to get into that research further." He shut the book, left his office, replaced it on the shelf, taking good note of its location, and took a walk around the stack of books to stretch his legs, wondering how long Maria's Pocklington family had potentially lived in the same villages as his early Sutton forbears.

Chapter 31
Memoir

I'd had another idea. I'd looked for the monasticon in a few online bookstores specialising in out-of-print books. One day, I received an email from one of those specialist bookstores, advising that the monasticon had been located. Hallelujah! It was going to cost me a sizable amount of money, but I felt it was well worth it. With delight, I responded to the email, only to discover it was, indeed, a monasticon, but not the one I sought. It was a copy of the first of several volumes of the *Monasticon anglicanum* published by Sir William Dugdale in 1655, thus far too late to be 'my' monasticon. I had read in Great Grandpa Charles Sutton's notes that Lord John Morley had advised him to read the *Monasticon anglicanum*. With dismay—as I always did—off I went out into my garden to smell the flowers and work off my frustration.

If I had the monasticon I searched for, I felt I could fill in some, or even many of the gaps in Great Grandpa's documents I'd inherited. The notes I had read were intriguing and there had to be so much more within the book that would enlighten me as to what happened to my ancestors in those long-ago times. I was grateful he'd jotted down so many notes about everything going on around him. I had no idea how he'd had the time with his busy job and all the committees he served on, but it was a real boon to me to be able to go through his notes to put together some of the story of his life.

Returning to my computer, I picked up the genealogical tree again where I read about a William de Pocklington in 1509 who'd had a dispute against someone called Robert de Lawethorpe about crofts. Years before when I'd been up to Yorkshire, I'd seen plenty of old crofts still scattered around the countryside. They were selling for a great deal of money when I was up there, and probably cost even more today. A croft in the

16th century was usually rented out as a small farm for it had land suitable for farming attached to it, and even the right to pasture one's animals on other nearby land, in common with other crofts or farms. Thus, a croft would have held good value in the 1500s. The land itself in this modern day would hold even more value, what with the burgeoning growth of construction going on in so many areas of England. Curious, I read on in the family tree and scribbles in Charles Sutton's own handwriting.

Chapter 32
1902

As it happened, deciding to research more about the Pocklingtons, Charles found that in many of the library books there were, indeed, references to the old Pocklington family. He read that in 1509 William de Pocklington had a dispute against Robert de Lawethorpe of Yorkshire, who was simply listed as a Gentleman. William and his wife, Elizabeth, won their suit and received a croft, fourteen acres of meadows for hay, eighty acres of cropland, and twenty acres of grazing pasture in South Searle, Yorkshire. Charles was curious as to what could possibly have caused William and Elizabeth to receive such a settlement offering, but he wasn't to find out. It would require too much time to delve deeper into this one particular facet of his literary adventure. "I've got an entire library filled already with thousands of gems to rifle through," he muttered gleefully to himself. "How lucky am I!"

Charles noted many Pocklingtons were baptised in the mid-17th century, and dutifully inscribed their names on his burgeoning family tree. Many of the family were vicars and various church leaders. Smiling to himself, he wondered what their ancestor, Walter Bishop Pokelinton from Gascony, would have thought of that. Maybe that it was something in the genes, passed down from Walter himself even though given up by himself. Walter certainly hadn't wanted to continue as a bishop once he'd left France, according to what Charles had read in the monasticon. If only all the conversations between Walter and the abbot at the monastery had been recorded, written down by the abbot's scribe. Charles would have found that very interesting indeed.

In another library book, he read that in 1637 William Pocklington became a constable in Chesterfield, Nottinghamshire. Said Charles under his breath, "A constable? Imagine that! Quite a different profession from a church position, indeed". Reading further, Charles read that the constable's son, a Dr. John Pocklington, M.A. got into trouble with the law, as well as parliament. Records show that this gentleman had a doctorate, was a canon of the church, and his books were burnt by the common hangman on parliament's orders. He was known as a 'fearful High Churchman in his day' and many people disliked his preaching. Charles muttered, "Wonder what old Walter Bishop would have thought of that?" Immersed in the story, Charles read that the good doctor wrote many books, which were placed in a pile in the centre of town and set fire to, with a crowd cheering from the sidelines. Dr. Pocklington had appealed parliament's decision to burn his lifework, citing 'injured innocence' and argued that they hadn't understood his contentions in his writing. His efforts to save his books were to no avail. Every one of his works went up in flames. The burning of precious books made Charles sick to his stomach. Finding a chair nearby, he sat heavily down, his mind swirling with grievous thoughts of England's parliamentary leaders in those days.

Immersed in this research, he stood up again and turned to even more of the books available to him, where he read more of the 'Sufferings of the Clergy', about nonconformist ministers who were silenced and ejected after the 1660 English Restoration, and of the deprivation and sequestration of these men of God.

As the 17th century wound on, Charles saw more and more Pocklingtons turning away from church professions and into academia. "Good thing, I reckon," said Charles aloud to the book stacks. Back in his office, armed with a pile of books to research, Charles continually drew his growing family tree toward him to make yet another entry of name, dates, profession, and spouse. The document was growing fatter and longer, each page written in Charles Sutton's own spidery but clear script.

One of the Pocklingtons worked at St. John's College, Cambridge, Charles discovered, and yet another at Merchant Taylor's School in Crosby, thus, they weren't all farmers or croft-holders. In 1690, a warrant was issued to the Earl of Manchester, Lord Lieutenant of the County of Huntingdon, to appoint John Pocklington as his Deputy Lieutenant. By 1710, this John Pocklington had become a lawyer, and permitted the use of Esquire after his name. He soon became a judge in Cheshire. Charles spoke aloud, "I suppose this could have been the same fellow whose books were burned, I think around 1670, but perhaps not; maybe a different John Pocklington." Hearing his voice through the dividing wall of their two offices, Percy glanced up from his desk and quietly told W.R., seated at the desk next to him, "The boss gets so involved in his research; he can't help himself talking out loud, and just to himself— funny chap, isn't he, Mr. Credland?" In response, the other gentleman said, "such a wonderful man," and gave a fond smile.

Charles continued with his research. The Pocklingtons were now involved in even more adventurous pursuits. In 1712, Captain Christopher Pocklington, who was sixty-four at the time and lived on Grafton Street in Dublin, was appointed in command of the 'Rippon' ship. She was a sixty-gun fourth rate vessel of the British Royal Navy's line. By 1744 the Rippon was cruising in the Windward Passage. She took a Royal Navy prize of a Spanish Man of War called the *Conde de Chincán*, bound for Vera Cruz, with eighteen guns, eight swivels, and one hundred and forty men, and captured under the Island of Tortuga. On board Captain Pocklington found twelve hundred chests of quicksilver along with a large amount of other valuable merchandise. Although originally very well fitted, by 1751 defects were discovered. The Rippon was therefore taken to pieces and a new sixty-gun ship was built to replace her.

More lawyers surfaced in the family. In 1789, Roger Pocklington, L.L.B. (Bachelor of Laws) taught at Jesus College, University of Cambridge. Yet by the late 18th century, many Pocklingtons had gone back to being church rectors, including one Thomas, who pastored his flock at Rotherby Church in Leicester for thirty-two years. He is interred there alongside his wife, Mehetabel. As Charles took a break from reading, he rose, stretched his legs and thought about how he loved the name Mehetabel.

He then left his office, saying a quick "Good afternoon, gentlemen" to W.R. and Percy. He proceeded down the corridors of the library happily whispering to himself, "Mehetabel, Mehetabel, how I do love thy name!" A passing junior librarian eyed him anxiously, nearly dropping the tray of cups of teas he was taking to the librarians' staff lounge.

"Alright then, sir?"

"Just fine and dandy, my boy, not to worry! Research is the thing, research is most definitely the thing, my boy!"

Back in his office, he carried on with his own way of filling his break-time, tracing the genealogy of the Pocklingtons. He paused at one point, wishing he were working on the Sutton tree. As much as the Pocklingtons' line fascinated him, he couldn't wait to unearth the past of his paternal family.

"Onward," Charles sighed, refilling his pen with ink from a pot dropped down inside a snug hole at the top right of the old wooden desk.

The last two decades of the 18th century saw a few Pocklingtons as aldermen in Nottinghamshire, Lincolnshire, and Bath, Somerset. By the turn of the century, a brave soul by the name of Joseph Pocklington, had left the area of York in the north and moved south, to become rector of St George's Church in Hanover Square in London. He knew that in the south of England, many would look down their noses at him with his 'oop north' accent, but nevertheless, he felt he could bring many of the lost souls down south into the Protestant fold.

But by the mid-19th century, the Pocklingtons completely left the ecclesiastic world to hold far more mundane professions. In 1856, Robert Pocklington was named Clerk of the Market. Also in 1856, Joseph Pain Pocklington was a music teacher, but by 1867 dramatically changed his career and became a butcher. Maybe it was a pain for him to teach unruly little boys so changed his tune, Charles smilingly said to himself, always enjoying a wee pun. In 1899, Thorston W. Pocklington decided to try his hand as a cattle salesman. That same year, Mrs. Agnes Pocklington turned her more delicate hand to dressmaking.

Charles Sutton, sitting at his library desk in Manchester, had heard of these London relatives, but even at fifty-four, in his middle years, he hadn't yet had the privilege of visiting the south of England. When Thomas, his father, had gone to visit Dickens in London when Charles was twelve, the youth had been given the job of staying behind to mind Thomas' bookstore in Manchester. Charles longed to see all that London had to offer, particularly its libraries and bookshops. In London he would have been able to visit his old friend Charles Dickens much more often and easily, but, and he sighed gustily again, poor old Boz had passed on so long ago, back in 1870. "My goodness, that's already thirty-two years ago!" He still retained all that his father, Thomas, had told him when he'd returned home from London from his visit to his good friend, Dickens.

Chapter 33
Memoir

I'd been reading so many of Great Grandpa's notes about Maria's and his ancestors, making notes for my own book about Great Grandpa's life, when my phone rang. Imagine my delight to discover the call coming in was from a newspaper in California. They told me they'd heard through their sources that I was looking for an ancient book about abbeys in and around York in the U.K.

The journalist said, "Look, this isn't going to be of much interest to the general public, nor sell our newspapers, but I just happened across this information and figured it'd be of particular interest to you. No idea why, ya know, but that ain't my business. If you want me to tell ya about it, just say the word, lady."

"Of course, I'm interested. Really interested. So, the missing monasticon has been found? Where was it? Who's got it? How do I get hold of it? Will it cost me? How did you get my phone number?"

"So many questions, lady. You want it then, don'tcha?"

"I do. How do I proceed?"

"Hang on, another call's coming through. I'll hafta call ya back." He abruptly hung up.

Well, well, it sounded like the monasticon had been found but not by me.

Sighing with frustration, all I could do was wait for him to call me back. I didn't yet have one of those modern phones that could show you the number of who had called. He had told me the name of his newspaper, though, yet for some reason at the time, I thought it prudent to wait for him to ring me again—as impatient as I was to find out. Now I think further on it, I could have just gone ahead and rung him...meanwhile, I went back to Charles Sutton's notes.

I shoved Great Grandpa's notes aside when I heard my phone ring again. Oh joy, it was the California newspaper man phoning me again.

"Still interested in that old book, are ya?"

"I most certainly am. Please don't hang up again; just tell me how I can get it?"

"It's gonna cost ya, you know that, right?"

"I expected as much. What's it going to cost me?"

"A coupla hundred dollars, lady. You can send it straight to me at the newspaper. Take down these details."

He then gave me the instructions for where, and how, to deposit my money. I asked him a few questions. There was something that didn't sit quite right with me. Something in his voice. He wouldn't tell me who had the monasticon or where it was being held. He wanted the money first. I had a bad feeling about this and simply said I'd take care of it, and we'd proceed from there. Instead of depositing the money into the account he'd told me about, I next dialled the newspaper. My suspicion was correct. The editor had never heard of this journalist; he certainly wasn't a member of their staff. I realised I was almost the victim of a telephone scam. Phew, I thought; that was a near miss.

Relieved I'd not sent him any money, out I went once again into my garden to walk around the flowerbeds until I'd got rid of my frustration. Where was the monasticon? How on earth had the man who'd phoned me known I was looking for it? Too weird, but by now many people did know about my search for that elusive book. I went back to my office and carried on writing, having to imagine what had happened in the lives of my Great Grandpa, his library underlings, and those listed in his family tree. Thank goodness I had so many jottings and notes he'd scribbled down.

I scrabbled around amongst the huge pile of Great Grandpa's notes—those masses of bits of paper covered in short remarks and sometimes longer sentences—I still supposed he'd written them all as his thoughts for a book it seemed he'd hoped to write one day. Aha! I found one that was quite interesting to me—saying he hadn't gone to London after all because the monasticon had vanished again! Again! Goodness me. I'd been wondering why he hadn't gone down to visit his relatives in the south of England when there had been a note saying he was going. This was the fourth occasion that the monasticon had vanished.

His note said that he'd taken the book out of his safe and was looking something up in it when he needed to go to the lavatory. He left the book on his office desk, knowing he'd only be out of the room for about five minutes. Upon his return the book had gone. W.R. said the only person who'd been in Charles' office was a young delivery boy, dropping off some paperwork for Charles. It had to have been this boy. Charles' secretary immediately phoned the delivery company. They spoke to the young man who, of course, denied any knowledge of it. By now, PC 39 was pretty much in charge at the Manchester Police Station. He was not happy to hear about the book having vanished yet again. Apparently, per Great Grandpa's scribbles, he agreed to write the details down on his Missing Items List and interview the boy at the delivery company. Another note paper-clipped to this note stated that nothing came of the visit by PC 39. The boy denied anything to do with it and PC 39 said he believed him—particularly because he knew the lad's father who was a perfectly good citizen. This time it looked as if the book really had vanished for good. My heart went out to Great Grandpa in his obvious distress.

Chapter 34
1904

By 1904, Charles Sutton was an important and influential man himself in Manchester. Thirty-nine years prior, he had entered the Manchester Free Library as an assistant librarian, and for the last twenty-five years he had been chief librarian. At almost fifty-seven years of age, he now held many bookish positions aside from his daily work. He was a vice-president of the Library Association, vice-president and treasurer of the Manchester Literary Club, a past president of the Lancashire and Cheshire Antiquarian Society, secretary of the Chetham Society, secretary of the Spenser Society, and honorary librarian of the Manchester Statistical Society (which was known to be able to prove both sides of any given question). He had already published many literary articles for organisations such as the Library Association, the Dictionary of National Biography, and had written *A List of Lancashire Authors*, plus he was the joint author of the *Life of Humphrey Chetham* (who founded the school) and wrote many other recondite essays. It was for all these somewhat abstruse works that in 1900, at the age of fifty-two, he had been granted the honorary degree of Master of Arts in recognition of his labours on behalf of readers of books. The Victoria University of Manchester[27] invited him to be presented with an honorary Master of Arts degree. Donning the

---

[27] The Victoria University of Manchester, usually referred to as simply the University of Manchester, was a university in Manchester, England. It was founded on 12th March 1851 as Owens College. In 1880, the college joined the federal Victoria University. (Charles Sutton attended Owens College as a young man.)

appropriate cloak and mortarboard, Charles proudly accepted his degree certificate.

By late 1908 it was obvious the library premises were far too small and greater space was required. Discussions had been going on for years by this time. A new building was finally to be erected. The committee in charge decided to acquire information that might be of use for the planned new Central Library. They decided to send the chairman (alderman Plummer), deputy chairman (alderman Abbott) and the chief librarian (Charles William Sutton) to the United States to study the libraries there. Charles was to much enjoy the visit, meeting old friends who had gone to America and creating new ones.

CWS at 52 years of age in 1900 received
his Honorary Master of Arts degree from
Victoria University, The University of Manchester.

Chapter 35
Memoir

A piece of paper lay on my desk with the titles of all the books Charles Dickens had written up to the time Thomas Sutton, Great Grandpa's father, had gone down to London to visit Dickens. I wrote my own 'Note to Self: Read all of these!' I'd read most of them in English classes at school, but not all of them. I'd not even been aware Dickens had written plays until I saw what Great Grandpa had jotted down; I made a list of those plays to read, too.

I rang my old friend in San Francisco. I'd heard she was going back to England to do further research on her own book she was writing. I got her up-to-date with my ineffectual hunt for the monasticon. She promised to make some more enquiries for me, including in the Manchester used bookstores. By now, I wasn't holding out much hope, but you never know, do you?

A couple of months went by when I received an email from my friend. She said she'd visited a large number of used bookstores, left flyers on windows and lamp-posts in areas with bookshops in general, but all her enquiries were fruitless. As I told her in my reply, she wouldn't have been able to visit every used bookstore in the Manchester area and I really appreciated her attempt to locate the missing monasticon. It sounded as if that was that now. I realised I'd done so much, along with all my many friends who'd helped, and I'd just have to give up the idea of finding it. It had vanished, and that really was that.

Chapter 36
1908

Charles William Sutton's only child from his second wife, Maria Pocklington, was a son called George William Pocklington Sutton. George was born in 1893 when Charles was forty-five. When George grew old enough, having attained fifteen years of age—at the suggestion of his father—rather than work in his father's library, he went to work at the John Rylands Library. One day, George was going through a stack of overdue books in the library that had accumulated large fees. George's job was not only to put all those books where they belonged in the library, but also to collect the fines as well. Imagine his surprise when he lifted a book from the huge pile of returned books that he was going through and saw that it was the monasticon, which had vanished yet again for the fourth time! Running to the telephone, he rang his father.

"Dad, I've found the vanished book, your monasticon", he shouted excitedly down the telephone.

"Oh, Good Lord, how marvellous!" cried Charles Sutton. "Any way of telling who the person was who stole it? We've always assumed it was a delivery boy who swiped it when bringing some paperwork to my office."

"No, the library card that may have been in the book with the name and date stamped on it has been removed, if it had even had one. I can't tell by looking at it. Anyhow, it shouldn't even have been out on loan, because of its incredible age, and, besides, it's a police matter, being stolen goods."

"I wonder..." said Charles. "I wonder if that delivery boy did swipe it from my office, then was making his next delivery to your library, and, realising a book about old monasteries was boring for him, just dropped it amongst a pile of books there. By the way, it's never had a library card in it. It didn't when I'd first found it, and I then decided it should never be loaned out, so we never stuck a library card in its cover. Just made a note on a library card in the file that I had it."

"Certainly could be that delivery boy, Dad. Maybe the beautiful colours in it had tickled his fancy, so he'd nicked the book...who knows, but anyway, I've got it!"

"George, please do me a favour and you ring Richard Marsden, now head constable at the police station and tell him it's turned up." As he lowered the phone, Charles reckoned the police wouldn't have spared the time to even look for his beloved book, with far more important matters to deal with, but it was always best to let them know, nevertheless. Doubtless the police were sick and tired of Mr. Charles Sutton, he thought to himself.

"Righty-ho, Dad, will do." George got off the telephone, made his next call to the police, then strode off to the library's cloakroom to put the book into a bag to take to his father.

Chapter 37
Memoir

I saw from Great Grandpa's notes that Mr. Sutton, Mr. Plummer, and Mr. Abbott had now arrived in New York City to research the American libraries and, perhaps, use some of the Americans' techniques to construct and run the new library that needed to go up in Manchester. I knew this was Charles Sutton's first visit there. A rush of memories swarmed into my head as I remembered the 13th January 1970, the date of my own first visit to New York City, in fact, the first day I set foot anywhere in the United States of America as an adult. I'd been to the States with my mother and sister at the age of nine and retained plenty of memories from my own youthful days. I could imagine how Great Grandpa felt, his excitement and eagerness to see everything New York had to offer. The delegation had rushed to see the New York Public Library first. I still had my own old library card from that superb library building on Fifth Avenue, having lived in Manhattan in 1970. For the hundredth time, I wished I had known my great grandfather. I was sure we'd get on like a house on fire.

Suddenly I got an idea for pursuing my hunt for the book. I'd pretty much decided to give up my own hunt for the old monasticon, but now...a new idea had sprung to mind for where to look for the ancient book!

I had a memory of reading somewhere in Great Grandpa's jottings that the monasticon had been pinched from his office. Apparently, that was the fourth time it had vanished. I read that his son, George Sutton, had found it at the John Rylands Library where he worked in his first job at fifteen. I now wondered whether Charles had perhaps taken it to the States with him; he loved that book. If that had happened, it could have ended up in the New York Public Library—say, if he'd dropped it. It was a far-fetched idea, but I'd been having quite a few of those! I went through my own notes to see if I'd already asked an old friend of mine living in Greenwich Village whether she'd enquired at the New York Public Library whether they had the book. Now there was a good idea I should have thought of earlier, I told myself. The library at 476 Fifth Avenue isn't that far away from her apartment. I found I hadn't yet asked her, so I set to and sent off an email to her.

Going back to read more of his notes about his trip to the USA on behalf of the library in Manchester, I also found more notes about Dickens' and Catherine's deaths I'd earlier put aside, plus I came across several memoranda he'd obviously kept to put together some sort of report for the committee in Manchester to read about the delegation's findings while they were in America.

Chapter 38
1908

isembarking from the ship at the port in New York City, the English library delegation of Messrs. Sutton, Plummer, and Abbott had unpacked their suitcases in their downtown hotel rooms, then gone straight to the New York Public Library. They'd heard that the building was in the Beaux-Arts architectural style and considered to be one of the most beautiful buildings in the City.

Finally, so many years after the idea was first raised, the committee put together to explore how American libraries worked, had decided to send a delegation from the Manchester Library to the United States. It had become patently obvious that a new library was needed in Manchester—a bigger, sturdier building.

Never having travelled this far before in his life, Charles was very excited to be in the United States and in the huge, smoky, noisy, exuberant 1908 City of New York. The three gentlemen gazed in awe at the Stephen A. Schwarzman Building at 476 Fifth Avenue in Midtown Manhattan that housed the books belonging to the New York Public Library. Preparations were already in the making for a grand opening that would take place in 1911, three years away. Known to the New York library's people organising the opening, the English delegation was permitted entry, have a look around, and hold discussions with those in charge. The delegation learned that the library was founded in 1895 and under its aegis had two other libraries. One was the New York Free Circulating Library and the other was the Ottendorfer Library. The Ottendorfer had opened its doors in 1884 as New York's first public library. Carrère and Hastings were the architects, and the building indeed was most attractive. It had white columns standing in front of three archways leading into the building atop sweeping stone steps, all guarded by two proud white stone lions.

A library already open to the public was the Astor Library. The three visitors had to see that library. It had opened in 1849 through a generous donation of a German immigrant called John Jacob Astor. When he died in 1848, he was the richest man in America. In his will he pledged $400,000 dollars for the establishment of a reference library in New York.

Another library was the James Lenox Library, with its consolidation of rare books, one being the first Gutenberg Bible in America. The English delegation was told that the public had access at this preeminent library to a vast range of studies in all areas of thinking, action, and experience, and was of great benefit to all scholars and lovers of books. It was free to the public, but one still had to have an admission ticket. Charles pondered on that idea for his new Central Library in Manchester. Having tickets would give him a way of counting how many visitors came to his Library. He'd think on that some more in his hotel room that night.

While at the Lenox, they learned that the very first library built in New York was the New York Society Library, which was founded in 1754. Inside were three storeys of book-stacks made of a mellowed, red-coloured, wood. Charles thought the wood was beautiful but didn't know enough about types of wood and made a mental note to investigate that, too. The ceiling was made of yellow glass in intricate designs, and the floor was richly carpeted. It had been built expressly for the use of the wealthy New York Rogers family but later was opened up to provide access to the public.

The three-man delegation hoped to have the time to get to Washington, D.C. because they'd heard that the Library of Congress was also a sight to behold, housing the bulk of Thomas Jefferson's book collection. He'd sold most of his collection to the United States in 1815 and, in doing so, that gave him the opportunity to get involved in designing the rebuilding of the Library of Congress.

After New York, the trio of English librarians took a train to Philadelphia in Pennsylvania. The first thing the delegation wanted to see wasn't a library. It was the cracked Liberty Bell. This notable landmark was forged in Whitechapel's Foundry in London but in February 1846 it cracked. The apocryphal story goes that it received its larger crack when it was rung after the death of Chief Justice John Marshall in 1835. Superstitious people were convinced it was to commemorate the loss of the great judge. It was originally called the State House Bell or the Old State House Bell, but after independence on 4th July 1776, the bell was adopted as a symbol of freedom by abolitionist societies, who renamed it the 'Liberty Bell'.

After thoroughly inspecting the Liberty Bell, the delegation visited The Library Company of Philadelphia. Benjamin Franklin had founded the Company as a library in 1731, and when the three librarians were there, it had already accumulated one of the most significant collections of historically valuable manuscripts and printed material in the United States of America.

That evening, after seeing The Library Company, Charles sat thoughtfully in his hotel room. Every evening he wrote reams of notes in his flowing cursive script about all he'd seen, what he thought of it all, and a consideration of how it could be of potential use in the construction of the new Central Library in Manchester.

He talked to many people, in all walks of life. His deputy librarian in Manchester, Mr. W.R. Credland, was of a more outgoing nature than Charles Sutton, but he wasn't in America, so it was up to Charles to question people. If Mr. Credland were by his side, Charles knew he'd step back and let W.R. do most of the talking. Yet he knew he had such an inquiring mind himself that he really didn't worry much about approaching people any longer. In that regard, he recognised that this trip abroad was good for him. If he wanted to know facts and information in general, he was just going to have to ask, and that's what he'd been doing more and more.

As he lay in bed that night, he remembered how he'd asked himself before leaving England, what was the United States of America going to be like in 1908? Here he was in Philadelphia and had already seen New York City. Was it what he expected? He would have to see quite a lot more, he thought. He'd done some research, of course, before leaving for the United States. He knew already that it was made up of forty-six states. He learned that ninety per cent of the country's inhabitants were white. Half of the entire population didn't live in the cities at all, but in the vast rural areas. He had heard about the south. He'd decided against traveling down to Florida because he was told that the bottom half of the state was full of swamps and alligators. No sir, he didn't fancy the idea of going there one bit.

People were telling him that the country was still new enough, in many of their minds, for people to go out to some of the wilder, still unsettled areas, to put down stakes and homestead. That sounded very exotic, very romantic, to Charles. He pictured covered wagons, bullocks or horses pulling them through land filled with extraordinarily-shaped hillocks pushing up through the earth. And Red Indians, of course! People told him you could still find places to homestead and pan for gold at the same time. He learned that Montana, North Dakota, Arizona, and New Mexico were mostly open to settlers. He found it all new and quite fascinating.

With his brain teeming and unable to sleep, he read through pamphlets he'd been given about what was planned for that year of 1908, checking to see if he and the other two fellows were going to still be there for any of the upcoming events. In his earlier research he'd somehow missed that 1908 was the celebration of the 225th anniversary of the founding of Philadelphia. Lots of events were planned, of course.

The Founder's Week celebrations not only brought fun and festivity to the locals, but it also brought visitors from all over to attend the events. Extra railway cars had to be attached to the trains to take everyone to the events. Each day of the celebratory week was devoted to a theme with a parade to match but interestingly, thought Charles, there was no mention of the arrival of immigrants and other ethnic groups after the American Revolution.

So much going on! Charles' eyes glazed over, and he slid down on his bed pillow and proceeded to have fabulous dreams. He wished Maria were there to share all of it with him. His sweet wife, how he longed for her plump arms around him, and his head lying on her full bosom.

On their travels back to New York where they'd be setting sail for England, the library delegation of Mr. Sutton, Mr. Plummer and Mr. Abbott stopped in Peterborough, New Hampshire, the site of the very first public library in the United States, opened in 1833. They learned that in 1881 Andrew Carnegie had started building more than 1,700 public libraries in the country. Then, to their amusement, they were told that America's real 'oldest' public library was The Darby Free Library in Darby, Pennsylvania, in continuous operation since 1743! But they gave that one a miss, not wishing to retrace their steps to Pennsylvania.

"But that can't be right," muttered Charles to the walls in his hotel room that night. "I remember reading somewhere, now where did I read that? It was about a clergyman from England called, what was his name? Ah yes, Thomas Bray (I remember thinking about a mnemonic for his name and came up with a donkey braying...not that all clergymen are donkeys, no sir!). Well, let's see, this Bray was the first to establish free lending libraries in the American Colonies in the late 1600s. Then, in the 1700s members had to pay dues if they wanted to buy a book from the libraries, yet they could borrow them for free. Silly idea, I reckon, letting people buy the library's stock. Bookshops are for that reason, not subscription libraries, for Heaven's sake."

Having remembered all of that, and knowing his brain was still able to provide facts when he called for them, he happily turned comfortably onto his pillow and was ready to fall asleep. His last thought before being caught in a web of dreams was about how tiring it was to travel. Constantly packing and unpacking in different hotel rooms. Soon he'd be back in his own curtained bed with his soulmate, dearest Maria Pocklington Sutton, and what a mouthful of a name, he smilingly sighed, turning over and hugging his pillow while planting a warm kiss upon her imagined lips.

During their time in the USA, the delegation ended up visiting most of the great American libraries across the country, and, once back in Manchester, Charles wrote up a valuable report, called *A Conspectus of American Library Methods* that was of great use in the decision-making process surrounding the building and stocking of the proposed Central Free Library in Manchester. He had started organising his *Conspectus* while sitting on a deckchair aboard the ship taking the delegation home to England.

⁓⊶⊷⁓

Charles sighed gustily, aboard ship to sail home, he had plenty of time to just sit, think and recall past events. The sigh came to him as he remembered the dreadful day that he learned Charles Dickens had died[28]. He got up from the ship's deckchair he'd been sitting on and walked to the stern of the ship. He stood there, looking down upon the wake of the waves left behind by passing under the hull of the ship. He remembered receiving an urgent message while at work to go over to his father's house immediately. That was on a Thursday, 9th June 1870. Charles was only twenty-two but already thought of Dickens as a dear friend of his, as well as of his father's, Thomas. Charles had been ushered

---

[28] I found this information on a note in Charles' writing that I'd put aside to deal with later. He had a lot of time aboard ship going home to remember much of the past.

into his father's sitting room where he found Thomas pacing up and down in obvious distress.

"My boy," Thomas said to young Charles. "Sit down, I have extremely bad news. Our old friend, Dickens, has left us. He was only fifty-eight years old. This is a complete tragedy. He's died, Charles, down in Kent."

"Father! My God! How? Boz?! What happened to him?"

"I received a telegram that he was at dinner at home at Gad's Hill last evening and was complaining of toothache. He then collapsed and fell unconscious. His raven apparently went berserk in its cage, screaming in a terrible way and biting the bars as if to try to get out and fly to its master."

"That would have been Grip, ah, poor, poor Grip!"

"Georgina sent me the telegram and..."

"Georgina? Miss Hogarth? Is that...? Oh, yes, I know, you mean the sister-in-law who lives in his house and helps take care of him."

"Yes, Georgina, that's the one. She said she sent for the doctor, and he tried different remedies but couldn't bring poor Boz back. It was a stroke, Charles."

"Father, the last time I spoke to Boz he was writing his novel, you know, the one he was calling *The Mystery of Edwin Drood*. Oh, my Lord, what will become of the book now, I wonder? Oh God, this is appalling news, father, just dreadful."

"Yes, he'd told me he was writing his novel while sitting in the garden each day. Miss Hogarth says he died today, just today, Charles!"

"It was very thoughtful of her to think to send you a telegram so quickly, how very kind of her. But what about Nelly? You'd told me about her..."

"Hmmm, Nelly, yes...well, he was still trying to keep his affair with her a secret, I suppose. I imagine Georgina wouldn't have tolerated the young woman living in the house, but I really don't know."

Charles recalled how he eventually left his father's and went back to work. How he tapped his fingers on his desk, reminiscing further about his youth and when he'd first met Boz. He'd pulled another old book toward him. He'd marked the place in this reference book where Dickens' book called *Hard Times* was mentioned. He recalled that he, himself, would have been only a whippersnapper of four, going on five years of age, when Dickens took the train north to see what was going on in The Great Strike. Charles was in the middle of considering writing an essay about those times including mentions, of course, of his old friend's book—hence it now lay on his desk with his light pencil marks throughout of ideas he'd had.

As the reference book stated, Dickens had gone up north from London to the Manchester area to research The Great Strike of 1852 for *Hard Times*, which he serialised and published in 1854. It was his only novel with no scenes set in London. It takes place in a generic Northern English mill-town called Coketown, probably 19th century Preston, or even Manchester, but smaller. Thus, he was in Manchester for the opening of the Free Library in Campfield, Manchester. It was quite a journey from his home at 48 Doughty Street in London.

By 1860, the reference book said that Dickens had decided he wanted to return to Chatham in Kent, where he'd lived from 1817-1822. Eventually he found a country house that suited him at Gad's Hill near Chatham. He loved the area and often wrote about it in his stories. Charles had hoped he'd be invited one day to see Gad's Hill for himself.

Still thinking back to those times, Charles remembered he'd read with interest a long note he found amongst all the paperwork on his desk. His father, Thomas, had written the memo about when he'd met Dickens on an earlier trip up north from London in 1838. Dickens was in Manchester and had stopped in at Thomas' father Robert's bookshop. Charles Sutton reckoned he could add to that story. Dickens was twenty-six at that time and ran into the boy who was helping his father out in the shop. That boy was Thomas, Charles Sutton's father. This encounter had a huge impact on Thomas who was thirteen at the time. Thomas went on to open his own second-hand bookshop in 1847 when he was but twenty-two years old.

Charles let out a deep sigh as he grieved the passing of his, and his father's, old friend Charles Dickens. He left the stern of the ship and retraced his steps back to his deckchair where he got comfortable and began to doze.

Still sitting in his wooden deckchair aboard the ship sailing home to England, Charles shut his eyes and thought of many things that had happened, prior to this journey he had recently undertook on behalf of the library. How he'd have loved to have talked to Dickens about the trip, but he had died already thirty-eight years earlier. Thomas, Charles' father, had been such a close friend of Dickens'. Charles now cast his mind back to what his father had told him about a visit Thomas had made to see Dickens in London in 1860, ten years before Dickens had died.

In 1860 when Charles was twelve years old, Dickens invited Thomas Sutton down to London to attend a lecture he was giving on his book-writing. The year prior he had published his *A Tale of Two Cities* and his adoring fans were keen to hear him speak about his visits to Paris and the Bastille for his research before penning the story.

Dickens had now started to write *Great Expectations*, inspired by the Cleveland Street Workhouse in London's Fitzrovia neighbourhood. The workhouse was also known as the Strand Workhouse.

Dickens enjoyed conversing with Thomas who was nearly thirteen years younger than he but they both enjoyed discussing the events of the day, and literature. Thomas left his Manchester bookshop in the safe hands of his twelve-year-old son, Charles Sutton, who helped out at the shop when not in school.

When his father returned to Manchester from his London visit, he told young Charles Sutton quite a lot about what Dickens had told him. Thomas left out some of the salacious bits, but Charles never forgot what his father had told him about his idol. Thomas felt it would be a good thing for his young son to learn of the social conditions of the time in London. It seemed Dickens had related a lot of his life story to his old friend, Thomas.

It was in 1837 that Dickens had written *Oliver Twist*, based on the poorhouse. The atrocious conditions had not eased, thus he was inspired to write another book about life in what were now called workhouses.

Dickens' own childhood home was less than one hundred meters (109.36 yards) from the workhouse, a grim area to grow up in. He knew the area inside and out and based many of his literary characters on the people he watched roaming the streets around his home.

One foggy, chilly morning, on Thomas' visit down to London, Dickens had taken him past the workhouse. Thomas stopped dead in his tracks when he heard a horrible low-pitched moan emanating from the filthy brick building. The sound grew louder and at a higher pitch.

"What the devil is that, Boz?"

"You'll need to ignore it, my friend. It comes from the workhouse and is a sound you'll hear day in and day out."

"But is it an animal? What kind of animal?"

"You could say that, or a person who has been, and is being, treated in that manner."

"A person? A human being?"

"Yes. And one who has reached the bottom of the barrel. One who has lost his strength, his belief, his very soul. One who is in such pain, both mortally and spiritually, that he has lost all hope. Death for such a one would be preferable to life in such a bootlicking piss-hole as that workhouse."

"Is it too naïve to ask why he cannot leave and go elsewhere?"

"He has nowhere else to go. He usually has debts to repay. He is expected to work in that god-forsaken place. He is poverty-stricken and has no other way to support himself and his family. Often his family is taken in there with him."

The moaning recommenced. At the same time, Thomas saw smoke rising from the chimneys and Dickens told him, "The women in there do laundry, hence the smoke you see. It's not coming from any sort of fireplace to warm their freezing bodies. Women also must scrub floors and walls, do sewing and weaving and any other kind of women's work."

"And the men?"

"If able-bodied, they go out to work in the nearest fields (not too many 'round here, you mind!), or break stones and chop wood, all that type of hard labour. Petty criminals not immediately sent to gaol serve out their short sentences in workhouses like this."

"What if a man's destitute, not fit to work and ill?"

"Then he goes to a poorhouse rather than a workhouse. Well, that is, there used to be poorhouses, but this one we're standing next to is an actual workhouse—although we've got too many of both the destitute unwell souls and the still able-bodied ones in London, as you can imagine—so the poor blighters who can't work are still thrown into the workhouses."

They walked along the cobbled street a little more.

"Ah Boz..." said Thomas, stopping for a moment.

"Still calling me by my old nickname, eh? But I don't mind," interjected Dickens.

"I'll call you Charles, if you want..."

"Not at all, old friend, Boz will do. Now, what thought of yours did I interrupt?"

"What you're telling me is heinous, indeed. I'm glad you're writing about it; the world needs to know what's going on with the poor and destitute."

Thomas shivered. Not only from the cold but from what he was hearing from Dickens. He pulled his long coat closer around him and turned up the collar. The outer top edges of the coat and the collar were made of a thick woollen astrakhan caracul lamb's fur. He wore it over a long woollen jacket reaching just above his knees. His trousers were chequered in black and grey, his gloves a soft grey leather, his shiny shoes were squared off at the toe and his top hat was equally shiny. A neat grey bowtie sat at his throat holding the two raised collars of his white shirt in place over his Adam's apple. He carried a thin walking stick, not that he needed it for walking, but to poke feral animals out of the way on his evening strolls, or for protection from evildoers, if the need arose. All-in-all, Thomas Sutton looked quite the dapper Victorian gentleman.

Charles Dickens looked slightly more unkempt only because his thinning hair was sticking out over his ears. His camel hair jacket had eight large buttons in the front, two large pockets either side and a breast pocket. His trousers were striped in navy blue and grey, his shoes identical to Thomas's. He favoured a larger deep red cravat style tie and a shiny deep blue waistcoat with gold straight, not round, buttons. Dickens loved his gold chain fob-watch which hung from one of the pockets and buttons of his waistcoat.

His walking stick was sturdy. He had the occasional need of it to raise up and threaten the plenteous street urchins running around his neighbourhood.

The pair walked on further then stopped beneath a gaslight. Even though it was daylight, it was still throwing a murky pool of orange light through the fog onto a circle on the pavement.

"We have gaslights now in Manchester, as you do here. Those old whale oil lamplights are fast being replaced," said Thomas, "and the lamplighters and the fellows selling the whale oil are losing their jobs, but you probably know all that, Boz.

Dickens knew a lot about gaslights, and about social conditions in general, because he researched things like that for his writing. He wasn't sure if Thomas knew how the new gaslights operated so he told him. Coal gas was heated up in an oven that was kept sealed to keep oxygen out. Workers also purified the gas in simple tanks of lime-water, known as cream or milk of lime, through which the raw gas was bubbled. The chemical bath removed around forty percent of inorganic sulfur in the coal. After that process, they filtered it, and pressurised it.

"As you can see, quite a job for the workers, and then," said Dickens, "they have to build pipes to move it into your house, your business and yes, into these very gaslights."

Dickens pulled his camel coat more tightly around himself.

"A trifle cold, don't you say, Thomas?" Followed by, "Harking back to workhouses, you've got 'em in Manchester, of course. I'm a tad surprised you're not that familiar with them?"

"Ah, well, I know the bare facts, but I can't say I've ever had the occasion to look inside one. I only know of that one on New Bridge Street, the Union one. I was told it's been there since 1792. I did hear that in 1855 it had become overcrowded. I think there's a new one in

Crumpsall just been built what, five years ago, I reckon, but as I say, I've not been in it."

"I see," said Dickens. "It's not the sort of place you'd choose to visit, is it? I go inside them, you know, for my research. I went into quite a few when I was writing *Oliver Twist*. Poor youngsters in there were dying of starvation. Same for the adults. I do know that Victoria's consort, Prince Albert, has been quite concerned and has visited these places here and there, and goes back to the Queen to convince her to change the system. Hopefully that will happen before too long. As a matter of fact, some thirty years ago, in 1834, he convinced her to change the poorhouses into workhouses, which was a start. The Prince has a good sense of social responsibility, even though he isn't even English!"

"I heard he's not that well, Charles. Let's hope he stays with us for some years yet."[29]

They both turned around at that point, feeling far too cold, not only from the chilly day but also from their sad thoughts, and made their way back to Charles Dickens's comfortable home at Tavistock House in Bloomsbury in the London Borough of Camden.

❧❦❧

Still resting in his deckchair on the ship, Charles thought further about his father's relationship with Dickens. Charles' capacity for remembering details of stories told to him by his father was extensive. He smiled as he recalled how his father had continued with the story of his visit to Dickens in London.

Seated by the fire in Charles Dickens' Tavistock House, Thomas and Dickens warmed up with a hot toddy. Thomas set his mug on a side table by his chair and, putting on a sort of Indian accent, asked Charles if he liked these Indian drinks.

"What on earth are you alluding to, Thomas? It's just a drink we Brits enjoy drinking on a cold day. And what's with the funny accent, you old dog, you?"

"You don't like my Indian accent, eh?! Don't you know about this drink? I'm surprised. It comes from India. In the early 17th century, the Hindus fermented sap from palm trees and called the alcoholic drink a 'taddy.' I happen to know that in the late 18th century the word was

---

[29] Queen Victoria's consort, Prince Albert of Saxe-Coburg and Gotha, died the following year on 10th February 1861.

154

officially recognised but altered to 'toddy' and is now made from hot water, spices, and, of course, sugar."

"And very good it is, too!" said Dickens. "I'll wager you got that information from one of those books in your bookshop, didn't you?"

"I most certainly did, old friend!"

"Thomas, you're a good man," said Dickens. "Listen, may I speak to you as an old, close friend, who will keep his lips sealed about confidences?"

"But of course. I'll be happy to give you advice if that is what you're looking for. We've known each other for a long time now. I only hope I can be of assistance or encouragement to you, Boz."

"Ah, but you're a good friend to me, Tom. I'd like to tell you bits of my life you may not be familiar with. It would help me to unburden myself to you. There aren't that many people I trust in that way."

Dickens took the poker and stirred up the coals in the fireplace. Bits of ash and sparks flew toward them, and they both leaned forward at the same time to brush them off their trousers and stamp out the hot sparks that landed on the oriental carpet before the fire, smiling at each other as they did so.

"So, Tom, you'll have noticed that occasionally I have this dratted 'falling down sickness?'"

Thomas nodded but said nothing, letting his friend pick up his tale when he was ready. He'd heard from others who knew Dickens that he suffered from some sort of disorder that would suddenly and unexpectedly come over him, causing him occasionally to fall to the ground.[30] Thomas had also heard that when he was little, Dickens used to have what they assumed were epileptic fits. Thomas' friends called these fits 'the falling sickness' because those suffering from it would collapse while experiencing a seizure. When Thomas read Dickens' stories, he saw that Dickens gave some of his characters in his books the 'fits'. He certainly knew enough about them to describe them well, if, indeed, seizures were what he himself suffered. He recalled the maid called Guster in 1852's *Bleak House*. She, too, suffered from 'fits,' as did

---

[30] Nowadays we'd call it OCD (Obsessive Compulsive Disorder). It's uncommon to find OCD in epileptics but medical research shows there is some sort of connection. Not only did Dickens write about epilepsy, but also other medical conditions. To this day, there are doctors who like to attempt to diagnose what was wrong with a Dickensian character by interpreting the symptoms that Dickens described so well in his stories, through having such an extremely observant nature.

Monks, a creepy and rather sick character in Dickens' much earlier work, *Oliver Twist*, which he wrote in 1837.

Twenty-seven years later, in 1864, when Dickens had published *Our Mutual Friend*, Thomas recalled their 1860 chat about fits because in this book, Mr. Bradley Headstone, the schoolmaster, also had 'fits'.

"Yes, I do suffer from periodic 'fits' and am quite an impulsive fellow, too, even compulsive, some might say; not good for my 'fits'. I'll relay more of my life to you, Tom, old chap. For example, you do realise, don't you, that *David Copperfield*, that I wrote and serialised in 1849 and '50, is about my own life? With more juicy bits added in, of course. And you know, Tom, to date I'd say I like it best of all my writing—probably because it's about me," Dickens said laughing.

Sitting there warming themselves up by the fire, Dickens began to tell his friend more of his life and things that had been troubling him. He told Thomas that in 1830, when he was a lad of eighteen, he fell in love for the first time with an older girl called Maria Beadnell, the daughter of a rich banker. Her father sent her to finishing school in Paris, and upon her return, Maria gave up Dickens and broke his heart. Then, as it happened, good fortune came his way.

Five years later, in February 1835, Dickens celebrated his 23rd birthday and invited Mr. Hogarth, the editor of *The Morning Chronicle*, to his party. As luck would have it, Mr. Hogarth brought his twenty-year-old good-looking daughter, Catherine, to the party with him. Word has it that she later wrote to her cousin, "Mr. Dickens improves greatly on acquaintance."

That same year, Dickens and Catherine were engaged and on 2nd April the following year, 1836, they married. Dickens told Thomas his love for Maria Beadnell had been deep passion, but not so with Catherine Hogarth. With her it was affection. Catherine had a younger sister, Mary, who came to live with them. Mary died at seventeen and Charles was devastated, which made Catherine jealous. What she didn't know at the time was that her husband would one day fall in love with Ellen Ternan, a girl of seventeen. Dickens wove Ellen into his stories over and again, further stoking the fires of his wife's jealousy.

Dickens sat musing in his comfortable chair before the fire. It had wings on either side of his head to protect him from draughts. It was a deep red velvet fabric with an antimacassar lying on the headrest to keep the oily pomade he wore from spoiling his favourite chair. He grasped a cigar between his front teeth. Thomas smiled encouragingly at his friend and whispered softly,

"Pray do go on, Boz; I find it all most enlightening."

156

Dickens continued. He said he'd made Mary his Little Nell character in *The Old Curiosity Shop* published in 1840.

"That's probably why I affectionately call Ellen Ternan 'Nelly'. Catherine hated it when I did that. She knew how much I, and my public, loved Little Nell. When Little Nell got ill in the story, I was asked by many fans not to let her die—and she was just a story character! But there you are. Shows how much people identify with some of my characters, don't you think? Oh, and I can tell you more about fans."

Dickens went on to tell Thomas how in 1842 he and Catherine had gone to America.

"I tell you, Tom, fame is all very well, and I won't say I'm not appreciative of all those people who enjoy my books, but really...in America we were literally crushed by throngs of admirers pushing up to us, wanting me to 'sign my John Hancock' they kept saying."

"Your what?"

"John Hancock. Lots of American fans said that to me. He was the first man to sign their Declaration of Independence, you see."

"Good Lord, I hadn't known that. Interesting, eh."

"And, Thomas, so many of them think slavery is just fine, especially those living in the Deep South. By the way, their mansions with white columns and trees with Spanish moss hanging from them are just magnificent! But I didn't admire their attitudes. They felt they were entitled to so much, the rich ones, that is."

"Did you sell books there, Charles?"

"Ah, now, that's another bone of contention. I don't have copyright protection over there. So many of my books are being sold there and I'm not making a single penny. Did you not read my American Notes? I let 'em know how I felt and, of course, I heard back in short order from some of 'em that they didn't like what I said one bit." Dickens followed that with a snort of derision.

"But, Tom, back to my chat with you about my domestic life."

Dickens told Thomas things about his family life that he knew already but Thomas patiently listened.

"You know Catherine gave me ten children, Charles. After that, she'd unfortunately grown fat, whereas Ellen, my Nelly, was quite the opposite—slim, young, and lovely."

Thomas interjected, "Well, as you'll recall, I married my wife, Martha, in 1845 when I was twenty-one and she eighteen, and we went on to have eight children. That gives us even more in common, old friend."

"It does, except you've still got your Martha. Catherine moved out two years ago, as I'm sure you must have heard. *Quel scandale*! She said she was unable to compete with Ellen, and with me having an affair with the girl right under her nose, she was moving out of our house after twenty-two years of marriage. She left all the children with me, as you'll probably recall. I do have Nelly in my life, as you've gathered, but we don't spread that around, yet more and more people do seem to know." Dickens sighed gustily. "Catherine and I just couldn't get along anymore; besides, Nelly grew to be much closer to me. She was in my world, you see, an actress, as you know, and I put her in my plays. Couldn't help it really. She's Flora Finching in *Little Dorrit*, and that was in '55, five years ago already. And she's to be the basis for my Estella in *Great Expectations*, which I'm working on now. I'm thinking of publishing it serially, Tom; probably next year. I think people are going to like it."

"You've modelled more of your characters in your latest books on Nelly, haven't you?"

Dickens stopped talking and gazed into the red and orange flames of the crackling fire, then added,

"Yes, well, it's hard for me to believe I've only known Nelly for a fairly short time. She's worked her way into my heart. I remember the moment, no, the very second that I first saw her on stage. Do you recall my telling you I'd gone to see a play at the Haymarket Theatre? In my 1857 play, *The Frozen Deep*, I went on to cast her, and her mother and sister. You saw that in Manchester, didn't you, Tom?"

"I did, and much enjoyed it, but wasn't the part supposed to be played by Katey, your seventeen-year-old?"

"It was but I gave it to Nelly to take over. Katey was not well pleased, Tom. Nor was Catherine. You should have heard the two of 'em rake me over the coals for that."

"Charles, thank you for sharing your home life with me. I empathise but won't offer you any advice since you've not asked me for any!"

"Thank you. Well, that is how it's all turned out, Tom, nothing can change it now, nor do I want it changed. Catherine's gone off and I've got my, um, hmm, secret life with dear little Nelly. Do you know what the last straw was for Catherine? No? Well, I'd ordered a beautiful bracelet for Nelly. The wretched jeweller had it delivered when I was out with Nelly, and Catherine opened the package. She read the note inside for Nelly that I'd left with the jeweller to include with the bracelet. The woman read it and that was it. Complete fireworks ensued. You can imagine!"

"Oh Charles, Boz dear, oh my dear man, what can I say? I'd heard there was some sort of scandal and now I know." There was silence while both men stared at the flickering flames in the grate then Thomas added,

"Dearest friend, I'll be off back up to Manchester tomorrow. I'll want to look at the train schedule before turning in tonight."

Chapter 39
Memoir

I wondered whether I myself was suffering from Obsessive Compulsive Disorder? All I could think of these days was finding the book. Where on earth to look next? Whom to ask? Somebody had to know where it had gone. That somebody was obviously the thief who'd swiped it the last time it had gone missing. Smiling, I knew I was probably taking this hunt for a simple book too far. Conversely, I knew I wanted the book badly, so I could read what else it said in it about my family's ancestors. If I had it, it would fill out the story of the Pocklingtons and Suttons that I surmised Great Grandpa had planned on writing. He'd left enough notes to prove that was the case. I felt I owed it to him. He'd done so much work but, in my opinion, had died far too early at just seventy-two. Good Lord, I would turn eighty years old in a couple of years, and had friends and relatives of that age and more who were still hale and hearty. But, because of my Parkinson's Disease, I didn't expect to live as long as those friends and relatives—at least able to function properly and to continue writing—that was another reason I wanted to get the monasticon into my own hands as soon as I could.

Chapter 40
1908

As Charles sat pondering in the ship's deckchair, he remembered more about Boz's passing, but first how Thomas Sutton had gone home to his Martha in 1860 after that wonderful spell he'd spent with Boz in London. Upon his return to Manchester was when he'd sat down with young Charles and regaled him with so many details of his time with Boz.

Charles Dickens had already published *A Tale of Two Cities* in 1859 (thus, one year before his intimate chat with Thomas Sutton), then he'd gone on to publish *Great Expectations* in 1860-61, *Our Mutual Friend* in 1864 and was in the middle of completing *The Mystery of Edwin Drood* in 1870 when he died on 9th June. He had still seemed so full of energy that people were completely shocked when he collapsed from an apparent cerebral haemorrhage—a stroke.

Charles Dickens was buried in Poets' Corner in London. Poets' Corner is in the South Transept of Westminster Abbey. The first poet buried there was Geoffrey Chaucer in 1400. Over one hundred poets and writers have been buried or have memorials in Poets' Corner.

Chapter 41
Memoir

I was immersed in reading more of Great Grandpa's brief jottings about the English contingent having returned from the USA, picking up information they could use for a new public library eventually to be erected in Manchester, when the familiar 'ding' came through on my computer telling me I had a new email. It was from my friend living in Greenwich Village in New York City. She'd been over to the New York Public Library on Fifth Avenue a few times to find out whether a book known as a monasticon—about monasteries in York, England, she'd told them—was listed as being available through their library. Every book they had in their vast collection was now easy to look up on their computers. They scrolled through all sorts of books in that vein, but not knowing the title or the author, it was a difficult research project. She told me they had been quite persistent and thorough but had come up empty. She'd had three young women looking for her; I thought that very kind of them.

This was an interesting conundrum. I had no clue as to what the title of the book was, or its author. Great Grandpa had made no mention of that in any of his notes or jottings—except it was written by a scribe at the bidding of his abbot. The only monasticon I'd heard of was the *Monasticon anglicanum*, and I already knew 'my' monasticon certainly wasn't that book, with its several volumes.

Sighing deeply, I turned back to see what more my great grandfather had written about his stay in the USA, now being in Pennsylvania. Having been there myself, too, I could picture just about everything he mentioned.

Reading Charles' papers about his fact-finding trip to America, I could see in my own mind's eye much of what he'd seen. Having lived in the United States for forty-one years before relocating to Australia, I'd seen many of the buildings Charles had seen, and I'd visited the Liberty Bell in Pennsylvania, just as he had done.

It occurred to me for the second time that he could have taken the monasticon with him to the USA, because it was his very favourite book. I didn't think he would have wanted to leave it out of his sight, since it had the habit of vanishing here and there, which drove him almost to distraction. Yet I had read in one of his notes of his distress that the book had vanished before he'd left for the United States, maybe stolen by a delivery boy, and had been found by his son, George, at the John Rylands Library, and returned to Charles. Surely, then, he would have left it safely behind in his safe? I couldn't find any note written by him that said he'd decided to remove it from the safe and take it to the States, but that didn't mean he hadn't done precisely that. Neither could I find any note that said he was lamenting its loss, for example, when he was on the ship sailing home to England. He was relying on his capacious memory as he sat in his deckchair aboard, thinking of the past, not mentioning whatsoever that he was looking at the monasticon.

Now, I told myself, if he HAD taken it to the States with him, maybe the book had vanished while he was over there, thus I reckoned I should at least investigate it—just to be sure. How to do that? I'd already asked my friend in Greenwich Village to pop into the New York Public Library to see if the monasticon had ended up there. She'd already let me know it wasn't.

I still had many other friends in many walks of life all over the place in America; perhaps one or two of them could help me. I wrote a letter to a few of those friends, asking for their help in locating the missing book. I'd already mentioned my search in previous letters, so a couple of them replied that they were still intrigued, and more than willing to help me. They contacted libraries and bookshops in many of the United States. One of them even contacted used bookstores. I couldn't believe how generous they were with their time. Another of them had the clever idea to contact Lost & Found departments of the railways, museums, and even art galleries.

Before long I had my own Friends Research Department, saving me much time. How lucky was I to have friends of this calibre. They told me they found the search to be great fun. One of them came up with the moniker for us all, calling us the F.R.D. Club. Someone else named our group simply FRED. It was wonderful to have this sort of moral support. Many of us contacted endless universities and colleges, to ask if the monasticon had turned up in their libraries. Of course, not only in America; eventually we sent out enquiries to every library we could think of in the countries where we respectively lived. I'd get endless emails, letters, texts, and the occasional phone call, updating me on what they were finding out—which was, unfortunately, usually nothing whatsoever—just lots of chasing down empty rabbit-holes. I began to feel like Alice in Wonderland. I was finding out all sorts of weird and wonderful information but nothing that was bringing me any closer to getting hold of the monasticon.

Chapter 42
1909

P eace reigned at the library. Charles had been home from the USA for a while now. The monasticon was stashed away in his office safe ever since his son, George, had found it at the John Rylands Library. Fortunately, Charles had had plenty of time to not only rest on the sea voyage home but also to write up his notes. Sitting on a wooden deckchair, the clean sea air blowing away any cobwebs lurking in his brain, he could muse, ponder, and think hard about his plans for the new library incorporating all that he'd learned in the USA. Many meetings were to take place in Manchester over the next couple of years led by the delegation to the USA and the rest of the committee in charge of building the new library.

By 1911 the erection of a temporary library structure was to go up in the Piccadilly area of Manchester and the Reference Library to move in. When that time came, thanks to Charles' foresight, all the books were classified, new presses were erected, and the rapidity of its removal constituted a record. He used much of what he'd learned from the American libraries' way of organising their collections. Interestingly, during his fifty years of working in the field, Charles was never to work in a permanent building erected for the express purpose of being a library. He began in the old Hall of Science, then in the Town Hall, and finished up in what could be called a big hut built mainly for storage purposes and, unfortunately, built in rather a flimsy manner.

Still in 1909, the library hadn't been relocated for a while and for that Charles was grateful. He loathed upheavals although was excellent at moving. Regardless of where the library was located, he did all his work in his office quietly, quickly and without fuss, drawing upon his vast knowledge of the literary minds enclosed in the library's books to provide requested information to all seekers entering his doors. Not only that, but he had his genealogical tree work, his duties on committees and societies, and his home life with Maria. Besides everything else he did, he always humbly felt it was his civic duty to take part in the Manchester events that he was invited to. He had always preferred a quiet life, but occasionally he joined other city leaders at various events. On 31st May 1909, at the age of sixty-one, and having been back from the 1908 United States of America trip for a while, he marched in a Church Sunday School Procession, decked out in his very best top hat. Being a cathedral leader and church warden, he felt he couldn't refuse. Besides, to a man like Mr. Sutton, it was not only an honour but a duty.

After the street pageant, he returned to his library office to do some further scholarly research on yet another subject with which he was fascinated. He'd been practising the Brazilian martial art of Jiu-Jitsu for a while. Speaking to the walls, as usual, he ruefully said aloud, "At my rather advanced age, I suppose I shouldn't be doing Jiu-Jitsu, but I much like the idea. It's another form of battle, which has always held me in thrall." He then took a few 'fighting' steps, punching his arms before him in undercuts and uppercuts, before remembering that Jiu-Jitsu is a ground-fight.

"You've got to take 'em down, control 'em till they submit. You've got to be the dominant one and use joint locks or chokeholds." The door opened and in came Percival, followed by a rather worried-looking W.R.

"Were you asking for something, sir? We heard your voice and saw you leaping about through the office window. We wondered, sir, at your age? Should you be...?"

"No, gentlemen, all's well, and thank you. Just expanding and developing my knowledge, don't you know? You don't need to fret about me!"

When Percival and W.R. had quietly left the room, they were still listening and surreptitiously peeking through their employer's glassed area of the wall separating their office from their employer's, where they watched Mr. Sutton bounding again around his office, chuckling to himself as he pretended to force his imaginary opponent to the floor. Shaking his head but smiling, Percival went off to regale his fellow librarians with his latest fond discovery about their beloved 'old chief', while W.R. sat back down at his desk thinking he'd never quite understand his employer, but how much he admired the good fellow.

1909. Charles William Sutton in his best top hat marching in a church Sunday School procession at the age of sixty-one.

༄

As the days passed, with the monasticon still safely stashed away in his safe—only being brought out when Charles felt he needed to research something—could he spend the free time he allotted himself each couple of days researching the library's books pertaining to the 13th through to the 19th centuries. That was a lot of books, giving him much pleasure to go through. He was enjoying penning the Pocklington family's genealogical tree in a fine, curving, spidery, script. Splotches of ink fell onto some of the pages, which annoyed him because he was a perfectionist.

He much enjoyed sitting at his desk, thinking back to the past, and ensuring he wrote notes about things he remembered. Occasionally, to his delight, he'd discover in one of the library's books a notation about one of his Sutton ancestors, and made sure he got that entry down, too. He came across an entry of the Sutton side of his own branch of the family that was in 1789, when Robert Sutton was baptised on 27th September. Robert was therefore Charles' own grandfather, father of his father, Thomas Sutton. Charles enjoyed the fact that he could discover the work his family members did, and enter that, too, on his genealogical tree. Robert Sutton's employment was as a fustian cloth cutter. It was Robert's son, Charles' father Thomas, who in 1847 purchased a used bookshop in Manchester.

After the horrid incident with the dratted raven when it had swiped the monasticon and flown out the window with it, Charles recalled that he had left Boz's place and looked up fustian cutters, not being precisely sure what they were, and partly to take his mind off his loss. He learned that fustian cutters were prevalent in the Manchester area. The fustian cutter tool, sometimes called a cord cutter, was what workers colloquially called a stitch cutter tool, or a button-hole cutter, attached to a long handle. Charles reckoned Robert would have preferred working around books rather than button-hole cutters; he himself certainly would. He must have been delighted when his son, Thomas, purchased the used bookstore. Yet, thought Charles, he hadn't been able to ascertain the date his grandfather Robert had died, so perhaps he hadn't even known his son had bought a bookstore. Charles left a quick scribble that it was something he still needed to look up.

Charles paused in his thoughts, remembering his dismay over the wretched raven incident, then smiled as he caught himself thinking 'Boz' when he thought of Dickens; that nickname for Charles Dickens always made him smile.

And, not as interested in fustian cutting as in battles, Charles sighingly confessed to himself—although, every detail about everything did fascinate him for the most part—his mind wandered to battles and then to historic castles. That was because all those years ago Boz had told him a fascinating story on one of their pleasant get-togethers.

Dickens said that when he was young, his family once went on holidays down to Robertsbridge in East Sussex. There was a castle there that the Dickens boys wanted to visit more than their female siblings did. He had told Charles, "I know you love hearing about combat, castles, and such, and I have a story for you that you'll enjoy from when I was young. It's about an ancient castle."

Dickens had continued, "Bodiam Castle was a 14th century moated castle near Robertsbridge in East Sussex. In 1385 Sir Edward Dalyngrigge built it, fearing Bodiam was likely to be attacked by the French. In 1372 the English had lost control of the English Channel. The important harbour town of Rye was attacked by the French in 1377, and some years later in 1380 Winchelsea would be attacked. By the way, Rye was burnt to the ground."

Dickens said, "In 1377, it was obvious to Sir Edward that Bodiam would be attacked. He was a knight of some standing, and rich. He'd served in the Hundred Years War against the French and loathed their guts. In 1377 he married Elizabeth Wardeux, heiress to the Bodiam manor. She had a French name that put him off, but only a little. She was beautiful, an heiress, and seemed not to mind that he was already middle-aged. He realised that since her manor was close to a navigable estuary it was vulnerable to a French raid. If he owned the vulnerable manor, he could repel the marauding French. The best way to accomplish that was to marry the lady of the manor. In short order, he married Elizabeth Wardeux, and the manor became his property."

Dickens continued, "My brothers and I explored Bodiam Castle from top to bottom. One warm day, we even removed our outer garments and went for a dip in the castle moat. If our parents knew, there'd have been trouble to pay! Luckily for us, the castle keeper had consumed one ale too many that afternoon and was taking a nap."

Charles Sutton was, indeed, fascinated, and begged Dickens to tell him more. Dickens went on to tell him that in those days castle-building was controlled by the monarch, so Sir Edward, as rich as he was, still had to obtain what was called a royal 'license to crenellate', which meant to build something and fortify it with crenelations, or battlements. One fine day in October of 1385, Sir Edward succeeded in getting this license from Richard II.

"By the way, Charles", added Dickens, "that was in 1380, when Winchelsea was attacked, so Richard II wanted to ensure Bodiam would be safe. Now, on a slightly different matter, five years earlier, Richard II had imprisoned some attorneys and proctors of the Augustine priories and churches for fraudulently coercing the churchmen to pay taxes that were illegal at the time. But you probably know all about those goings-on, did you?"

"Indeed I did, Boz, but do get back to your story. Forgive me, but I'm afraid you've gone off on a bit of a red herring, you see."

"Where was I then? Ah yes, when my brothers and I returned the next day, the castle keeper told us about a clever escape."

Dickens said, "I and my younger brothers, Frederick, Alfred, and Augustus (you'll recall, Charles, it was Augustus who called himself Moses, which had morphed into Boses then shortened to Boz because of that snotty nose the wretch always had—and which name I swiped for some of my earlier works), had climbed up the ancient stone steps to a higher level in the castle and come across a room which had a private area with an ancient lavatory in it. The castle was never put to the test in the end to help defend the south coast of England because by 1388 the English had regained control of the English Channel. One could say that Sir Edward Dalyngrigge had married Bodiam manor's heiress for no reason, but that wasn't the case, for she did give him much happiness throughout his life."

Dickens added that the castle was, however, sometimes used to imprison local miscreants with criminal deeds behoving a trip up to the London courts and possible imprisonment in a gaol such as Newgate. They'd languish in Bodiam Castle until word was sent to East Sussex that the London courts were ready for them.

The castle keeper had related to the Dickens siblings with relish how two highwaymen had been caught and imprisoned on the topmost level of Bodiam Castle. One day they simply disappeared, "Evaporated into thin air, like," said the old man relating the tale, "never to be seen again, you mind."

Young Dickens said he had asked, "Do you know how they escaped?"

The castle keeper responded, "Aye, that do. It took a while for Sir Edward and his cronies to work it out, but eventually they did. Seems them highwaymen had climbed into their lavatory 'ole and, with legs up on one side and pressing their back against t'other, they wormed their way down to the bottom. Must 'ave got well and truly covered in smelly, slimy muck, I reckon."

He went on, "The lavatory, which is still there, consists of an 'ole in the floor, which is what you squatted over, see. Seems them two crims was young enough and thin enough to climb into the 'ole with their arms 'eld straight up in the air above 'em. The lavatory's shit emptied out into one part of the moat what 'ad a sort of netting around where it come out, if ye get me drift. All they 'ad to do was 'old their breath while tearing the netting apart, swim through and off they went. Dropped outta sight, so to speak." The old fellow chuckled. "Never seen again, them two."

Hearing Dickens' memories about playing at Bodiam Castle had inspired Charles to take a look at his monasticon again, which was stuffed with fascinating tales from the past, mostly relating to abbeys, but not all of them. He'd taken to reading parts aloud to Maria when at home of an evening, seated in front of the fireplace on a cold night, nestled up to his cuddly, voluptuous, wife.

"Maria, listen to this. I know we've read this part before, but it's so romantic, don't you think? I still wish I knew whether it was true, or whether the abbot made it up. Or, as I thought earlier, maybe it's just the scribe's salacious imagination."

"Can't be the abbot, Charles dearest."

"Why not?"

"Because he was a man of God, an abbot, a monk of the highest order."

"Well, he was still a man, and practised celibacy, and we know what that can do to a man. I happen to think it was all in his imagination."

"Well, dearest, read it aloud to me; I do enjoy it. I find it not only sweetly romantic but rather titillating and," she'd added coquettishly, "it's bedtime for us shortly anyhow, so..."

I had my drink of mead with the Knight of Poke and discussed France and my life as a bishop before moving to England by now a couple of months prior. The knight was most interested and asked me what my plans were for when I left the monastery. I told him I had enough money to build myself a home and was thinking of perhaps acquiring some land and doing some farming, but no firm plans were yet in place.

Putting down my tankard, I saw Eleanor had re-entered the Great Hall, having left it when her father presented me with the tankard of mead and sat down to converse with me. Eleanor asked me to walk in the garden with her. With alacrity up I bounded, took her arm and we walked and talked for a long time. She told me how drawn she was to my French accent. She led me to a bench under a bower of white Madame la Jolie Sœur climbing roses. I knew my roses and that impressed Eleanor. I told her she was the prettiest white rose I'd ever seen. She leaned toward me. We hadn't sat down. Electricity ran between us, pulling us toward each other. I took each side of her face in my hands, stared deeply into those violet eyes, and kissed her. I felt her body go limp in my arms. I almost swooned with the ecstasy of the first kiss of my life. My heart began pounding as my body responded to the deep kiss. Everything around us was gone, just our lips pressed together under the bower of roses, the scent of them now swirling around us. We strained against each other, my hand pulling at the golden threads of her bodice until I had loosened it enough for it to fall open. We literally disappeared into each other. I knew not what I was doing, it all being new to me, but instinctively I knew I wanted, nay, I had to touch those soft breasts, white as the down of a bird. She cried out, saying "Walter, oh Walter" again and again...

Maria's hand in his, Charles led the way by candlelight to their bedchamber.

The next day, Charles arrived at his office with the express intention of devoting the day to the Pocklington genealogical tree that he'd started so many years ago. Climbing up on a chair with a heavy encyclopaedia he'd placed upon it, Charles reached up to the topmost shelf of one of the many bookcases in his office and felt around for his beloved monasticon.

"Damn and blazes! It's not here. Oh, maybe I locked it in the safe; that's what I would have done—silly me, am I getting senile?" He climbed off the chair and opened the safe. No monasticon. He felt around in it twice then sat on his haunches scratching his head.

"Where in the name of God is the book?" he said aloud in exasperation. "How can it not be here? Now, did I put it in the safe or on my top shelf? Oh dear, I must be getting senile. Oh dear, oh dearie me. I must ask the cleaning lady if she has moved it." This he did immediately, only to learn that she knew nothing of such a book; indeed, he surmised she never even cleaned the top shelves of his room. The book had gone, vanished completely. How could anyone have got it out of the safe? He knew the only bastard who'd made a key was that Tommy Duckworth fellow and HE had been locked up since 1898. "Well," Charles said aloud, "He deserved the long sentence. Eleven years! I heard the judge said the police had discovered he'd broken into some pubs and robbed the tills after closing, so that's why he got the long sentence. Maybe he's been let out already and slipped in here to have another go at swiping my book and selling it. No, surely not! Did someone else have a key without my knowing it? Not possible, I just don't believe it so I must have left it on the top shelf in error, like I used to do before I got the safe in." Up he climbed once more to check his top shelf but it wasn't there.

He then called a short meeting of all the assistant librarians and administrative staff to inquire about the misplacement of one of the library's most ancient and treasured possessions. Nobody confessed to borrowing the tome. Nobody knew anything about it. Nobody had even read one page of it. Charles then realised it was only he, himself, and the nun, who had ever dipped into the valuable book, and now it was gone, completely evaporated. Yet again. Charles was decimated. He grieved for the loss of the monasticon and once again reported its alleged theft to PC 39.

Charles always thought of Richard Marsden as PC 39 even though the policeman had held the rank of chief constable for some time now. Over the last many years, he had been promoted to superintendent, and had then gone on to take the exams for one of the highest levels of policemen, aside from detective. Richard was dismayed to receive the news of the loss.

"Again, AGAIN? WHAT DO YOU MEAN IT'S VANISHED AGAIN? This is the fifth time according to my records? And you'd got it back; we nicked the bastard who took it from you and that was years ago, for

Heaven's sake. And then when that delivery boy allegedly pinched it, well you got it back after that, too!" he said loudly to Mr. Sutton in exasperation. He was having a bad day at work, and the last thing he wanted was for that damned book to vanish again, with him expected to find the wretched thing. The chief constable called out to a junior constable to bring him the Missing Items List. He apologised profusely for yelling at poor Mr. Sutton, thanked him for his call, hung up the telephone after saying he'd take care of the matter, and hopefully in short order. Uttering one of his gusty sighs, he commanded the junior constable to write down the details as he dictated and to do it 'right proper' because this was an item belonging to "one of Manchester's premier citizens, the chief librarian of our most prestigious libraries, don't you know". He felt embarrassed to have yelled at the chief librarian like that.

Charles returned to his office this time with a strong library ladder. "It can't be gone, it just can't. I must be mistaken. It has to be here. I just don't understand. It can't be that dreadful Mr. Duckworth because he's already been copped, as PC 39 says and as I well know, and PC 39 tells me he's still in gaol, the dammed thief. AND I got it back the fourth time, when dear George found it at the John Rylands Library. Yes, I know, I should say chief constable Richard Marsden now, but never mind, I know who I mean, he's still PC 39 to me." Muttering away, up the ladder he went for the third time, searching yet again in vain for his precious book, for to his great chagrin, of course, it wasn't there.

That evening at home he took a ladder from its cupboard under the stairs and searched on top of all the bookcases in the house, thinking he may have mistakenly put it up on one of his private book stacks and that is when he fell from the ladder and broke his wrist. All that for nothing, he told himself, for the precious book wasn't at home, either. He received many well wishes from the public, both in letters and even newspaper mentions.

> Anxious inquiries were made by members of the Manchester Libraries' Committee, to-day, as to the condition of Mr. C. W. Sutton, the city librarian, who met with an injury at home last week. Mr. Sutton broke his wrist through falling from a ladder.

Charles' wrist got better in quite short order. This was one of those strange occasions when the monasticon turned up in a most unexpected place. He was most impatient with himself about having little 'turns' as he called them. Apparently, his balance had gone off, even with all the exercise he continued to do each morning, including his Jiu-Jitsu practice when he'd shadow-box pretend foes, leaping around his office, driving W.R. and Percy mad with alarm. Every now and again, he'd stumble and almost fall. W.R. begged him privately to 'take it easy', to also stop climbing up ladders, but Charles simply responded it was all good for him and besides, he still had pretty good balance. Charles jotted down in a diary he'd started that he thought both W.R. and Percy were molly-coddling him. Both those fellows had worked for him for the past many years now and knew him well; indeed, one could say they loved their employer. They'd both started work at the library in 1870. That meant they'd been in Charles' employ for thirty-nine years! No wonder they both sported rather grey hair and lined faces.

The cleaning lady came into the library every night after everyone had left the building to sweep and dust the bookshelves throughout the building, and to give the two rooms of the chief librarian, his deputy and private secretary a particularly good once-over. She was most precise about her work, and you could never charge her with leaving a speck of dust anywhere. Percy referred to the sweet older lady with her hair up in a turban as 'our dear Mrs. Mop'.

One morning, while Charles was issuing instructions to his secretary, and standing next to Percy's desk, all of a sudden he literally tipped over. Both W.R. and Percy leapt up, ran around their desks, and heaved Charles up off the floor. He came up grinning, not hurt one bit, triumphantly holding the monasticon in his hand.

"Ha!" he cried with glee, "there's a reason I fell over just now. No idea what made me fall, no reason for it, but, dear colleagues, look what I discovered!"

All three gentlemen stayed somewhat late after work that day until Mrs. Mop appeared, bucket, brush and broom in hand, smiling her usual beatific smile. Of course, they asked her if she had seen the book last night when she's swept under Percy's desk.

"No sirs," she said in surprise. "I'd 'ave told you, 'course I would. I knows what it means to you, Mr. Sutton-sir, that I do. Now, 'ow on earth would it 'ave got under Mr. Bastowe's desk, eh?"

They all agreed it was, indeed, quite a mystery, what with the monasticon vanishing then re-appearing, now turning up in such an unexpected place. Percy even claimed the building must have a poltergeist, but Mr. Sutton and Mr. Credland claimed there were no such things.

Charles was obviously quite happy with himself for finding his precious treasure. He literally danced back into his own office. Seated back at his desk, he pondered on how the book had got under Percy's desk. Whispering under his breath, while staring at his treasure in his hand, "I suppose we'll never know how this literary rascal comes and goes. I rather like that, as much as it annoys me when it does vanish. The thing is, it always reappears. That's the thing, the important thing!" Up he stood, marched over to his safe, and locked the book up—a satisfied smile creeping up under his bushy moustache.

Chapter 43
Memoir

I came across a note Great Grandpa's had written about himself feeling so wretched when the monasticon had vanished, and how relieved he'd felt when it had shown up again, and proud that it was he who'd found it that time. He noted that he'd been feeling wobbly and seemed to be aging, although he wasn't about to confess that to his two principal employees. I confess to being a tad worried about him falling over—even though I knew this happened over a century ago. To me, it felt as if it had all happened only yesterday.

Great Grandpa was naturally not to know what would occur in the future, which descendants of his and Sarah's, and of Maria Pocklington's, were going to be born, or what they'd all become. He'd know nothing about his granddaughter, my mother Molly Sutton, nor about his two great-granddaughters, her two girls—Pam and me—and nothing about the Second World War military exploits of his son, George William Pocklington Sutton—all still in the future. He had known what had happened to his son—my Great Uncle Oliver Jepson Sutton— because Oliver died in 1918 at the very end of the First World War.

Charles had been long dead by the time this book you now read was written. The last he knew about anything to do with his family tree was when he was seventy-two, but he did enjoy a fabulous ceremony held in his honour on his 68th birthday, four years before his death in 1920. I'd read about that big bash for Charles Sutton somewhere. I shuffled the notes he'd written this way and that on my desk and found one pertaining to the party. I put it aside so I could mention it when 1916 came up in my timeline in the book I was putting together on Great Grandpa's behalf.

And what about my hunt for the actual old book in these days? Nothing. Nada. Zilch. I gave a long sigh and got back to my reading of Great Grandpa's papers. I must confess I suddenly became quite exasperated. I actually swept all the neat piles of his notes off my desk in one frustrated sweep of my arm. Looking at the papers now strewn across my office floor, I actually laughed out loud. "This won't do," I said to myself. "I'd better go outside and walk this off." After my usual turn around the garden, feeling a lot calmer, back I went into my office, cleared up the mess I'd made, and went back to reading Great Grandpa's notes.

Chapter 44
1914

Charles was sitting quietly in his office in mid-1914, thinking about the late Charles Dickens, good old Boz, and musing upon how much he'd enjoyed Dickens' entrancing storytelling, the day he'd told him about his family's trip to Bodiam Castle—and how much he loved history in general. He also mused on his dear wife Maria's sadly never having had the privilege of meeting Boz. She'd died in 1911 at the early age of forty-nine. After all, he'd not married Maria until 1892 and by then, Boz had been gone twenty-two years. Charles got up to take some history books down from one of his office shelves, when he heard Percy's rather raised voice outside his office. Head down, deciding to stay concentrated on the task in hand, he began some more research on Maria's Pocklington forbears in the Middle Ages. He then heard Percy saying, "No, sir, no, you can't, sir. He won't want you to have it, sir. Alright, then, I'll ask him, just wait please, sir."

Not two minutes later, a knock came at his office door. Percy poked his head around the door. Both he and W.R. were always keen to help keep Charles' precious monasticon staying firmly on the premises, in the safe—that is, until the day Charles received that knock on his door and was asked to lend it to an academic professor of his acquaintance.

"Sir," said Percy, "I've been trying to tell the professor you won't let the monasticon out of our, erm, that is, out of your sight, but he insisted on talking to you in person."

Charles sighed gently. "That's alright, Percy, show him in."

With a certain hesitance, but being a kind, unselfish, gentleman, Charles said he would lend the monasticon to the professor, with the caveat to take the utmost care of it. The academic wanted to show it to the young men studying *The History of the Printing Press in England 1415 to 1492*, with reference to the historiated initials at the beginning of each special section or chapter. Charles trusted this professor but still insisted more than once in their conversation that he keep a sharp eye upon it and return it as soon as the lecture sessions were over. Both Charles and the history professor spent a delightful hour or so discussing Charles' latest research.

The two men, of course, talked a little about what was obviously on everyone's minds, The Great War that had started on 28th July 1914. Then they talked about battles, with Charles telling him that he'd be able to read about some of the ancient ones in the monasticon he was borrowing.

Talking about Maria Pocklington's forebears, Charles explained to the history professor that whenever he came across a Pocklington who had been in a battle, he became enthralled. The history professor agreed, saying he, too, loved reading about the old battles. Charles told him that in his perusals of the 15th century, he discovered a notation in a manuscript in this very library about two brothers, Ralph and Roger de Pocklington, who were at the Battle of Wakefield on Christmas Eve, 24th December 1460. They'd both survived, Roger settling in the county of Nottingham and Ralph moving farther west.

Charles fished around in his desk and hauled out the manuscript he'd been speaking about and read a part of it to the history professor. The history professor was quite delighted and begged him to read on further. As Charles read out more about the Battle of Wakefield, he stopped for a while to tell him how he envisioned Ralph and Roger de Pocklington in their suits of armour, horses prancing, the clanging of sword against metal shield, the shouts and screams of the soldiers and the injured. He imagined himself in a suit of armour, charging into battle. The history professor grinned and said he, too, was envisaging himself in a suit of armour. This battle was part of the War of the Roses and took place next to Sandal Castle near Wakefield in Yorkshire, where the Duke of York and his 10,000 men awaited reinforcements at the castle built upon a Norman *motte*[31]. They were surrounded by some 24,000 Lancastrians. Richard, the Duke of York, nevertheless decided to sally forth into the fierce battle, where he fell, along with one-third to one-half of his men, after Lancastrian forces ambushed them on 30th December 1460. His death didn't end the War of the Roses, though, and

---

[31] *motte* is the French word for a huge mound with a keep/castle built on top, which attackers would have to climb up slowly to reach the keep or castle above, making it easier to defend. [A moat is a ditch surrounding a *motte* or castle, with water in it to deter attackers.]

more battles were to follow. Aside from the Duke of York's death, perhaps more significant was the death of the Earl of Rutland. The Earl of Clifford killed him, presumably in revenge for the death of Clifford's father in the First Battle of St. Albans. Many prominent leaders in the Yorkshire area and members of their families were killed, or captured, then executed.

The final significant civil fight between the House of Lancaster and the House of York took place on the 22nd August 1485. This was the Battle of Bosworth, also known as Bosworth Field, and represented the end of the Plantagenet dynasty in that Richard III's loss meant the end of the War of the Roses. Richard III (Richard Plantagenet, the last king of the House of York) died during the battle for want of a horse. The last line he ever spoke was, "A horse, a horse, my kingdom for a horse!" as he fought on foot, having lost his horse in the battle.

"Ah yes," said the history professor, and I'll add to this true tale. He then regaled Charles with more history. The Tudor dynasty began in England because of the victory at the battle of Henry Tudor, the Earl of Richmond, who went on to marry Elizabeth, a princess from the House of York, who became his queen. The newly-crowned King Henry VII married her in 1486, thus both their symbolic roses, the red and the white, came together, creating the Tudor dynasty. Now that the two houses of York and Lancaster were joined, it was hoped peace would reign. Elizabeth of York gave birth to Henry, who would become Henry VIII (being the son of Henry VII). It was Henry VIII's second wife, Anne Boleyn, who gave birth to a girl also called Elizabeth, who in turn became Elizabeth I. Queen Elizabeth I was Elizabeth of York's granddaughter[32].

Charles put his manuscript back in his desk and then handed over the monasticon to the history professor with yet another warning to take great care of this most valuable book, both because of its sentimental value to him and because of its antiquity.

After the visitor had left, Charles mused on roses in general, particularly those he grew in his own garden—always tended with delight by himself—specifically the roses representing the Houses of York and Lancaster in the War of the Roses. He knew the white rose represented the House of York and the red the House of Lancaster, and that these colours became the emblems for both sides contending for the throne of England. Making another of his cursory jotted notes to himself to research which species of roses were used for these emblems, he concluded it was just the white and red colours that held significance.

---

[32] Queen Elizabeth II was a direct descendant of Elizabeth of York.

Once Henry VII of the House of Lancaster married Elizabeth of York (daughter of the Yorkist king Edward IV of England), the two roses thus combined to form the Tudor rose. King Henry's mother was a direct descendant of the Lancastrian branch of the House of Plantagenet. This new rose symbol now represented the union of both claims to the throne. The newly bred rose had five white inner petals and five red outer petals. Charles smiled as he jotted down yet another note, 'Why five petals of each colour? Must try this graft on my own roses!'

Growing up in England, Charles himself, along with other children, had all learned the order of the colours of the rainbow from the mnemonic phrase 'Richard Of York Gave Battle In Vain' (red, orange, yellow, green, blue, indigo, violet). This was Richard, the third Duke of York. Historians claim it was wrongly believed that he was the Grand Old Duke of York who had ten thousand men, or mistaken for Richard the Third, his youngest son. The Grand Old Duke of York is now believed to have been Prince Frederick, Duke of York and Albany from 1763-1827, thus much later than the War of the Roses.

"Well", said Charles aloud to the walls of his office, "so much history, so many battles. Ah, if I were a young man again, how I'd love to wear a suit of armour, and even ride a huge horse into battle. How fine that must have been!"

With more clangs and crashes of metal swirling in his imagination, Charles Sutton sat back in his chair, imagining all the conflicts from 1455-1485 that were centred on the House of York and the House of Lancaster, both struggling for the English throne. And, tugging thoughtfully on his full, rather shaggy, brown moustache, he thought how lucky that Ralph and Roger de Pocklington survived the bloody conflict, in order for his Maria to be born from one of their line. Now thinking of infants, Charles found himself humming the traditional old nursery rhyme called The Grand Old Duke of York who marched his men up a hill and down again. Charles had learned in his early history lessons that the rhyme signified the futility of battle, for the Duke of York took his men half-way up the hill only to realise they were technically half-way down, so they were neither up nor down, were they?

After some days, Charles received the history professor into his library office. The gentleman looked distraught.

"My dear Mr. Sutton, I regret," he stammered, "I most seriously regret..."

"Out with it, sir, what has happened?"

"The book", wailed the professor, "it has gone, Mr. Sutton sir, completely gone from my study, disappeared; in effect, I would say it has absolutely vanished, sir!"

Charles pressed his hands hard on either side of his cheeks in absolute, total dismay. This was the sixth time the monasticon had vanished. Back in his office, he picked up his telephone and rang PC 39.

House of York.

House of Lancaster.

Chapter 45
Memoir

I adored roses and sniffed my white *Madame Alfred Carrière* rose and white *Madame la Jolie Sœur* rose in appreciation of their glorious scents, making a mental note to be sure to get some red climbing roses into the garden as soon as possible. I loved it that there'd been a mention in the monasticon of a *Madame la Jolie Sœur* rose when Walter Bishop was courting the daughter of the Pocklington knight. Thus, my rose here was descended from a very, very old strain. When I'd come to Australia, I'd ordered it online and was told it was considered quite rare.

Returning to my office, I continued reading Great Grandpa's notes to discover whether, or when, he'd got the monasticon back from the history professor; I certainly hoped so after all his warnings. Now, if only I could step into a time machine and step out in Great Grandpa's office; what a thrill that would be. Maybe I could just 'borrow' the book to bring forwards to my day, to delve into for writing my book! Yet, if my hunt for it now were successful, I wouldn't have to bother, now would I?

As I smilingly mused on this thought, the smile left my face as I came across a terse note on a torn piece of paper, half-stuck to the memorandum about the history professor losing the monasticon. I'd read on Great Grandpa's genealogical tree the date of her death but seeing his writing on the note somehow choked me up. All the note informed me: 'Maria died 1911. God help me.' Per my habit, I ran out into my garden to shed a tear or two. These ancestors of mine had become so very real to me.

Chapter 46
1914

Y et more time passed, as it is ever wont to do. Charles worked hard at his job at the library and loved every minute of it. It distracted him from the huge loss of his second wife.

It gave him great satisfaction to reflect upon how much he'd achieved over all the time he'd been working. Before 1865 when he'd first started at the library and begun his cataloguing, the library had held 31,000 volumes, but by the end of 1865 the collection had more than doubled to 70,000.

Thirteen years later in 1878 libraries were open on Sundays, and circulation had expanded exponentially. In May of 1879, when Charles was only thirty-one years of age, the libraries committee promoted him to chief librarian of the Manchester Free Library. Now sitting musing at his office desk, with great satisfaction he again went over all he'd accomplished during his tenure leading up to 1879. He was particularly proud that in those first fourteen years of his work, he'd increased the number of branch libraries from six to sixteen.

Many journalists agreed that the growth of libraries was due to Mr. Charles William Sutton. They attributed it to his enthusiasm, ability, careful cataloguing, the entirety of his library equipment, and his overall management. He cast his eye over some newspaper cuttings with rather silly caricatures of himself drawn in them. They always made him smile.

On Monday, 2nd March 1914, *Manchester Evening Chronicle* reported that in 1912, at the time of the library's removal to its Piccadilly location, the library had 170,000 volumes, up from the 70,000 in 1865, at the end of the first year of Charles' tenure at the library. By 1914 there were 24 branch libraries and 450,000 volumes. Charles had a lot to smile about, yes indeed.

Maria had had her own achievements to smile about before she'd passed on in 1911. She had satisfactorily brought up Charles' and the late Sarah's four children as well as her own only son, George William Pocklington Sutton. When Charles thought of his happy homelife, he knew he owed it all to his dearest Maria, the best helpmeet a man could have. Smiling, he said to his office walls, "Behind every successful man is a good woman. I couldn't do all I've done without Maria's ever-present support."

Newspapers celebrated Manchester Library's clever chief librarian, whom everybody admired and loved. Lord Morley had pleasing things to say, too, especially regarding Manchester having the best library of all provincial cities. Lord Morley spoke about his memory from 1865 when he joined the Libraries Committee, and how there were but three branch libraries. Charles Sutton was quoted in several newspapers that the Free Libraries Act was adopted in 1850. He said that, on that day, there was a town meeting in which 4,000 citizens voted in favour of the City Corporation to take over the new library in Manchester and make it free to the public. A mere forty voted against the plan. The Manchester Library was the first to operate a free lending service without subscription. Thus, Manchester was the very first to offer a rate-supported public lending and reference library under the Free Libraries Act. Charles made a wee joke that in 1850 he was but two years old, so hadn't been allowed to cast a vote himself!

Lord Morley also noted in the 2nd March, 1914 *Manchester Evening Chronicle*, that under Mr. Sutton's librarianship the Manchester libraries rose in stature and were considered next in line of importance, after the Chetham Library, the British Museum, the Bodleian at Oxford, and the University Library at Cambridge.

Charles was quoted in many newspaper articles about the opening of the Free Library in Campfield, Manchester on Thursday, 2nd September 1852, which was rendered notable by the presence of three famous writers—Charles Dickens, Edward Bulwer-Lytton and William Makepeace Thackeray. In reading about the event in the papers from that day, Charles smiled, thinking how he would have loved to have been present but was only four years old in 1852. There was a slew of other notable attendees, but their names meant little to Charles William Sutton, being so young. One of his first memories, though, was the excitement at his home on that auspicious day. He was also much pleased to read that money had poured in from everywhere for the new library, including from Prince Albert of Saxe-Coburg and Gotha, Queen Victoria's consort.

Reflecting further, Charles recalled that in 1877, when he was twenty-nine, the Library had moved from Campfield into the old Town Hall. By 1912 it was moved again, this time into temporary buildings in the Piccadilly area of Manchester. A bank building housing Lloyds Bank at 53 King Street was built on the site of the demolished Town Hall but eventually the bank moved into a more elegant Grade Two listed building in the exclusive banking district of Manchester. Other free public libraries had existed in different parts of the world prior to Manchester's, but it was generally acknowledged that none of those libraries held a candle to the library run and managed by Charles William Sutton over his tenure in Manchester. It was Charles' library that became known in history as the first free public library in England in the 19th century.

Chapter 47
Memoir

Charles Sutton had four sons with Sarah, his first wife: Charlie, Frank, Oliver, and Bernie. He then had a fifth son, George, with Maria. I thought how frightening it must have been for him when World War I, known as The Great War, started in 1914. Charles must have realised his sons were likely to be called up to serve in the forces. The only countries that didn't participate in conscription were Australia, South Africa, and India. Frank and Oliver joined up voluntarily, as did George.

Both George and Oliver fought in Gallipoli 1915 to 1916. The Great War raged for four years, with Oliver sadly going missing in action in 1918, presumed dead. George fought in both World War I (1914-1918) and World War II (1939-1945), ending up a Brigadier with three medals: Commander of the British Empire, Distinguished Service Order, and Territorial Distinction.

Chapter 48
1916

It wasn't until January 1916 that the Military Service Act was passed. This meant that all single men between the ages of 18 and 41 were conscripted to serve in the forces. The only exempted individuals were those who were medically unfit, clergymen, teachers and certain classes of industrial workers. Several young men had been able to claim exemption through poor eyesight or even flat feet. One of these, a student in his university professor's history class rode a penny farthing bicycle down the bumpy cobbled street from the college to his home. He didn't notice the book he'd 'borrowed' from the professor's classroom desk had fallen from his wicker bicycle basket behind his seat. He planned to show it off to his family and bring it back to class the next day. Surely the 'old prof' wouldn't mind. Not only had he borrowed the book from the professor, but also the old-fashioned bicycle. The student knew penny farthings had gone out of style in the 1880s and he'd listened often enough to his professor touting the charm of the old bike, and how pleased he was that he still had balance enough to stay seated on the old machine.

A seaman on leave from his ship in Port Salford stumbled across the monasticon on the cobblestones while on his way to visit a girl. "Every man needs a girl here and there, and this 'ere's a pretty-enough-looking present for my girl, innit?" he chuckled aloud, pocketing the book. "She'll like the pretty coloured bits in it. I can't read it, and nor can she, I wager, but 'tis the thought that counts."

When he gave it to the girl, the strumpet eyed the gift with suspicion.

"What's I supposed to do with this, then?"

"I dunno. I thought you'd think it pretty."

"Well, aye, that it is, but I can't read, nor can you neither, you daft sailor."

"Give it to someone else then, me feelings won't be 'urt."

"Ha, daft as a brush, you are!"

The next day the woman did exactly that. A student came to her room as usual, always for his regular mid-week visiting day. After they had consummated their friendship, she gave him the monasticon.

"I don't need this daft thing. 'Ere, you 'ave it. Maybe you can read some sense out of it."

The young student gawped. His jaw dropped. He realised at once that it was the book his professor had been using to teach his class about the historiated initials in ancient tomes. His fellow student with the penny farthing bicycle had told him he'd borrowed the book and lost the dratted thing, and how furious with him the old prof had been, and angry, too, that he'd used the professor's pet bike. Ooooo, the young student thought, but he'd be getting extra points for bringing the book back to their professor, and that's for sure. With glee he returned to the college and handed the book over to the old prof. The teacher, as soon as the lecture was over, placed the monasticon into his own rear basket behind his seat and climbed onto the old penny farthing. It was a windy day. He pulled his hat well down over his ears to hold his spectacle arms safely atop his nose. His heavy black professor's cape flew out behind him as he bumped along the cobbled street heading toward the library.

Out of the side of his eye, he noticed workmen had set up a coarse hessian material barrier around a sewer manhole. The manhole's heavy metal cover lay next to the hole. Four men sat around on old milk crates smoking or getting a bit of a shut-eye. Four men to do a job? Good heavens! thought the professor. What a waste of time and money. Two to do the actual job—whatever it is—one to ensure they're doing it right, and the fourth one to make sure the other one checking up on the first two is doing his job right. "Good heavens!" he said aloud, bumping toward the crew of workmen. A thought flew through his mind. There were very few manholes in Manchester, so maybe it needed all these workers to do whatever it was down the hole.

A strong gust of wind caught his cape. In turn, it caught the edge of the book. Next thing, just as he cycled past the manhole, the monasticon flew off the penny farthing, and right across the barrier. No reaction whatsoever came from any of the four men, who continued smoking their pipes, resting, or simply staring in the other direction. Obviously, not one of them had seen the book tumble straight down the manhole— this became the monasticon's vanishing event number six.

The history professor arrived at the library and immediately asked for Charles Sutton. Percy took the call from the foyer receptionist and told his employer to run downstairs, for "a college professor has something very important to give you, sir." The library receptionist didn't need to ask why the academic was bringing his penny farthing bicycle into the library foyer; he well knew there were street urchins about who'd think nothing of swiping the bike.

Down the stairs went Charles, looking forward to receiving the monasticon back from the professor he'd loaned it to. There stood the bespectacled teacher in his black cape, holding his bicycle with its large front wheel and small rear wheel.

"You'll never guess, sir, no, you wouldn't, but it's true, sir, completely true! No, you just wouldn't believe it..."

"What's true, professor? What wouldn't I believe? For God's sake spit it out, man! Last time you came here you said my monasticon had vanished. What now, sir, what now?"

"Your monasticon, sir, the book, the BOOK, sir, it's found. It came back to me. I have it here, in my bicycle basket. Take it, sir, oh, you'll be so pleased. You are, aren't you, sir? Yes, of course you are! I can see it in your face." He turned to his bicycle basket. "No! What? Wha? Wha? Where's it gone? Oh, my dear sir, the monasticon, it's vanished! Again? What? How? Oh, my good Lord, I had it back, sir, I did! A student had borrowed it with no permission and lost it. Another student found it, Mr. Sutton; oh, 'tis a bit of a saga, but I got it back and was bringing it here, and now, oh my good Lord, where HAS the darned thing gone?"

Sweat now beaded on the poor man's brow as he stood there gawping in dismay at his empty bicycle basket. Charles sank into a foyer chair, gripping its armrests with white knuckles. Why, oh why, did I even consider lending it out to this man? I must be mad, he thought, almost ready to shout at the academic, he was so frustrated. Taking a deep breath, he calmed himself and remembered his manners.

"I'm sure it's not your fault..." but was interrupted by the professor.

"Look, I'll cycle back the same way and see if I can find it, Mr. Sutton. Oh, my dear sir, I am so sorry. I don't know what could have happened. I had it, I really did, sir, and..."

"You do just that, Professor, yes indeed, you go ahead and do just that. Please retrace your steps, erm, your bicycle route."

Charles stomped back upstairs to his office to relay to W.R. and Percy what had just happened. Next, he picked up his telephone and told PC 39 the latest news. Sighing, as usual, the chief constable said he'd fill out the details on his Missing Items List and told Charles he would walk that way on his next rounds and see what he himself could see. "You never know," he said, "maybe I'll just find it meself this time. With any luck..." he whispered under his breath. After hanging up the phone, he said to his desk sergeant, "This is the sixth bloody time it's vanished, according to me records on this 'ere Missing Items List. When Mr. Sutton told me t'other day that professor had stopped by the library to tell 'im the book had vanished then 'e rang me, I confess I didn't even write it on me Missing Items List. I 'ad an idea the wretched thing would show up like it always does, but not this time it seems. What the 'ell is going on with that book? It vanishes then it reappears. Me wife tells me it's haunted. But that's plain daft, innit?"

⁓ᘓᘓᕟᕽᕙᘗᘗ⁓

The assistant librarians heard the news in the library's staff lounge that Mr. Sutton's most precious book had vanished. They had heard he was most upset and advised each other to stay clear of their employer in case he flew off the handle.

One whispered to the other, "Watch out for Old Buggerlugs[33], 'e might bite yer 'ead orf today!"

A young fellow said since it was no longer inside Mr. Sutton's safe, that was a big boon for him to act as a detective and try to find the book for their employer. Certainly, that would result in a bonus for him if he found it; wouldn't it? Now all he had to do was find out who'd pinched it and waylay its return to its rightful owner—who was now going to be ME, he chuckled to his friends. How to find out where it had gone? They'd all heard a history professor had borrowed it so all the would-be detective had to do was find out from which university the professor came from and go from there. The young sleuth fancied himself in the role of Sherlock Holmes. He marched off into the Gentlemen's Lavatory where he preened in front of the mirror, imagining how he'd 'interview' the history students until he found out where the monasticon had ended up.

---

[33] Buggerlugs is Mancunian slang for referring to or speaking to someone in a friendly but insulting way, especially someone you are fond of.

It shouldn't be a hard task. He was a clever young chap; everybody said so.

When he returned to the staff lounge and told his friends his plan to go to the university as a detective, his colleagues all burst out laughing, telling him he'd be arrested by PC 39 himself for impersonating a stalwart member of the law. AND, further, if he wasn't careful, the cops would arrange to get him conscripted sooner than later into the Army for the war effort, wouldn't they? They wouldn't buy it that he had flat feet...he'd got away with that one once, but not a second time, for sure! The young man's mouth immediately turned down at the corners from dismay at such a barmy plan he'd had and said he'd only been trying to help his much-admired boss—and ran out of the room to the continued loud guffaws from his colleagues.

Chapter 49
Memoir

As I read more of Great Grandpa's notes, particularly the one about the manhole, I could now really feel his total frustration and dismay. Poor man! I related to his feelings completely, now that I was on the hunt myself to find the precious book. Chewing on a carrot and sipping coffee, I started thinking about how few manholes there were in Manchester in the 1900s, according to my own research. Manholes? What did they have to do with the missing monasticon? What a strange thing to be researching, indeed, but his notes led me in that direction. I knew England in general had problems dealing with human waste effluence. I knew London had The Great Stink in 1858, with cholera prevalent and no knowledge at the time of how to treat it.

The problem of getting rid of human urine and feces arose when we first started living in settlements. In Manchester, up until the middle of the 19th century, people still used outhouses, pits, and chamber pots within their homes. Effluence was discarded into the rivers in the Manchester area, such as the Irk, Medlock and Irwell—just as it was in London into the River Thames. I did some more research. It wasn't until 1840 and 1850 that 25 kilometres (15.53 miles) of sewerage pipes were laid within one kilometre of the Manchester Town Hall. There were hardly any manholes for access to the sewers in those days, and many workmen were not yet well trained in working in the relatively new infrastructure of sewerage. That's probably why Charles had noted down that the professor on his penny farthing bicycle wasn't too surprised to see four workmen around a single (rare) manhole—even though he obviously disapproved of the number of men required to do whatever it was they were up to.

The pipes transported the sewerage to the rivers instead of to treatment plants, which hadn't yet been invented. This was obviously a bad idea for the rivers. 19th century Manchester was an industrial city with many textile factories, cotton mills and warehouses, going into the 20th century. It was growing in leaps and bounds and any infrastructure in place was already deteriorating as the populace grew. Manchester gained a reputation as one of the most filthy, overcrowded, and unhealthy places to live in the country. Death rates soared and your life expectancy by 1837, according to the Manchester Statistical Society, had been the extraordinary figure of only seventeen years of age! Cholera was rampant in London, but in Manchester, typhoid and dysentery were also spreading rapidly. In 1832 and 1849 Manchester had also been badly hit by outbreaks of cholera.

In 1830 the factories particularly on either side of the River Irwell discharged their industrial waste into the river and by the 1860s it was so polluted, it was rising by three inches a year. Manchester's three main rivers were regularly flooding, culminating with The Great Flood in 1872. The city's early sewer work was inadequate and designed to deal with surface rain water only. Not only was the network haphazard but the clay pipes continued to discharge untreated effluence into the rivers.

There was much inequality, with the middle class eventually receiving plumbed toilets, but not the lower classes. They still relied on buckets which were collected daily by carts, which then transported the buckets to the rivers. By 1880, the middle class was investing in attractive toilet pedestals within their homes, decorated with painted flowers and leaves, and all the effluence deposited into them plumbed into the sewerage pipes. Conversely, the densely populated centre of Manchester didn't receive a proper system of sewer pipes until between 1912 and 1914—pipes that would bring the waste to a treatment plant. Its system was operated by gravity, having the human waste flow to a pump station along Manchester Harbour.

After thinking about all this rather unpleasant subject, I searched around in Great Grandpa's papers to see if there was any clue as to what happened next, in the year of 1916. Did Charles get the monasticon back? Had it really gone down a manhole? And what state would it have been in, lurking down a sewerage manhole?

Besides those questions about that era, where was the precious book NOW—in my world?

Chapter 50
1916

PC 39 had walked his beat down the cobbled street where the professor had apparently lost the monasticon when it must have flown off his bicycle. Being a chief constable, he was not required to walk the beat any longer, but in certain instances, such as this one, he preferred to do just that. He noted that the new department in charge of sewerage was working on this street. He strolled over, saying "ey oop then" to the workmen and "'ave any of you seen a book blow over 'ere in this godforsaken wind?" The four workmen all asked the constable what they'd want with a book for none of them could even read. "Bloody daft question, weren't it?" they all said, snorting with derision.

PC 39 had one of his 'funny feelings' about this manhole the four fellows were gathered around. He asked the supervisor whether he could go down, "Just to take a wee look, know-wot-I-mean?"

The supervisor just shrugged, saying, "Ecky thump, whatchawanna go down there for, me 'owd lad?" followed by, "Sounds like bobbins to me, but down ye go, if that's whatchawanna do. You're the bobby, so you can do what ye wants, eh? Bloody angin, that 'ole is."[34]

---

[34] Mancunian slang:
Ey oop = hello.
Th'owd lad = the devil (or 'old mate').
Bobbins = rubbish.
Ecky thump = an exclamation of surprise.
Bobby = policeman.
Angin = disgusting.

PC 39 squeezed his rather portly figure down into the manhole. He thought to himself, what on earth am I doing? I'm in me early seventies, but I reckon it's the least I can do for our Mr. Sutton. I'm a wee bit fat, but I can still climb down a bloody 'ole! I'm not ready to retire yet, and nor is 'e, so we got to 'elp each other, is wot I think.

There was a one-in-one vertical ladder down to the murky bottom. The stench rising up from the miasma below made him retch. Urine, feces, and god-knows-what was silently and slowly moving along just below his heavy policeman's boots as he stood on the lowest rung of the ladder, just above the stinking putrefying thick liquid beneath him.

One hand firmly on the ladder, the other on his torch, he shone it all around him in the darkness. A head blocked the light above him for a minute.

"You awright down there? Find anything? We don't go down ourselves, mind. We're just mending the top part of the 'ole, where the 'eavy lid goes. It's takin' a month of Sundays, but it don't bother us none."

PC 39 thought, I bet it doesn't, you lazy rapscallions. You've been 'ere for days already. So the workmen haven't even been down this ladder. Hmmm, I wonder...shining his torch up and down and all around him, he stiffened. Waitaminit, there's something there, hanging over that bit of old wood sticking out just above the sludge. Hooking his left arm around the metal ladder, he put his torch between his teeth and swung his big body toward the piece of wood. There! He reached for it. Felt like paper, felt like a...book! YESSSSS! Grabbing it with his right hand, he swung himself safely back onto the ladder and stuffed the book carefully into his wide uniform pocket. Gotcha, he crowed inwardly, and started the climb back up toward the light.

<hr/>

PC 39 marched straight to the library, flashed his badge at the receptionist in the foyer and approached the staircase. The receptionist immediately telephoned Percy Bastowe, who ran into Charles' office to advise him that the police were on the way to see him.

"Richard! What brings you here?" asked Charles.

"Mr. Sutton, sir. I found it. Your book, sir. It is with the utmost delight I'm handing it over to its rightful owner. And, sir, I must say as 'ow very pleased I am to say 'tis the first time I meself 'ave found this 'ere precious item. With the greatest pleasure, I shall be crossing it off me Missing Items List, sir, aye, and that's a fact!" The policeman then added,

"And it don't even stink, sir. Looks awright, too, not even dirty for wot adventure it's been on down that there 'ole!"

Percy and W.R. filled the door, their eyes almost starting from their heads.

Charles sank heavily into his desk chair, this time with the greatest sigh of relief, his thoughts tumbling over themselves one after the other. What an extraordinary book, this monasticon. It vanishes; it returns. And here it is again, safe in my own hands once more. A huge thank you, dear God, for that, I swear! He got up and placed the book into the safe and locked its door.

The policeman admired the safe. "I'm glad you bought one of them there safes, sir. That was a good investment, yes sir, a very good investment, indeed."

"Where was it, Richard? How did you find it?"

PC 39 then spilled out the whole adventure of climbing down the manhole and retrieving the poor old monasticon.

Jumping up from his chair, Charles took an unexpected step toward the policeman and embraced him. PC 39's face turned crimson from embarrassment—or was it from prideful pleasure?

On his 68th birthday in 1916, Charles William Sutton was the guest of honour at a magnificent ceremony to honour his fifty years of dedication to the library. A bronzed plaster bust of him sculpted by John Cassidy was placed in the library's foyer during the celebration. Cassidy was an Irishman who had moved to England to study at the Manchester School of Art. He created a slew of public sculptures, war memorials, and exhibited broadly. He was much sought after to commission sculptures of famous personages in many cities. The Manchester Corporation commissioned Cassidy in 1896 to create a large hexagonal Jubilee Fountain for the city's Albert Square to mark the Diamond Jubilee of Queen Victoria. On 7th June 2020 a group of protestors called Black Lives Matter pulled Cassidy's statue of merchant Edward Colston from its plinth in Bristol's The Centre, pushing it into Bristol Harbour, because of its controversial connection to the Atlantic slave trade. That statue was rescued and in June 2021 exhibited at the M Shed Museum in Bristol, in its damaged and disfigured condition.

Each morning after his statue was erected, as Charles Sutton entered the foyer to start his work day, he couldn't help himself from giving the bust a little wink. As a humble man, it quite amused him that anyone would want to put a bust of him anywhere, but then, he owned, it was quite flattering.

Not four years later, on 24th April 1920, Charles lay on his bed in his home at Higher Broughton near Salford suddenly feeling tremendously tired. He'd had to work even harder than usual in these latter years, because his reliable, conscientious, and committed deputy librarian, William Robert Credland, had unexpectedly died in 1916.

Sun streamed through the window of Charles' bedroom. He thought, I'm glad I stopped working at the library a few days ago. And no work for me even in the garden today. It's a Saturday, and I think I'll lie abed for a little longer.

For the first time in his life, he felt relieved he could lie late in bed. Glancing up at the window, he drifted back in his mind to his first day at work, when the sun had similarly poured through his mullioned office window at the library with dust motes flying through the rays.

He thought of his early life. For the first twenty-five years he had been a vegetarian. To his dying day, he'd remained abstemious and moderate in both drink and food and had retained a sympathy for suffering humanity and animals. He smiled gently, remembering his recent adjudication on essays on kindness to animals written by school children.

So much, so very much had happened since that happy day in September of 1865 when he'd first sat at his desk at the library, a young man of seventeen thrilled to be in his first permanent job.

His mind wandered to his first wife, Sarah, devoted mother of four of his sons, and he remembered with pain her accident and death at only thirty-six years of age. Oh, that distressing day of 29th September 1889 when he lost her. It had been a cold, dry autumn but that Sunday she died it was cold and frosty. He'd stood at the bedroom window looking out. The moon draped a shimmering veil of silver over the black shapes of the trees at the end of the garden. He needed air. Opening the window, a bitter blast of cold blew in. Slamming it shut, he saw a curl slightly move from below Sarah's nightcap. Hurrying to her bedside, he placed his hand on her neck, searching for a pulse. Maybe she was still alive? But no, it must have been the wind. Such pain clutched his heart that he sobbed.

His mind then leapt to three years later when he married Maria, dearest, plump, jolly Maria Pocklington, mother of young George. What a joy and helpmeet she'd been to him, but oh, such sadness when she'd died at only forty-nine years of age.

Charles grimaced, remembering that awful day of 13th June 1911 at 323 Great Clowes Street in Broughton, near Salford, when her spirit had finally given up the ghost. Then he saw himself but three days later standing in the Southern Cemetery, black hat in hand, tossing a handful of earth upon her coffin. He buried her in the same consecrated area as dear Sarah. Twice he'd stood at that same graveside, black hat in hand. Oh, the pain of it all!

He'd lost both of his beloved wives but had still gone on to accomplish much. A satisfied smile crept slowly across his face. Yes, he'd accomplished much, particularly for the library, his beloved library. Plus, two of his own sons had worked in libraries. Oliver Jepson had been an assistant, first in the reference library, and afterwards in the John Rylands Library, before joining the Army, becoming a captain, and winning the Military Cross for services in Gallipoli. But, alas, wounded in March 1918, Oliver had been 'missing, presumed dead', nothing having been heard of him since.

And how about George, Maria's only birth son? Now there was another remarkable soldier. He'd formerly worked at the John Rylands Library, and eventually in Charles' reference library, then became an adjutant of a Lancashire Fusiliers Territorial Battalion and become a very great soldier, as had dear, lost, Oliver. And the other three boys, now successful men, all doing well. Yes, all was well.

"I'll just sleep a little more now," he gently spoke aloud, "then I will do some gardening after all. Maybe. Maybe not. Oh, how tired I am. No, first I'll read a little more of my favourite book." He reached out his right hand to draw the ancient monasticon book from his bedside-table toward him. He held it almost reverently now in both his hands. The illuminated first letters of the chapters danced before him. Smiling gently, his eyes closed. His right hand let the pages fall softly, one after the other, until they all fluttered to a stop. His breathing slowed, and with a final rasp, stopped. Charles William Sutton was gone.

Charles William Sutton in his later years.

Charles William Sutton, Chief Librarian
of the Manchester Free Library. Sadly,
this bust was smashed in an accident
by a lady called Lillian wielding a book trolley.

Chapter 51
Memoir

After John Francis (Frank) Sutton's death in 1953, my sister, Pam, and I used to raid the cupboard where our grandfather kept his Masonic Lodge regalia and dress up in it. We found the outfits quite hilarious. There was a white tunic with a cross on the front, an apron with all sorts of decorations sewn onto it, huge decorative cuffs to wear on the wrists, a necklace with a medallion hanging from it, white gloves, and all sorts of medals Grandpa pinned to his jacket.

As I typed the lines about dressing up in Grandpa Frank Sutton's masonic regalia, I suddenly thought of a couple of places in Great Grandpa's notes where he'd written in the genealogical tree and other documents about the clothes sewn by some of the Pocklingtons, those working at the royal courts of the times who created gorgeous outfits for the royal retinue. Could the missing monasticon in any way at all have ended up in the world of couture or even in the theatre? I emailed or rang up my FRED Club, those great buddies helping to find the monasticon—my Friends Research Department, to get them interested once again in finding the missing monasticon. Soon our group was sending out enquiries to all the fashion houses in Europe, and to contacts some of us had in the theatre and opera world, where clothes were designed and sewn. I smiled as I organised this grand search, knowing how far-fetched it all doubtless was, but there was always a small chance somebody might know something about an old book that had described rich clothes sewn for royalty. You just never knew.

While I waited for responses to flow in from all our many enquiries, I made my own notes of Charles Sutton's other sons, and their children. It filled my days and brought me an equal measure of joy and sadness as I researched the Sutton family tree, thinking how Great Grandpa Sutton would have approved of my additions to his genealogical tree, which had started in 1202 and burgeoned to page after page of Pocklingtons and now Suttons.

Opening my computer one morning, there was an email from a member of our FRED Club who lived in Paris. She'd been going through clothes used in theatrical productions that had landed up in a used and vintage clothing shop in the quarter of *Le Marais*. In the inside pocket of a gentleman's winter coat was a book. My heart skipped a beat. Was it? Could it be? Reading on, she said it was very old and written in 'quaint' English and appeared to be about monasteries somewhere in the north of England. I couldn't bear the suspense, leapt up from my office chair and paced for a while. She said the shop-owner made her buy the coat to keep the book and would I please send her a reimbursement for her costs as soon as possible! Of course, I would. Who wouldn't?

While I waited for the mysterious book found in the vintage clothing area of Paris to reach me by post, I went back to researching Great Grandpa's descendants.

The youngest son of Sarah Evans and Charles Sutton, Oliver Jepson Sutton, was born on 29th July 1882. When he was only seven, his mother died. Three years later in 1892, his forty-four-year-old father married Maria Pocklington and, the following year, at the age of thirty-one, she gave birth to Oliver's half-brother, George William Pocklington Sutton.

As Oliver grew, he developed an interest in the belief and practice of magic skills and abilities by people or groups, simply known as witchcraft. The Central Library in Manchester holds the collection gathered by Oliver of books, pamphlets and magazine articles covering topics from history to superstitions and philosophies.

In 1914, at the age of twenty-two, Oliver joined a Manchester Regiment of the British Army to go to Egypt to fight for England in the Great War. By 1915 he was a lieutenant and sailed off with his battalion to Gallipoli on 9th May 1915. On 10th July, volunteers were called for to make a reconnaissance of newly dug Turkish trenches. The moon was barely bright enough to see, but out he went with his sergeant to make observations. Oliver's sergeant later reported that he and Oliver went out two nights in succession. They tied a length of rope to their wrists and crept along the parapet of their trench to the new Turkish trenches to measure the distance between the British and Turkish trenches. When the Turks saw them and started firing, Oliver and his sergeant ran for a few yards then lay down amongst some dead Turks to pretend they'd been shot. Fortunately, bullets from the Turks missed them and they were eventually able to creep back to their headquarters' trench where they were congratulated by two British generals.

Oliver took two platoons under him back into the trenches on 7th August to reinforce the firing line but unfortunately got wounded in his shoulder by shrapnel and had to return to the British casualty tent. He was then evacuated to Cairo and couldn't get back to his battalion until 21st October 1915. At that point he was promoted to captain.

By 28th January 1916, Oliver Jepson Sutton was back in Egypt serving with his battalion. He received the Military Cross and given leave to return to England for a little over one month. Oliver went on to fight in France with his battalion as an adjutant to the company commander. On 22nd March 1918 the men in the trenches were barraged by fire, which they mistakenly thought came from their own forces. A pigeon basket was despatched to ask the British artillery to cease fire. Captain Oliver Jepson Sutton was hit and severely wounded by a direct hit on his battalion, and the battalion was forced to retire from their position under heavy enemy machine gun fire. Oliver's body was never found. He had only just turned thirty-six years old. There's a commemorative memorial to him at Pozières Memorial in France.

Oliver Jepson Sutton, in the
British Army. Born 29th July 1882.
Presumed dead in action on
22nd March 1918.

Sitting at my desk, thinking back to those days about a century ago, I wished I'd known my great grandfather. If he was anything like his son, my mother's father Frank, Charles must have been a gentle soul, with a winning personality, and a high intellect. I sat there, pondering on what he'd written in jottings, notes and memoranda about the later years of his life.

Not only had Charles been lauded for his much-appreciated work at the library by notable citizens in England, but he was also doing well at home. His broken wrist had healed eleven years earlier in 1909. The monasticon had been found all those years ago, and he'd had the joy of holding it in his hands even as he lay dying at the age of seventy-two. Not the same for me, though, as I still needed to find the 'dratted book,' as jolly Maria had often called it—and it was with grief that I'd read Charles' note about her untimely death in 1911 at only 49—what could have taken her life? I found no clue to that.

Charles' children, meanwhile, had grown into successful young men working in different walks of life. I knew quite a lot about those great uncles of mine already—Oliver and George. I knew less about Charles' two sons who had gone to make their fortunes in Chile, so was grateful for the notes he'd left, and hearing a little from my second cousin, Barbara Sutton, who was born in Chile.

Charles Sutton's first-born son, born in 1875, Charles Evans Sutton ('Charlie'), had moved to Chile to make his fortune as a merchant. He worked in England for the merchant bankers Huth & Company, then was posted to open a branch of the company in Chile. Some years later, Charlie was followed to Chile by his brother, twelve years younger than he, called Albert Bernard Sutton (Bernie). Bernie was the last of the four sons of Sarah Evans Sutton.

I did unearth more details about the Chilean side of the Sutton family; it grew exponentially. Charles' eldest, Charlie (born 1875) married Annie Cutter and they had three children, Anita Mary, Charles Henry, and John B. Sutton. Charlie's daughter-in-law, Jean Fowler, tragically died after she had an abortion. Her husband, Charles Henry, was devastated and took to drink. He'd been a real party boy, a good dancer and storyteller. He contracted nephritis and eventually died in 1945 in the Royal Navy Hospital in Havant, Hampshire. His mother, Annie Cutter, was so upset by his death that she sold the house so full of memories and bought another in Viña del Mar, not far from Valparaíso in Chile. Annie Cutter had also had kidney problems. According to Nita, 'poor Auntie Annie Cutter' had one kidney removed as a young woman by a surgeon performing the operation without anaesthetic on the kitchen table. She was warned that if she ever had a child, it would kill her. Then Nita appeared a short time later at ten pounds in weight!

John B. Sutton married Jane Stewart and had two girls, the beautiful Barbara and her sister, Jennifer. Anita Mary (Nita) was my mother Molly Sutton's cousin and Robert Barber's grandmother. Nita's daughter Alice Barber was struck and killed by a car on the tarmac of an airport in France. Her son Robert Barber was then brought up by his grandmother, Nita. Nita married twice, the first time secretly. She lied about her age, and eloped with Mr. Donall K.L. Sim, to Gretna Green, Scotland. That marriage eventually failed. She later married her second husband, Mr. Ted Ovington.

I recalled my older sister, Pam's, twenty-first birthday party in 1963 at The Prospect of Whitby pub on the Isle of Dogs in the East End of London. It lies in the Tower Hamlets borough, part of Wapping. This tavern dates from 1520 and used to be called The Devil's Tavern, because of its shady reputation. In the old days, sailors, smugglers, cut-throats, and footpads all liked to gather at the pub set beside the Thames.

Little ragamuffins still haunted the area even in the 1960s. As my mother, Molly Sutton, parked her car to attend Pam's birthday party, some street urchins accosted her and said, "Give us yer money to guard yer car, missus, or slash yer tires!" Ted Ovington had parked near her, saw what was transpiring, bellowed and shooed the urchins away. He carried a hearing horn with him, as he was extremely hard of hearing by then. He'd hold the hearing horn up to his 'good' ear to catch the conversation. I watched the urchins running off, pointing at him, mimicking him and his horn, and cackling with laughter as they disappeared around a warehouse corner.

Nita died in 1993 and has been sorely missed ever since by her grandson, Robert Barber. Robert became a photographer. One of his principal assignments was private photographer to the American actress, Faye Dunaway. I met with Cousin Robert, in Malibu near Faye Dunaway's exquisite home. It was located on the expensive stretch of Malibu sand called Broad Beach. Faye liked to say it was a contemporary hideaway influenced by her visits to Bali. I've seen the truly striking photographs he took of the gorgeous Faye, which hang in his home in England.

I doubted the Chilean side of the family knew much about Charles William Sutton's obsession with the monasticon, or anything about their ancestors. Why would they? Unless they'd read the paperwork Great

Grandpa had left after his death, because he was writing his notes about his ancestors and compiling his genealogical tree while in England. There was something that gnawed at me: how was it that so much of the paperwork I now had copies of, ended up in a trunk under one of his sons' beds in Chile? Had the son gone to England for his father's funeral and brought it all back to Chile? I knew all Great Grandpa's books were left in his will to my grandfather, Frank Sutton, so this was something I doubted I'd ever find out.

———————✳———————

I felt it was now up to me to carry on entering names and dates of Great Grandpa's descendants. My maternal grandfather, second son of Charles William Sutton, was John Francis (Frank) Sutton, a journalist and scholar (1877-1953).

Searching around in Great Grandpa's piles of notes and memos, I looked for a note that might show that Frank knew about his father's favourite book. Surely, I thought, Frank had to have been privy to many of those dire occasions when the monasticon had gone missing from his father's office. But then, it seemed to me that Great Grandpa was mostly a mild-mannered, non-complaining, quiet sort of fellow, so perhaps he kept his grief away from his children when he suffered the book's vanishing episodes. Alas, my search was in vain.

I wondered for the hundredth time, where was the monasticon NOW? Who had it? Surely it was time it turned up again into the family— that is, ME! Alas, I wondered yet again in vain and went back into penning Great Grandpa's descendants into the family tree and noting their work and achievements.

Frank also became the director of the first waste paper business in England called Lendrum's Company. Not only was Frank a company director, but he was also invited to join the same Masonic Lodge to which King George VI belonged. There's an old photograph somewhere in my house that sadly I have been unable to locate. It shows the King in a big black car inside the gates of Buckingham Palace where the Changing of the Guard takes place. It's either Grandpa Frank Sutton behind the wheel, and the King standing on the running board, leaning into the car window, or *vice versa*. I can't quite remember. It must be somewhere in my home because my husband, Horst, remembers seeing it, too. Frank Sutton most certainly was encouraged to be a Freemason by his father, Charles William Sutton, who was an enthusiastic and prominent Freemason. I have a small pewter jug with the insignia of one of the Freemasonry meeting places where King George VI and Grandpa Sutton used to meet in London. The insignia is a shield that says Alexandra Palace Lodge Number 1541. It has several lions depicted on it. The Freemasons also used to meet at the United Grand Lodge of London on Great Queen Street.

Frank married twice. First, to Charlotte Hannah Hallet, with whom they had one son, Harry. Harry became a dentist by profession and a fisherman by preference, owning two large fishing ponds in Somerset. Harry was also a good watercolourist and painted many scenes of the area around his Somerset home. During WWII he couldn't get hold of enough paper to paint on so painted on both sides of many of his paintings. When I inherited some of these, I had to decide which side to frame.

When Frank's wife, Charlotte, died in 1908, at the age of only thirty-three, he married Edith Ford two years later. Edith had been a nurse, and a dancer, yet, in my memory, she was a dour, strict woman. She was born in 1880 and was almost three years younger than her husband, Frank. I was terrified of my grandmother. Edith Ford Sutton was tall and slender with very dark hair until the day she died. Her hair parting was combed exactly in the middle and her long hair twisted into a neat bun at the back of her head. She wore round, gold-rimmed spectacles and was always dressed in black. Grandma Sutton had one edifying feature. Her skin was like peaches and cream, right up until she had a stroke and died at the age of seventy-two on 24th August 1952. Frank had two daughters with Edith Ford, Edith Marie Sutton (Molly) and Olive Minna Sutton. Both girls were sent to Heath House boarding school. The school was so cold that Olive developed chilblains each winter and eventually ensured she got sent to Australia as a 'Ten Pound Pom'[35] where she spent the rest of her life in the warmer clime.

My mother, Molly, married a half-German and half-English spy, with whom she had two children, my sister Pamela Read-Jahn Bailey and myself. I have written much more about my parents in a book about my

---

[35] Ten Pound Poms was the name given to the million British people who emigrated to Australia under a government scheme between 1945 and 1972. The long sea voyage cost them ten pounds sterling. They were promised jobs and better weather.

Author's note: POM (or POME) originally stood for Prisoner of Mother England, referring to British prisoners sent from England to Australia as punishment.

father's spying work for MI-19 in WWII in the Soviet Union and in England, and in the two volumes of my memoirs.[36]

Olive never married. She had one unsuccessful romantic relationship in England before leaving the country forever. She was known in her area of Sydney as 'Auntie Privet' because she developed an eccentric passion for cutting down privet bushes. Every day she donned her safari-like gardening clothes and went out to attack the privet. The story goes that a gentleman took a fancy to this eccentric woman and proposed to her over the garden fence, but she turned him down in short order. It was Olive who was given the monasticon by her parents' maid when her grandfather, Charles Sutton, died and the book had fallen under his bed.

A.E. Searle.

In the First World War (The Great War 1914-1918),
at the age of 27, John Francis (Frank) Sutton was in the
2nd Battalion of the Manchester Rifle Bicycle Brigade.

---

[36] My father's work is described in my book *Hidden in Plain Sight, a British Military Agent's Story*, published on Amazon in 2019. My memoirs are called *Dancing Through Life, Volume I* and *II*, published on Amazon in 2020 and 2021, respectively.

John Francis (Frank) Sutton, Freemason and King George VI
(1895–1952), in the United Grand Lodge of England, the governing
body of Freemasonry in England and Wales.

In The Great War: John Francis (Frank) Sutton & family
with second wife Edith Amy Ford Sutton.
Standing: Edith Marie (Molly Sutton, my mother, 1910-1987).
Seated is Frank's half-brother, George William Pocklington
Sutton (1893-1971).
On his knee is George's niece, Olive Minna Sutton (1915-2007).

Charles William Sutton's 2nd wife and family.
Left to right:
Top row: Maria Pocklington Sutton, John Francis (Frank), Oliver Jepson Sutton.
Bottom row: Charles William Sutton, Albert Bernard (Bernie), George William Sutton, Charles Evans (Charlie).
Children of Charles William & his late first wife, Sarah Evans:
#1 son: Charlie (moved to Chile),
#2 son: Frank (stayed in England),
#3 son: Oliver (joined the Army; presumed dead in action),
#4 son: Bernie (moved to Chile).
#5 son: George William Pocklington Sutton (became a Brigadier; child of Charles Willliam Sutton & his 2nd wife, Maria Pocklington).

Finally, the book arrived from France. With trembling fingers, I tore open the brown envelope and carefully removed the book. It wasn't 'my' monasticon. One after the other, emails or phone calls came in from my FRED Club pals. As I'd rather expected, sadly none of our enquiries throughout the fashion, theatre, and art world brought in any positive results about the vanished monasticon.

What to do now? Back to the drawing board. I thought some ideas would surely come to mind, but meanwhile I'd just get on with updating the genealogical tree and book I believed Great Grandpa had intended to write.

Pouring myself another cup of coffee, I thought not only about Oliver Sutton but also about my Great Uncle George. George William Pocklington Sutton, the only son Maria Pocklington had borne for

Charles William Sutton. I'd known Uncle George quite well in his later years of life, and I much admired him.

George became a great British Army man, fighting all over the world in World War I and II, eventually attaining the rank of brigadier with the Lancashire Fusiliers, earning himself three prestigious medals. He was wounded in World War I, shot through both legs, but survived to tell the tale. He also fought at Gallipoli. George was one of the last men to leave the beach at Dunkirk in World War II. As an old man, George got gangrene in one leg, and had to have the toes of that foot amputated. I adored my great uncle George, as did my mother before me. He was fair, never scolding, and quite funny. He liked to twirl his military moustache.

Uncle George never married. His last years were spent living in a boarding house in Lewes, Sussex. Molly's two daughters, my sister, Pamela Frances (born 26th September 1942) and me, Shirley Ann (born 22nd November 1944) were sent to St. Mary's Hall boarding school in Brighton, Sussex, at the age of eleven and nine, respectively. It was George who'd made the arrangements to get my sister and me into what was in 1954 known as the third best school for girls in England. It was a Church of England school in Brighton, Sussex and I was a boarder there for seven long years. St. Mary's Hall was sold to Brighton Hospital some years ago and the girls still attending were relocated to the other great school in the Brighton area of the south Sussex coast called Roedean.

I recalled seeing a memo in Great Grandpa's collection of notes about his children for the genealogical tree. I carefully went through his papers until I found the one about my Great Uncle George. With those notes, I could put a chapter together about the great British Army officer. I recalled that Charles's monasticon had once again vanished and it was his son, George, who had found the missing book, just as he had on an earlier occasion when it had vanished. There was a tale to be told about that. Tossing Great Grandpa's notes and memos this way and that, I unearthed the one I'd seen before about George William Pocklington Sutton.

I reread Great Grandpa's note about his son George finding the monasticon at a library where he worked. I sighed, thinking that was terrific, but where was the book in my world? It seemed that none of my friends could locate it, nor had they any more ideas on where to look. Everyone had now seemingly given up on the hunt for the monasticon, nor were they probably even thinking about it any longer, why would they? But it was out there; it would surely come back to the family—wouldn't it?

Meanwhile, I still had the note to write more about Great Uncle George and the second time he found the missing monasticon.

Great Uncle George William Pocklington Sutton, wounded in the first World War.

1950s. King George VI and Great Uncle George Sutton, CBE, DSO, TD directly behind him. Hyde Park, London, inspecting servicemen who had fought in WWII.

212

So many stories; tales I thought I'd forgotten now came crowding back. I'd always loved palaces and castles. I remembered my favourite uncle, Great Uncle George, taking me one day in 1962 to the local castle in the area where he lived. He said he had a story for me about his father's favourite book. I knew he'd been the one to find the missing monasticon at one time when he'd worked at the John Rylands Library as a young man. Now he told me it turned out he was to find it yet again when it had gone missing, and how serendipitous that occasion had been.

First, he wanted to tell me about Lewes Castle, which was built in the eleventh century. After the 1066 Battle of Hastings (I smiled as I typed, thinking how 1066 was one of the only dates I could remember from history class without having to do research), loyal supporters of William the Conqueror built Lewes Castle, along with many other castles along the south coast of England.

After my fun bonding session with my favourite uncle—where I showed off for him doing somersaults on the grass in front of the castle and showing him the judo moves I'd perfected—he took me to see the outside of the old prison in Lewes. I loved seeing places like that, too, especially if my companion could tell me the sad, often gruesome stories of the prison's inmates. Uncle George sat on one of the Lewes Prison committees managed by Her Majesty's Prison and Probation Service Board. As we stood and stared at the forbidding grey, square-box structure of the Victorian prison, with its huge dark red door and windows surrounded in red brick, Uncle George told me about a strange experience he'd had there involving a rare book.

"Let's go to have a cup of tea and sit comfortably while I tell you about it. Besides, it's starting to rain and that's when my old war wounds begin to act up."

Sitting inside a pretty teahouse with a tray of scones and a pot of hot tea in front of us, Uncle George told me the story.

In 1791 Lewes Gaol was built at the corner of North and Lancaster Streets. It was enlarged in 1818 to hold seventy cells for males. In 1853 the Admiralty bought the gaol to house prisoners of war from the Crimean War.

"That's the building we looked at today, Shirley. It's in poor shape and I expect it will be demolished soon. They'll have to move its current prisoners while constructing a more modern facility. More tea, my dear?"

"Was anybody famous held in the gaol, Uncle?"

"Funny that your Aunt Olive wondered the same thing. She was interested when I related this tale to her because of her decision to move to Australia."

"The story is that George Ramsdale Witton, an Australian from Warrnambool, Victoria, was a Lieutenant in the Bushveldt Carabiniers in the Boer War in South Africa. He was sent back to England where he was imprisoned for nearly three years in His Majesty's Prison at Lewes after being convicted for shooting nine Boer prisoners."

George went on, "Winston Churchill had also been a prisoner during the Boer War. When in parliament, Churchill questioned the Colonial Secretary about the ongoing incarceration of this Witton fellow, and a campaign for the man's release ensued. On 10th August 1904, King Edward VII pardoned Witton who immediately left England to return to Australia. Alfred Deakin was the Australian Prime Minister at the time, and he welcomed George Witton home with open arms."

As I typed up this story, recalling the details of what Uncle George had told me, I remembered Breaker Morant, a film about the Boer War I'd seen in 1980. It related the story of Witton's court-martial and the conviction as well as that of a fellow soldier called Hancock.

A plate of Bakewell tarts, a specialty from Bakewell in Derbyshire, was placed before Uncle George and me. The young waitress proudly announced that her mother was from Derby so knew how to make these treats. These were small round shortcrust pastry tarts with a delicious, layered filling of jam and frangipane, topped with a hard white icing, flaked almonds, and a half glacé cherry. We each ate one of the delicious morsels.

"And what about the rare book story, Uncle?"

"Ah, yes, the monasticon. This was a book much loved by my father who came across it in his Manchester Free Library long ago in 1867. It had an extraordinary story attached to it whereby it kept disappearing and then turning up again."

"A monasticon—THE monasticon that your father absolutely loved?"

"Yes, that's it, the very one; the book that gave an account of monasteries in a certain area—York, in this case."

"The book that vanished then reappeared? A sort of magical book, as some people have claimed?"

"No such thing, no, not magical my dear—although my half-brother, Oliver, was into magic and he'd certainly claim it had magic attached to it—but it certainly seemed to become that way over all the years of its existence."

"Doesn't it exist anymore, Uncle? I know it went missing, didn't it?"

"Ah, well, therein lies the tale. I'll tell you about it because this part of its story involves our Lewes Gaol."

He then told me how part of his work on the Lewes Gaol Committee was to listen to prisoners and former prisoners' perceptions of how the prison education system was working. He had been a librarian in his youth, before his long, successful career in the British Army that culminated with his promotion to Brigadier.

My great uncle said, "At the end of the nineteenth century there was a change from the Victorian prison system of punishment to where prisoners' needs and rehabilitation were to be considered. This was a true reform. Younger prisoners were now kept separate from adults and ones below the age of twenty-one were sent to separate penal institutions, called borstals. In 1948 they abolished penal servitude, hard labour, and flogging."

"Flogging was used in the Royal Navy for years, you know, where a sailor who was considered to need it, was tied to the deck or to a ship's mast and whipped with a cat o'nine tails. A nasty multi-tailed whip or flail. Come to think of it, Shirley, we used it in our British Army, too."

"And the monasticon?" I quietly encouraged Uncle George.

"Ah yes, it ended up for a while in Lewes Gaol. Before the youngsters were separated from the adults, they were all put in together. You know, the population has grown and grown in our prisons, my dear. Even with the reforms. In fact, as the reforms in prisons have grown, so have the number of prison inmates.

"Yes, I felt like I was in prison, too. It was your fault I got sent there, Uncle. You suggested St. Mary's Hall in Brighton for me and Pam. I know, I know, we were certainly in need of some strict obedience training, but did you see the high stone walls with broken glass on top, Uncle? I never knew whether it was to keep us in or keep boys out!"

Uncle George smiled and patted my knee. "As I was saying, the number of inmates grew exponentially."

———※———

On one of my visits to Australia before I moved there for good in 2011, I met up with my Auntie Olive, who told me she had a memory from 1920 when she was five years old and was still living at home in England before being sent off to boarding school to join her sister, Molly.

The story goes that Olive's grandfather, Charles William Sutton, had been reading the monasticon in bed in his home in Manchester. It had fallen off the bed and slid underneath it when he died on 24th April 1920. The cleaner, a lass called Mary, found the book when she went to clean Mr. Sutton's house. She reckoned it was just an old book. Besides, she could barely read so had no concept of its contents or historical value. She did notice its pretty colours in the illuminated first letters of each chapter.

When her sister Bessie visited her in Manchester, Mary showed her the monasticon that she'd got tucked into her big handbag, and said, "Some child would like this book. When I found it under Mr. Sutton's bed, that's what I thought. Some child would like this 'ere book 'cos it's pretty."

"And, Bessie," added Mary, "Now 'e's gone and died, I'm going down to work at 'is son Frank's 'ouse in Surrey after this weekend 'aving you up 'ere. 'E moved down there from Manchester with 'is new job, you know. 'E's got two young 'uns, Frank does, as you 'eard, them girls Molly and Olive. Maybe the littlest girl would like the pretty colours in them words."

"Good idea," said Bessie. "Glad you didn't tell 'is wife, that Mrs. Sutton. She don't need to know you got it. It's just an old book, after all. And don't you call Frank by 'is first name. 'E's your new employer so you 'ave to call 'im Mr. Sutton, too!"

Mary took it down to Frank Sutton's home. When she showed it to my auntie, young Olive, and the child said she wanted it, Mary gave it to the youngster. Olive did, indeed, like the pretty illuminated first letters of each chapter but wasn't at all interested in the subject matter, herself knowing only a little of her ABCs at her age. She put the ancient book away in a drawer in her bedroom. Olive didn't get on very much at all with her mother, Edith Ford, Frank's second wife, or her older sister, my mother, Molly, so declined to tell them about the book. Besides, the cleaner had given it to her, and a gift is a gift just for yourself, isn't it? It was Mary, the Suttons' cleaner, who tidied up Olive's room, not Olive's mother, so neither of Olive's parents ever knew the book had fallen into Olive's hands.

———————✲———————

Great Uncle George told me the quick version of how the monasticon had been stolen by a young thief who ended up in Lewes Prison. It seems his mother was a cleaner called Mary. When her employer, Charles Sutton, had died in Manchester, she had found a book under his bed. She'd gone down to the south of England to work for his son, Frank Sutton. It was little Olive, Frank's younger daughter, to whom Mary had given the book.

Mary and her sister, Bessie, had talked further about the book and, even unable to read, they'd worked it out that it must be old, because of its medieval pictures in the historiated initial letters of chapters. Mary came up with the idea to have her young son come to Frank's house and nick the book. This was vanishing number seven of the monasticon. The boy had it in his pocket, along with some other stolen items from the house, when he went to a pawn shop to try to turn his loot into money. The pawn shop owner got suspicious and pressed his alarm button connected to the police. The boy was caught and his bag of loot taken from him. The book remained in his deep jacket pocket and it wasn't found until he arrived at Lewes Prison, when it was removed and placed on one of the prison's library shelves.

That was the monasticon book, the very book that Uncle George came across when in the library at Lewes Prison. He'd then taken the book to one of the Sutton uncles who ran a bookstore. He, in turn, had given the book to Molly Sutton to give to her sister, Olive, and Olive took it to Australia, where it was stolen from her luggage at Sydney customs when she got off the ship in 1957. That became vanishing number eight.

Now I'd got the order clear of the vanishings of the monasticon in 'the old days', all I had to do was find the book nowadays. ALL? I must be mad to think I could now find it. It seemed as if it had gone completely into hiding.

I got up to stretch my legs and rest my eyes from my computer and took a walk out into my garden. Sitting on my wooden Lutyens bench, with my much-loved nearly thornless creamy-white *Madame Alfred Carrière* rose clambering up a trellis behind me, I cast my mind back yet again to the chat with my Uncle George in the early 1960s. The book, I remembered, he'd been leading up to the book, what had happened to the precious monasticon. He'd told me how more and more prisoners filled Lewes Gaol. The prison offered rehabilitation to its prisoners by way of job-skills, numeracy, life and social skills, and, most importantly, library access for all. Because Uncle George had been a librarian as a young man, he told me that he was particularly interested in the books Lewes Gaol provided for the inmates to borrow.

On one of his committee visits to the gaol George went into the prison library. He planned to write an investigative report about the status of prison education at that time. His superiors would, in turn, present his findings to parliament.

As George stood before the bookshelves that day, there, right in front of his nose, was the monasticon. The very book that George's father had held so dear throughout his life. With a shaking hand, he took the book from the shelf and went straight to the prison warden. This was just too strange. He'd found the very same book once before, as a young librarian in Manchester. It had vanished and then turned up in the John Rylands library where he was working, and he'd telephoned his father immediately. And now, here he was in a similar situation. He hadn't remembered, even if he had known, that the monasticon had gone missing again, yet he was the finder of it once more. How extraordinary!

"How do you come to have this rare book on your bookshelf in the prison library, Warden? You know it's about monasteries in and around York?"

"Oh, that dog-eared old thing. One of our remand boys from the local courts had it in his pocket when he was brought in. He said he'd pinched it along with a lot of other stuff that he'd got done for. For some reason, the cops hadn't taken it off him, but we found it when we patted him down and before he changed into our prison overalls. He didn't know anything about the book, and nor do I, for that matter, so we stuck it in the library. Maybe somebody will read the old thing one of these days, but you don't get much interest in stuff like monasteries in this place, as you can imagine. Look, if you fancy it, you can take it away with you."

So, as George told me, he'd got permission to carry the monasticon away with him from Lewes Gaol. All of that had taken place in the mid-1950s before Auntie Olive had set sail for Australia. With George not having been told that the book had originally been given to Olive as a present by the housemaid—after her grandfather had died and dropped the book by his bed—George now gave it to one of the Sutton uncles who happened to run a bookshop. It was the bookshop uncle who had deciphered the faded pencil signature inside the book. Strangely to me, George obviously hadn't noticed the faded signature in the front or hadn't been able to decipher it. It was my mother Molly, who had been handed the book by the bookshop uncle and it was she who had returned it to her sister, my Auntie Olive. My mother had told me that the scribbled name of her sister inside the book was, indeed, almost faded out. Perhaps Uncle George's eyes were also somewhat faded by that time. I worked it out that in the mid-1950s he would have been in his sixties.

Knowing the young thief in Lewes Gaol had stolen the book from my grandfather's house in Surrey, it was another case of the monasticon vanishing but luckily turning up again. The young thief himself had long ago done his time and gone out into the world once more, never to be seen again.

When the monasticon had vanished for the seventh time but had eventually shown up—as was its habit—I remembered Olive telling me the story of how that happened, which Molly had told her. Molly had an uncle who ran a bookstore in London. My fingers were poised over my computer keys. The story came rushing back to me and I began to type. Red, orange, yellow, leaves turning to brown swirled down from the trees. Hanging onto her red beret as she entered the bookstore, Molly pushed against the wind holding its door shut. The bell on the door tinkled as she forced the door open and was just about blown in. The old bespectacled man looked up expectantly.

"Molly!" cried her uncle in delight, "What brings you here?"

"Hello, Uncle, I'm looking for a book on Australia. Olive's off to Sydney in a few weeks as soon as spring arrives. You remember about her chilblains? A warmer climate she reckons will cure her."

He smiled, came around the counter and led Molly down a steep, narrow, staircase lined with musty smelling books.

"Here you are, Molly dear, take a browse through these. Not too many on Australia, but enough to keep you interested." His bent-over body creaked its way back up the staircase. Molly found a travel book, knocked the dust off the top of it, sat down on the stairs and started to read. The photos were in black and white, but every one of them so exotic to Molly.

"Hmmm," she said to herself, "maybe I'll go to visit our Olive one of these days, after she's all settled in. Lots to see, kangaroos, emus, koalas, oh, and look at those gorgeous sandy beaches. How I love to swim!"

Soon Molly's eyes glazed over reading about such an exotic country. She began thinking about how she would truly miss her younger sister. They didn't get along that well, but Molly was fond of the old stick, as she called her, even though she was five years younger than Molly. Olive always seemed too old for her young years. Leaning her head against the bookshelves, she felt tears begin to roll slowly down her cheeks.

"I must be daft, I can't be crying over the old stick popping off to the other side of the world," she said aloud. "She'd laugh herself silly if she saw me."

A mother and her child passed Molly's crouching body on the stairs. The little girl hesitated then said, "What did you say? Why are you crying?"

The mother turned right into an aisle at the bottom of the stairs and soon disappeared, calling behind her. "Hurry up, come on, Flo dear, I think I know where that story we're looking for is."

"Wait a minute, mum, I'm talking to the lady crying on the stairs."

"Hmmm, well darling, don't be long," the mother responded with disinterest, intent of finding a book she herself wanted for her child.

"But why are you crying?" the little girl asked Molly, concern etched into her big blue eyes.

Molly couldn't answer at first. She hiccupped, then took the child's hand and said, "My sister's leaving England and sailing far away, to Australia, and I'm a bit sad."

"Don't be sad. I expect you'll find a good book today to cheer you up!"

Looking very wise, she smiled at Molly then ran off to join her mother.

Standing up, Molly replaced the travel book she'd been looking at.

She found herself quite cheered up by the little girl's optimism, and felt a smile crease her face. She climbed back up the musty steep stairs.

"Find what you wanted?" Uncle asked, cleaning his half-glasses, and peering myopically up at Molly from his stool behind the counter.

"No, wait, sort of, well, yes, I suppose I did, but it's nothing I can pay for, at least, this time, I'm afraid."

"Never mind, see you next time you stop in," he called out to her as she went out into the sparkling light of a now much brighter autumn day, hearing the tinkling of his door as it swung shut behind her. With a loud creak and more tinkling, the door re-opened. Turning around, Molly saw Uncle standing there, holding out a book toward her.

"Meant to remember to give this to you. Give it back to Olive, will you, Molly dear?"

Molly's mouth dropped open as she saw what it was. The monasticon!

"What on earth? How? It can't be! Where was it? How did you get it? It's been vanished for ages, Dad told me; nicked from our house with some other valuable stuff! He described what it looked like—this is it, isn't it?!" Molly spluttered.

"Your Great Uncle George found it in Lewes Gaol's library, of all places," Uncle replied. "Go on, take it to Olive. I heard it had vanished. She'll be pleasantly surprised. I know it's hers because she scribbled her name in it in pencil. It's almost faded out but I can see it says O.M. Sutton."

"That's right; it was given to her when she was very little, after our grandpa died. She told me about it recently. Grandpa Sutton's maid went to work at our Dad's house, and that's when the maid gave it to my sister. When Olive was leaving for Australia, she said she wanted to take it on the ship to read on the long voyage, but she couldn't find it when making out her list of what to pack. She wondered whether Mother had found it in her room and chucked it out without telling her; sort of thing we reckoned she just might do. She's not that fond of our Olive and is a bit mean, Uncle, you know her!"

As he went back into his bookshop, the door's bell tinkling behind him, Molly clutched the monasticon to her breast. She marched along, thoughtfully kicking at a pile of red, orange, and yellow leaves with her boots. They flew up around her, swirling as the wind caught them, like sprites, fantastical fairylike creatures from another realm. They glowed in their autumnal robes, teasingly blowing around her head till she found that any remaining sadness she'd had earlier was now completely gone and, with one last kick tossing the autumnal leaves high into the sky, she knew how pleased Olive would be. That, too, brought a satisfied grin to her face. Once home, she handed the monasticon over to her delighted younger sister. Olive grabbed it, telling Molly, "It's quite fantastical that this book vanishes then reappears over and over. Magical, in a way, don't you agree, Moll?"

So here I was, now sitting at my desk in Shoalhaven Heads, compiling all the information I could find about the Pocklington and Sutton families' history. I researched for hours online. I read books I had shipped over to Australia when I'd married Horst, books about the Sutton family on my mother's side; books I'd never given much time to until now. I'd continue to incorporate the Suttons into this book I had now started writing, of course I would. Story after story flew into my mind, told to me by various relatives over the years.

———————※———————

I now knew I was hardly likely to find the monasticon, so what was I going to do? Get on with writing the book about the family, of course! I'd made a mental promise to the spirit of my Great Grandpa that I'd finish the book for him, so that's what I felt compelled to do. Rustling around in his notes and memos strewn across my desk and in the plastic box, I found more pieces of information that gave me clues as to what had happened in the lives of those now departed ancestral souls—once I'd matched them to their names, dates and occupations he'd written on his family tree.

My heart started to beat even faster as I now typed more and more about my ancestors. My grandfather, Frank Sutton, had told me how his father, my Great Grandpa Charles William Sutton, had started the family tree in his free time when he was chief librarian at the Manchester Free Public Library—the very tree now lying on my desk in my office. Grandpa Frank Sutton had mentioned much about a monasticon, how it was his father's favourite book that Charles had used to enable him to write about the Pocklingtons, the old family he'd married into after his beloved first wife had unexpectedly died. I'd taken little notice at the time—not until I'd started on my own hunt for the same book.

With determination to get on with the job of writing the book, yet again I lifted the lid of the plastic box I'd brought from California and started to pile onto my desk the remaining documents within that were in my Great Grandfather's writing. Soon I was swimming even more in paperwork. I wrote more and more of his story in Charles Sutton's voice, which I decided to tuck inside a memoir in my own voice of the circumstances of this almost magical book, which seemed to appear then vanish repeatedly.

I included the tale in my book that Olive had told me about her sister giving her the book because I saw it as pertinent to the whole story. It appeared that the monasticon vanished then reappeared, countless times, and Olive's tale was about one of those times. The book always seemed to find its way back to the Sutton family. Always—so...maybe I shouldn't be so convinced it had well and truly disappeared. Maybe, just maybe, it would show up...

Meanwhile, my sister and I decided to fly to Chile to visit our second cousin. We had the same great grandfather. I wondered about her memories and couldn't wait to talk to her about so many family stories.

———————✤———————

In 2007 my sister, Pam, and I flew to Chile to visit our second cousin, Barbara Sutton, Pam flying from Australia and I from the United States, where we'd respectively made our homes. Barbara's grandfather was Charles Evans Sutton, who, with his brother, Albert Bernard Sutton, had settled in Chile to make their fortunes, Charlie leaving England first, and Bernie following him some years later. Charles Evans and Albert Bernard's father was Charles William Sutton of the Manchester Free Library.

An old trunk was found under the bed of one of the Sutton relatives. It was filled with photographs and letters from the past. My sister, cousin and I spent some exciting days going through the papers. Some of it referred to the fact that Charles William Sutton owned two of the English Romantic printmaker and watercolourist, William Turner's landscape paintings. Charles requested that they be given to the Manchester Library after his death. The will states that they were to be left first to his youngest son, my great uncle, Brigadier George William Pocklington Sutton, to distribute per his father's wishes, but it's unknown what became of the valuable paintings. Paperwork in the trunk also showed that there were two other paintings, one of which was a life-sized painting of Charles William Sutton himself after he received his honorary Master of Arts degree from the Victoria University in Manchester. This was painted by Grace Esdaile, otherwise known as Mrs. Montague Tabor Pickstone, a student artist with an admirable skill in reproducing a true likeness of Charles. You could just imagine the twinkle of his hazel eyes behind his *pince-nez*, and the twitch of his mouth under the thick brown moustache, when the chief librarian of 53 King Street was about to let fall some quip or pun. Another painting was listed, but it is unknown what it depicted. Unfortunately, nothing is known of the current whereabouts of any of those four paintings.

As the years passed, Auntie Olive grew up into a rather plain and sad young woman with horrible chilblains on her hands, had a brief unhappy love affair, and finally convinced her parents, Frank and Edith Sutton, that it would be a good move for her to leave cold, damp England and go to live in Australia where the hot sun would clear up the painful condition of her hands. She learned there was an Assisted Passage Scheme to help populate Australia whereby you could travel there as a 'ten pound pom'. A doctor had told her she'd do much better in a warmer clime. Here and there, Olive drew the old monasticon out of her bedside table and glanced at parts of it. She noticed that it recorded the family history of her grandfather's second wife in it, Maria Pocklington Sutton, so she packed the book in her luggage, thinking she really ought to read it one day.

One fine day in 1957, Olive's luggage was loaded onto the Orient Line ship 'Orontes' sailing from Tilbury Docks on the River Thames in Essex. It was mainly carrying passengers migrating to Australia under the governmental scheme. Olive had been promised a secretarial job and other assistance when she started a new life once in Sydney. As she walked up the ship's gangplank, children pushed and shoved past her.

"Leave the young lady alone, Georgie, don't push people!" called a mother to one snotty child excitedly squeezing past Olive on the gangplank as she plodded upwards, hanging onto the railing with one painful chilblained hand and holding her overnight bag in the other. Her main trunk of possessions had been loaded onto the ship by the stevedores.

"'E's travelling for free, miss, wonderful, innit? And I only got to pay ten quid for me for this journey. Bloody marvellous, I say."

"Yes," replied Olive, "me, too. They call us ten pound poms. Funny, isn't it? Can't wait to get out of this horrible weather in England."

"Almost four weeks at sea, lovely, innit? Just hope Georgie don't fall overboard, eh miss?"

After their ship steamed into Sydney Harbour, Olive started her new life in the warm, sometimes very hot, humid, climate of Sydney in the summer. She delightedly noticed that her chilblains had, indeed, already begun to clear up. This amazing discovery made her feel relieved and much happier.

The only problem, minor in her opinion, was the loss of just a few of the contents in her luggage. She assumed a thief had been at work when all the luggage passed through Customs at Sydney Harbour. The book, the ancient monasticon book, where was it? She should never have packed it in her trunk. She felt so silly. She knew she wanted to read it while aboard on the long trip to Australia so why hadn't she packed it in her overnight bag? Stupid! Molly always said she was a silly goose. And now where was the darned book? Gone? Surely not? As she rifled yet again through her belongings strewn over her bed in the hostel she had been put into temporarily, she realised it was indeed gone. Completely vanished. Maybe it was valuable, she thought. She muttered aloud to nobody in particular, "I never was terribly interested in family history, anyway, so, really, who cares. It's gone. Family never really liked me, either, so...a shame, though, in a way. I should have read it, I suppose, to find out about the Pocklingtons. Would have been more interesting to me, I expect, if it had been about the Suttons..."

Before I'd moved from the States to Australia in late 2011 and brought the box of Olive's grandfather's papers and documents with me, I'd not looked through them much at all, and hadn't even picked up that a monasticon even existed. Thus, when I'd had lunch with my Auntie Olive in Sydney on one of my visits to Australia prior to my move, I'd had no idea what she'd been talking about regarding the treasured book. It was at that lunch at her club that she'd told me about it going missing from her luggage when she'd moved to Australia from England in 1957. Olive had died in 2007 without my having discussed it with her ever again. I'd been a little interested when we'd looked at family papers at my cousin's in Chile and made photocopies of some of them. After that trip, I had dismissed it from my mind and was only interested in it so many years later when I started working on Olive's grandfather's (and my Great Grandpa's) genealogical tree.

The next person I thought about—after looking at my own notes just as for her sister, Olive—was my own mother. Of course, I'd already heard many stories straight from my mother to me about her immediate family.

Her father was John Francis (Frank) Sutton. He was Charles William Sutton's second son, born of Sarah Evans. My mother was born in 1910, her sister Olive's senior by five years. Molly would have known her grandfather, Charles Sutton, who died when she was ten. Molly married Fred Read-Jahn, a naturalised Brit, born to a German father and an English mother. He worked for British Army Intelligence in a highly secretive department of the Foreign Office called MI-19.[37] They had a rushed courtship and married on the 31st March 1940 because Fred was going away shortly to Moscow in his spying capacity. Fred's father, Friedrich Ludwig Jahn, was a journalist in Berlin. Fred's mother, Clara Read, was an English hatmaker from Luton, centre of the millinery trade. Her father, George Read, was a plait bleacher—a much sought-after trade in the 1800s.

---

[37] See note at end of Chapter 97 regarding my books that have more information about my mother and my father, and his espionage work in WWII.

Molly Sutton and Fred Read-Jahn married in 1940, just before he left England for his espionage job in the Soviet Union. They had two children, Pam and me, conceived on Fred's brief visits home from the Soviet Union and when he was working in England at the end of World War II.

Pam had four daughters, each delightfully different from one another. I bore one child, a boy, Samuel Sutton Kline.

My husband, Horst Reimann, moved to Australia from Germany with his family after the war. After a long life in Australia, Horst then met me on one of my visits from California to see my sister, Pam, in Sydney. In late 2011, Horst flew to the United States and brought me back to Australia, where we married and settled into Shoalhaven Heads, a small boating and fishing village in New South Wales only a couple of hours' drive south of Sydney.

While I sat in my office, musing on how far away I now was from England, and the USA where I'd been living since 1970, it hit me how far I now was from where the monasticon was probably lurking. Perhaps lying forlorn and forgotten on somebody's bookshelf, or in a library somewhere, and doubtless with nobody keen to read about monasteries around York in England. Who knew where it was? I most certainly didn't, and that fact continued to bother me. I concluded I was going to have to let it go. The book was not likely to ever be found. I'd searched and searched, as had all my generous friends in different parts of the world. I felt we'd come to a complete dead end. Standing up, I marched outside to my garden, as was my wont, and soaked up the scents of all the flowers in bloom, until I'd come properly to terms with the idea that there was nothing left for me to do, that I could think of anyway, so I'd better forget the monasticon—just let it go and get on with my life...

———————�֍———————

One day I took the train from my village of Shoalhaven Heads up to Sydney. A friend invited me to attend an auction with her. I was handed a numbered paddle. My friend told me to raise the paddle in front of me if I wished to bid on an item. A set of silver spoons was offered, then a framed collection of exotic blue glittery butterflies from the Inca Trail in Peru. Next from China came an exquisitely carved ivory box within a box within yet another box. Then a carved soapstone white rhinoceros from Africa. The auctioneer said it was a Kisii soapstone from southwestern Kenya, considered unique, and this rhino was particularly rare, being carved in white. I fell in love at once with the six-inch-long rhino, raised my paddle and outbid another lady in a row behind me. The auctioneer made each item sound more intriguing and exotic than the previous one. I was enthralled with the whole experience.

As the afternoon progressed, the auctioneer offered more and more expensive items, and some of a great age. People in the audience held phones to their ears, muttering into them in secret whispers, then raising their paddles to outbid each other in not-so-friendly 'auction wars'. Near the end, the auctioneer called out, "Next, a book. Could be rare, hence in this section. Not sure about its value. Quite old, I'd say, but its cover has gone, so I reckon it lacks much of any value it could have had. Plus, some of the pages have been torn out. Frankly, looks like the dog ate some of it for its dinner, a bit daggy, you know? But maybe one of you might be interested? Just got dropped off today by someone who shall be nameless. Looks like he found it in the skip", he said below his breath.

"Well, anyway, any interest? Anyone?" A shaking of heads ensued. A few derisive snorts were heard, but I was intrigued. A book? What kind of book, I wondered? I loved to read.

"I'll start at twenty-five dollars. It is rather old...just twenty-five dollars, anyone?"

An old man raised his paddle.

"You, sir, twenty-five dollars, okay. Anyone else? No? Oh, yes, I see you, the sheila near the back, yes, you lady. What's that? Thirty dollars? Okay, thirty dollars. Sir?"

This went on, backwards and forwards, until it reached fifty dollars.

The man didn't raise his paddle. I timidly lifted mine up for the auctioneer to see.

"Fifty dollars, missus. Anyone else interested? You sir? No? Okay then, right you are, missus, fifty dollars, going, going, gone! See my assistant at the end, missus, and thank you."

The old man scowled at Shirley. The woman in the seat next to her said,

"Don't worry about him. He's a retired teacher comes in here to see what's up for grabs but never goes too high. Pleased for you, my dear. Hope you like it, 'though I think I'd prefer that rhino you got, myself!"

I collected the sorry-looking, dog-eared book and put it in my bag. The front cover had indeed gone. I decided I'd start to read it tonight after dinner with Horst. A thought flitted through my head: could it, could it possibly be, maybe, golly, COULD it be the monasticon for which I and many of my friends had searched? It did have now-faded historiated first initials in different sections and chapters. Don't be daft, I told myself, there's no chance whatsoever a book like the monasticon could be in an auction in Sydney, Australia. Oh my God, but if it WAS...well, then I'd be all set to continue writing Great Grandpa's story. I already had my own notes started on my computer, and some of the writing done, but if...oh, if it were indeed to be THE book, well, I was all set to have a real go at it!

As calmly as I could, I told the lady from the next seat, "It could be interesting, you never know," as I pushed open the door of the auction room to let her exit before me, "that's why I bought the ratty-looking thing. It's obviously very old..."

"Let's have a look at it then," said the woman. "Look at it, mate, it's in lousy shape. And you paid fifty dollars for it. Well, hopefully it'll be a good read."

I took the train from Sydney all the way down to Shoalhaven Heads, flipping through some of the book's pages to get an idea of what was in it, and still legible. Some of it was illegible and some bits of its pages were torn out or apparently damaged by moisture.

Once home and after dinner, I sat down to have a better look at the book. It had looked boring at first, when I'd looked at it on the train, all about monasteries in the northeast of England, mainly around York. Still the niggling, persistent question sat in the forefront of my mind. Just maybe, could it be? I'd need to read through the old book much more carefully, seeing if I recognised anything Great Grandpa had written about.

Taking a deep breath, I put it aside while trying to calm my now pounding heart. I threw my mind back to York itself.

I had been to York and had walked atop some of the city's surrounding walls. It was founded by the Romans and had a beautiful thirteenth century Gothic cathedral called York Minster, with bell towers that still rang bells, and stained-glass windows from the Middle Ages. I loved history and read on. I suddenly started straight up from my chair. By then, I had looked through the plastic box of my Great Grandfather's papers and documents and already knew quite a lot about the vanished monasticon book from some of his jottings and notes. I now recalled the conversation with Auntie Olive about just such a book having vanished from her luggage when she'd sailed to Australia in the fifties. What a fool I was, what a dunce! This was the missing book, it had to be! Springing out of my chair, I ran to my husband. "Horst! This book is a monasticon, you know, a book that tells you about the history of monasteries—in the York area in this case. It incorporates the story of one of the Pocklingtons! It does! I found something about it in this book! You remember, I told you bits about it all. I think, oh I think it could actually be the missing...oh!"

I couldn't believe it, as the understanding of what I was now holding in my hands hit me between the eyes and my excitement grew in leaps and bounds.

"Horst, Horst, oh, and listen to this!" I cried out to my husband. "This book includes some history about that Pocklington man, that Walter Bishop, oh, you remember, I told you, the man from that old, old family one of our Suttons eventually married into, you know, my mother was a Sutton. Wait, I remember! It was my great grandfather's second wife who was a Pocklington. I've read bits about it in Great Grandpa's notes in the box. Good Lord, Horst, I think this is that very book that Auntie Olive Sutton said had been stolen from her luggage when she came through Customs off that ship bringing 'ten pound poms' to Australia!"

I showed him the ancient book, pushing it right under his nose, pointing out the faded illuminated first letters of each chapter. "For Heaven's sake, can you believe it, Horst? This is it, the actual missing monasticon! It IS, it's talking in places about the Pocklingtons so it HAS to be. It IS, Horst, oh my God, it's vanished no longer. I'VE GOT IT, darling, oh my God!"

"This book could be worth a bloody fortune, Horst! And I only paid fifty dollars for it! Oh, I'm going to have to write to my FRED Club, you know, my Friends Research Department Club, to tell 'em the book's been found!"

The next day I took the book to a bookseller in my local provincial town to get his opinion on its worth. He looked at the book carefully, squinting at it through an enlarging glass.

"It's very, very old, missus," he said. "I expect I could sell it for you, if you like? I could buy it off you? Or, maybe you'd want to take it to one of the university libraries up in Sydney? Up to you. Not worth that much anymore, though, 'cos it's lost its cover and some of its pages. Up to you, as I say."

Hmmm, I'll bet. You're not getting this from me, I thought. I can see that you think you know very well what it's worth.

"No thank you, I'll hang on to it for a while, anyway," I said, pressing my treasure to my chest. I walked out of the bookseller's shop, thinking hard and with great excitement about what I'd do next.

Sitting in my office, with the monasticon at my side (Hallelujah!), I carefully went through many of Great Grandpa's papers again, to familiarise myself with what he'd said about the monasticon. Obviously, the book had remained at the abbey for many years after Walter-from-Gascony, the original abbot and his scribe in York had died. Friar Alberic had made a final entry. He sounded quite as lascivious as the earlier scribe. No wonder Great Grandpa had found this book so fascinating. I wondered how it had finally left the abbey and turned up in Great Grandpa's library? That was something I knew I'd never find out. I would love to know that part of the story but recognise that it will probably be forever shrouded in mystery. To my absolute delight, I now read what the new scribe had written.

I took it upon myself to read everything in this monasticon about our old town of York and its many abbeys and priories. I had met, on my walks around our different districts of our locality, one or two gentlemen and men of the cloth from the village of Poke, even a young squire called Richard Hugo Pocklington. He was thus, in a long tradition, called by the name of his estate at the village of Poke. This gentleman had a lady upon his arm, dressed in the latest of fashions, and most fetching to boot, although before God, it would be most profane of me to speak in such a vein. What I would have been more advised by our abbot to write, if he were to be alive (may his soul rest in peace with our Lord), was that the lady I mention was the squire's wife and was introduced to me as Marguerite Cecilia Sutton. I wondered about her name in that I knew that the word Sutton meant a farmstead in the south. I dared to question the provenance of this lady, not having myself heard such a surname mentioned in our parts. She advised me in a most becoming, shyly sweet way, that her family hailed from one of the villages around the town of Manchester, south from our York. She had met the young Squire Pocklington at the yearly Grand Farmers' Market, when she had accompanied her father up to our area. Myself exclaiming in surprise at the long distance, she said they had spent nights on the way at roadside inns in Huddersfield, Leeds, Wakefield, and Castleford. It took them many days in their cart, but well worth the annual event whereby her father sold much of his produce, reaping a rewarding amount of silver to take home to the farm. She smilingly added, squeezing her husband's arm most coquettishly, that as Squire Pocklington's wife, she was now considered a real lady, which, Brother, said she to me, you can see for yourself, as she twirled a parasol up and around beside her. It was not easy to twirl, I could see, being rather heavy; made of bamboo, cloth, and some feathers. The young squire's wife obviously felt herself to look a lady with such an accoutrement. Look at her I did, indeed, it was hard to look away, and with my heart pounding, I decided to...

Those were the last lines in the monasticon; the following page, to my dismay, torn out of the book. Regardless, I walked quickly to my husband, to share with him my vast excitement in discovering that a Pocklington had married a Sutton a long, long time before the first entry in our family tree of one Robert Sutton, father of Thomas Sutton, born in 1825. Robert was therefore my great great great grandfather.

Now, what on earth should I call this book I was writing? I stared at the monasticon. Of course, it was the monasticon that spoke to me, lying next to my computer, a tatty old tome, speaking to me through its ancient pages, nagging at me to get on with the tale. It had existed then vanished, reappeared, then vanished again, and again, and again. Suddenly I knew the title of my book. And...the book, how lucky was I— I had the monasticon itself! I stared at my computer screen then, with a satisfied, happy, smile, I carefully typed three words, *The Vanishing Book.*

EPILOGUE
Memoir

There are other strange, unexplained, even mysterious 'vanishings' that have occurred in my life. There's the photograph of King George VI and John Francis Sutton, in their freemason regalia in a black car outside Buckingham Palace, and the photograph of Charles Dickens telling Thomas Sutton about his novella, A Christmas Carol. Both photos have completely vanished.

There's another photograph that has mysteriously disappeared. In my mid-twenties, I visited the Holy Monastery of Great Meteoron at Meteora on the Plain of Thessaly in Greece with my first husband, William Luther Grenoble, IV. Women were never welcomed into the Meteora monasteries in the old days and in the 1960s only welcomed if their arms were covered up. At that time, there were but five monks still living in the Grand Meteoron monastery. It was perched high up at the top of one of the strangest geological formations in the world. Meteora is on the northwest side of the Plain of Thessaly, near the river Penios and the Pindos Mountains in north-western Greece.

I entered one of the empty monastic cells and stood near the window. My husband stood inside the cell near the door. The cell window had no glass and was just a smallish opening at eye level cut into the wall of the cell. It had a fantastic view of the other suspended monasteries on neighbouring massive rock formations. A monk entered and offered us both some homemade Turkish Delight. He said, "The rocks you see thrusting up out of the Plain were formed millions of years ago of stone, sand, and mud flowing in streams into a delta at the edge of a lake, then further shaped by natural phenomena such as wind and rain. People often tell me that the mountains are made from volcanic plugs of igneous rock, but not so, they're of sandstone and conglomerate."

The monk passed the plate of homemade sweets again to me and my husband, then added softly, "It was an eagle sent by God that flew with the first rope up to the top of one of those mountains to allow the original monks to begin their construction of the first monastery." Then, he left the cell.

We finished eating the delicious morsels of Turkish Delight then my husband photographed me standing before the window opening. When we eventually got the slide back, my face was backlit from the window light, and the image showed the arm of a man clearly holding a hammer above my head as if to bring it down upon me. Mystified, we went back to the photography shop where the slide had been developed. The man who had personally developed the pictures said there was no 'bleed' either side of the image. In his opinion, it was a ghostly apparition of a long-dead monk's arm holding a hammer, doubtless unhappy about having a woman standing in his cell.

Fifty years later my former husband was cleaning out his attic. He went to find the slide from long ago, having promised to give it to me, after I'd told him I'd like to use it in a book I was planning to write. He pulled out the slide carousel and started searching. All the slides were in the carousel in their proper order. All save one. The slide of the monk's arm with the hammer over my head had gone. Disappeared. Gone. Just vanished completely into thin air.

A REQUEST

Good reviews are important to a book's success and will help others find *The Vanishing Book*. If you enjoyed it, please be kind and leave a review on Amazon.com or Goodreads.com.

I'm always delighted to receive email from readers.
Email: shirleyreadjahnbooks@gmail.com

ABOUT THE AUTHOR:

Shirley Read-Jahn is a writer and illustrator, having published nine children's books since 2018, an historical biography of her father's story of his work as an MI-19 spy in World War II, plus a memoir of her own eventful life, comprising two volumes. Shirley has a chapter in three anthologies to date.

The Vanishing Book is her thirteenth book. Shirley was born in World War II and educated in England before becoming a hippy and living in an ancient Roman burial tomb in Matala, Crete. She has enjoyed various colourful careers, including swimwear model, interpreter, landscape gardener, paralegal and events organiser. She also co-founded the highly-successful San Francisco Jazz Festival (SFJAZZ) as well as running her own landscape business in the United States. Shirley has belly-danced since her thirties, still teaches dance, plays table-tennis, and practices tai chi. Now living in partial retirement in Australia, she has finally found time to devote to her passion for writing the books swirling around in her head, including this latest publication.

Email: shirleyreadjahnbooks@gmail.com
Facebook: https://www.facebook.com/srjpublications/

ALSO BY THE AUTHOR

BOOKS FOR ADULTS AND CHILDREN

ALL of my books may be purchased by clicking on amazon.com/author/shirleyread-jahn and clicking on All Formats.

BOOKS FOR ADULTS

The following memoir is about my father's spying work during WWII.

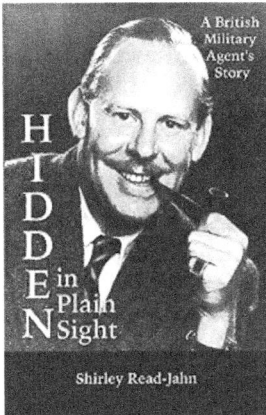

Hidden in Plain Sight, a British Military Agent's Story.
When World War Two splits Fred Read-Jahn and his English bride, Molly, she is forced to face the Blitz alone while he carries out secret missions on an epic journey from London to Moscow, travelling through North America, Canada, and much of Asia to the USSR. Only recently has it been released that he was working as an undercover intelligence agent for MI-19.

The following two memoirs are about my own eventful life. I suggest reading volume 1 before volume 2.

Dancing Through Life, Volume 1
Straddling the century, this colourful memoir tells of a childhood with an English rose and an English-German spy as parents, the confusions of a Dickensian schooling, coming of age in London's legendary sixties, before becoming a cave-dwelling hippy on the Greek island of Crete. We follow Shirley to exotic places where she lived and loved. Her new knowledge about men, her marriages, triumphs, and misfortunes, are laid bare. This is one woman's story of her time, but all women will see reflections of themselves.

Dancing Through Life, Volume 2
Still breathless after the whirlwind of Shirley's early life as she grapples with growing up and maturing, we follow her youthful footsteps to the next stage. We learn more of the men, the marriages, the triumphs and misfortunes that threaten to trip her. We are given an insight into Shirley's travels, her work, her glamourous life and her celebrity friends. But, as her twilight years approach, where has Shirley chosen to end her days, and with whom?

BOOKS FOR CHILDREN

All my kids' books may be read independently or as a sequential story, if there's more than one book in a particular series. I am the author and illustrator of all my children's books. The age group is around 5-10 but it really depends on the maturity of the child. They may also be used as READ ALOUD books for younger children, from 2 years old upwards.

The Prince Oliver Penguin Trilogy SERIES (based on a true story).

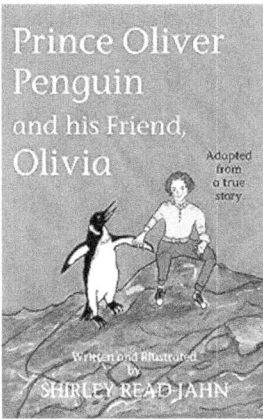

Prince Oliver and his Friend, Olivia. Many years ago, when Olivia's family moved to the Falkland Islands, she unexpectedly made friends with a persistent young King penguin. She named him Prince Oliver and the pair adored each other. They did everything together and were never apart. But what will happen when Olivia's father announces that the family must return to England and Olivia must leave Prince Oliver Penguin behind? This beautiful tale, based on a true story, will charm both 5 - 7 year olds and adults alike.

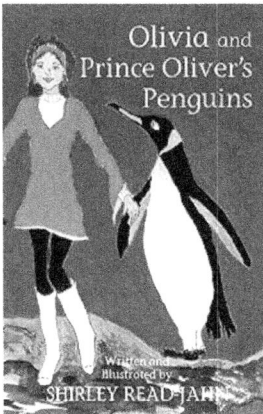

Olivia & Prince Oliver's Penguins. There's a king penguin dynasty happening at the Penguin and Seabird Sanctuary on the Falkland Islands. What do you think will happen to Princess Olivia, Olly and Olivette, and to Piper-the-Penguin? What about the grown-ups, Olivia and Harry? What excitement will happen next? This beautiful tale will charm both 5-7 year olds and adults alike.

Olivia, Prince Oliver and the Penguin Chicks. More characters, both human and penguin, enter this final story of the Prince Oliver Penguin trilogy. Love is in the air, but everything is set to change with the occurrence of the 19–2 Falklands War. What will happen to Olivia's much-loved Princess Olivia, who started life as Prince Oliver? This beautiful tale will charm both 5-7 year olds and adults alike.

Wally the Water Dragon Duology SERIES (fiction)

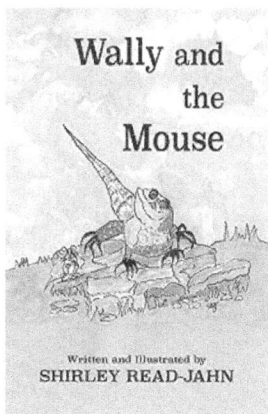

Wally and the Mouse. Wally, a young Australian water dragon, meets Pinky, a little pink mouse. Will he eat her for dinner, or become her saviour, when a venomous red-bellied black snake slides into the billabong? What will happen when all of Pinky's mouse family rush down to the billabong? This delightful, educational, tale will charm children of 6-10 years old and all adults who love stories about Australian animals and nature.

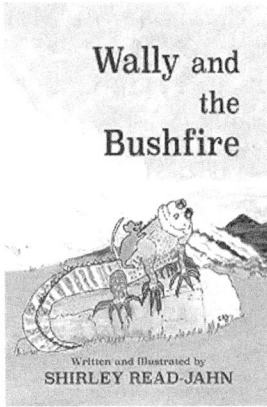

Wally and the Bushfire. Ideal for children transitioning from picture-books-only to text-only books. Wally, a young Australian water dragon, and his beloved friend, the little mouse called Pinky, are caught in an emergency. A terrible bushfire is raging and threatening to kill all in its path. Can they outrun it? How can Wally and Pinky help rescue all the creatures, great and small? What about the humans in the red-roofed house, and the mice living in the flowerpots on the deck? Will everyone be saved? This delightful, educational, tale will charm children of 6-10 years old and all adults who love stories about Australian animals and nature.

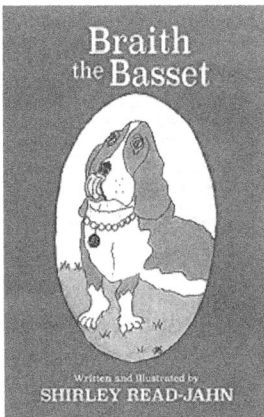

Braith the Basset. Sir Frederick Braithwaite, the basset hound, was born in Kansas, USA in 1971. He had bright, inquisitive eyes, a lolling tongue, and simply terrible breath. He was adorable, warm and friendly, and travelled in his owners' car throughout eleven of the United States as they pursued various work assignments. But why did Braith have a garment specially designed for him? How did he break the law? And why did his poop sparkle? Find out in this true tale of Braith the Basset.

Hello Snail. Sally and her brother, Max, love snails and keep them as pets. Their mum, a snail expert, is keen to tell the children all she knows about these amazing creatures. But when a friend does something horrid, how does Sally react? Can she save her snails when lightning strikes her aquarium? This charming tale educates children about the life of snails and also how to behave in a crisis. Suitable for children aged 6-8, transitioning from picture books to text-only.

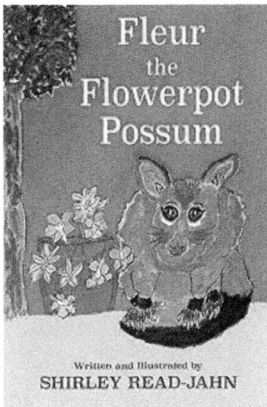

Fleur the Flowerpot Possum. An Australian brushtail possum sets up home in a flowerpot on a verandah after her tree-den was flooded by winter rains. When she refuses to leave her new snug flowerpot home, the wildlife rescue man is called. What will happen when Cranky is set free? Will Pete the Pelican become her friend or enemy? Will Fleur claim her old den back? Or has somebody else moved in?

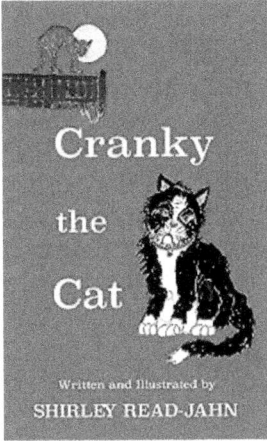

Cranky the Cat is very bad-tempered. Although she lives with a loving owner next to a beautiful flower garden, she's always mean. She scratches her owner and fights with the neighbouring tom-cat. Will Cranky always be the worst cat in the neighbourhood? Or will something happen to change everything in this true story?

Printed in Great Britain
by Amazon